Hare Kṛṣṇa!

I offer my sincere thanks to you for kindly helping me to publish my books. I hope you like the book!

With best wishes,

[illegible]

Flagler Beach, Florida

26.11.16

Praise for
Quest for Justice: Select Tales with Modern Illuminations From the Mahabharata

"Based on a series of *Mahabharata* lectures, *Quest for Justice* is a one-of-a-kind book. The speaker, H.D. Goswami, is obviously learned, and also possesses an uncanny knack for turning the story into a very entertaining presentation, captivating the reader by its "page-turner" quality. All in all, it is definitely the best "popular" version of the *Mahabharata* I've ever read. It is very well told and the language of the text is exquisite. For those interested in India, Indian literature, and/or Indian religion, this is definitely a 5-star introduction. It is beautifully written, like a thrilling adventure story, with a cliff-hanger at the end of every chapter. Once you start reading you just can't stop – and that goes even for someone like me, who is basically familiar with the text."

Dr. Åke Sander
Professor of Psychology & Sociology of Religion
Department of Literature, History of Ideas and Religion (LIR)
University of Gothenburg, Sweden

"*Quest for Justice* is based on a collection of lectures on various themes and episodes from the enormous *Mahabharata* Epic. Paralleling the rhetorical style and delivery of the Epic itself, the book's tone is one of oral transmission, as it reworks ancient narratives into an appealing, comprehensible contemporary idiom. Delivered with frequent good humor, the talks are easy and entertaining, even as they clearly confront the deepest meanings of the text. In this, the speaker benefits from his devoted, decades-long engagement with the text in the original Sanskrit. Indeed, H.D. Goswami skillfully and profoundly depicts the psychological depth of the characters and the existential dilemmas they face in a very vivid and immediate way. Put differently, *Quest for Justice* is something of a continuation of the Epic tradition – the perpetuation, contextualization and rearticulation of ancient narratives and *dharma* teachings for a contemporary audience. H.D. Goswami combines his trademark wit, erudition and insightful analysis, breathing new life into the most compelling episodes of this ancient literary masterpiece."

Edwin Bryant
Professor of Hindu Religion and Philosophy
Rutgers University, USA

"Anyone familiar with the *Mahabharata* knows that following, much less explaining, this complex tale of fraternal enmity and fratricidal war is a daunting task. Yet, in H. D. Goswami's *Quest for Justice*, we are treated to a deft and captivating retelling that practically places us inside the drama as it ravels and unravels. At the risk of sounding cliché, the millenia that separate us from these ancient events *do* seem to fall away as we are invited to recognize the very real human emotions that motivate the heroes and the villains of this celebrated Indian epic. Reading *Quest for Justice*, it is easy to understand that we are dealing with one of the great, enduring works of world literature, not a period piece from some forgotten age.

Kenneth Valpey Ph.D., Oxford Centre for Hindu Studies, UK

About the Cover

The five Pāṇḍava princes, heroes of the *Mahā-bhārata*, began their lives high in the Himālayan Mountains, where they lived among sages and *yogīs* during their formative years. When their father, King Pāṇḍu, tragically passed away, followed by his second wife, Queen Mādrī, their remaining mother, Queen Kuntī, brought the bodies of the legendary king and queen back to the capital city of Hastināpura. That procession – featuring Kuntī, the five young Pāṇḍavas, and four pallbearers – is depicted on this cover, coming from the mountains to the foothills below. The Pāṇḍava princes are at the very beginning of a long quest for justice.

(For a more complete explanation of this particular version of the tale, see Chapter Six, pages 101-102.)

Quest for Justice

Select Tales with Modern Illuminations from the Mahabharata

H.D. Goswami

Published by

KW

Krishna West, Inc.
1515 NW 7th Place
Gainesville, FL 32603
www.krishnawestinc.com

ISBN: 978-0-9862403-17
Library of Congress Control Number: 2017934788

Readers interested in the subject matter of this book are invited to write to:
bookinfo@hdgoswami.com

Text design and formatting by Polgarus Studio
Cover design by Daniel Laflor
Original cover art by Vrinda Gleeson

Contents

Acknowledgements

Quest for Justice is based on thirteen *Mahā-bhārata* lectures, given by H.D. Goswami in April-May 2010. Transforming these lectures into a satisfying written work that simultaneously retains the charm and spontaneity of the original oral presentation was challenging, to say the least. It took a real team effort and we'd like to thank everyone involved.

Our process started with the transcribers, Prema-manjari dasi (Fiona Macphee) and Fred Grave, both of whom did a really fantastic job. Then the text went to our assistant editor, Sara Crow, who did much to prepare the text for its final editing. Our senior editor, Aja dasa (Allan Andersson), performed the final editing and refinement of the text. Candrabhanu dasa (Jon Kaufman) then conducted the first proofreading of each chapter, adding a number of interesting footnotes along the way; he also finalized the book's chapter titles. Vrinda Gleeson contributed the original artwork for the cover and Danesha dasa (Daniel Laflor) designed the cover's text and formatting. Revati Prema dasi (Marianne Laflor) then conducted a second proofreading, catching a number of missed errors and typos. Finally, Polgarus Studio's Jason Anderson formatted both the print and the e-versions of the book.

Once again, many thanks to everyone involved.

– The Publishers

A Note to the Reader

Even with decades of editing experience, each new project presents different challenges. To create *Quest for Justice*, we worked with transcriptions of thirteen *Mahā-bhārata* lectures given by H.D. Goswami at a *yoga* retreat in 2010.

The task of creating a written work from a series of lectures requires a transformation of the original speech to a new medium—taking one type of experience and largely shaping it into another. In this particular case, our aim was not to polish the transcribed lectures to sterile perfection, but rather to craft them into a type of literary hybrid: something that reads clearly and elegantly as a written work, but that simultaneously retains the mood, tone, and spontaneity of an informal lecture. This often required us to reorganize, refine, and embellish the original material, and thus involved a fair degree of creative license.

For instance, with the permission and often the collaboration of H.D. Goswami, we have added material here and there that fills out the lectures, enriches the written work, and further illuminates Goswami's points. We also chose to sacrifice the strict rules of grammar, punctuation, and standard non-fictional style in order to retain the casual character and overall spirit of the original lectures. Finally, to highlight H.D. Goswami's various humorous asides and set them apart from the main discourse, we present them in italics.

We hope that we have achieved our goal, and that reading this text will be nearly as delightful as listening to H.D. Goswami speak in person. Even if you've heard the lectures before, *Quest for Justice* should provide a uniquely charming and satisfying experience in and of itself.

One final point: In India, there are numerous recensions, or manuscript traditions, of the *Mahā-bhārata*. Thus details of the stories may vary, though the basic narrative remains the same. H.D. Goswami has therefore selected details and versions that, in his view, reflect the most historically probable and spiritually instructive representation.

Setting the Stage

Thousands of years ago, according to ancient sources, a series of extraordinary events took place that transformed our world both culturally and spiritually, and carried consequences that stretched far beyond this planet. Indeed, these events were so singular and powerful that great *brāhmaṇas* described them to their students, parents taught them to their children, and wandering sages (bards)[1] traveled from village to village, narrating what had happened. Thus passing from one generation to another, these narrations were eventually preserved as text and remain accessible even today, known as the *Mahā-bhārata*. It is this *Mahā-bhārata* that will be the focus of our attention twice a day for the next week. We can start by exploring the Sanskrit term *avatāra.*

All spiritual paths begin with the assumption that the world as ordinarily perceived is not the highest truth. They begin by assuming that there are profound, inconceivable, wonderful truths about the universe, and things beyond that, which can only be understood in higher states of consciousness. In this way, spiritual paths lead *upward*, and thus the *avatāra* is "one who crosses down." Sometimes it is God Himself and sometimes it is a very great soul, but the *avatāra* always descends from that higher plane to ours, bringing guidance, strength, light, and restoration.

---

[1] The ancient Sanskrit word is *sūta*.

The suffix *tāra* (crossing) in *avatāra* comes from the same Sanskrit root as the word *tīrtha,* which means "sacred place of pilgrimage"—a place one commonly visits for spiritual inspiration and renewal. The idea is that when either God or a highly elevated soul crosses down to our world, wherever that *avatāra* "lands" or lives or performs activities becomes a place of pilgrimage, a *tīrtha*. This is because the *avatāra* opens a channel between our world and that higher plane. Thus, while visiting a holy place, we can, in a sense, ascend (experience the divine) through that same channel. This explains why holy places are called *tīrthas* as well as the linguistic connection between *tīrtha* and *avatāra*.

Now, according to the *Mahā-bhārata*, it was no ordinary *avatāra* that descended to our plane thousands of years ago; it was actually the *avatārī*, which means "the source of all *avatāras*." When, for example, this *avatārī* briefly spoke to Arjuna, His teachings became the *Bhagavad-gītā,* perhaps the greatest spiritual work to come out of the East, and certainly one of the most famous texts in the world. Of course, that *avatārī,* that speaker of the *Gītā,* is Kṛṣṇa.[2]

In fact, Kṛṣṇa's descent to this world was so significant that another *avatāra*, Bhagavān Vyāsa, came down simply to record

---

[2] Kṛṣṇa is the speaker of *Bhagavad-gītā*; His name literally means "the all-attractive person." In the *Mahā-Bhārata*, *Śrīmad-Bhāgavatam* and other Sanskrit works, Kṛṣṇa is understood to be the chief and most intimate name for the supreme monotheistic Godhead, the original cause of all causes. The *Śrīmad-Bhāgavatam,* for example, states, *kṛṣṇas tu bhagavān svayam*: "Kṛṣṇa is the original Personality of Godhead" A.C. Bhaktivedanta Swami Prabhupada, canto 1, ch. 3, v. 28 of *Śrīmad-Bhāgavatam* (Los Angeles: Bhaktivedanta Book Trust, 1972), 175. The ancient *Brahmā-Saṃitā* also proclaims, *īśvaraḥ paramaḥ kṛṣṇaḥ, sac-cid-ānanda-vigrahaḥ,* "The supreme controller of everything, who possesses an eternal form, is Kṛṣṇa" Bhaktisiddhānta Sarasvatī Goswami, *Brahmā-Saṃitā*, Calcutta: Sri Gaudiya Math, 1932, ch.5, v.1.

what was happening. Veda Vyāsa, as he's als[illegible] extremely famous within Indian civilization as the auth[illegible] the *Mahā-bhārata* and the *Bhāgavata Purāṇa*.[3] He also [illegible] and organized the *Vedas* for the present age, and person[illegible] participated in the events he described. In other words, he was not only the observer, the witness, and the documenter; he was integrally involved in his own narrative. And the story he told of those immortal events was called the *Mahā-bhārata*.

The Sanskrit word *mahā* means "great." From this, by the way, we have the well-known Latin word *magna*, as in "magnify" or "magnificent" *(so* Magna-bhārata *also works!)*. Bhārata is the ancient name of India, but not necessarily the India of today. Today's India is a modern political invention, whereas the principal region in which the *Mahā-bhārata*'s events took place stretches from Afghanistan in the west all the way to Bengal, or perhaps even Burma, in the east. So this narrative took place over a vast area known as Bhārata, and to this day India bears that name—especially among members of the Indian population.

Let's now turn to the text itself. What is the *Mahā-bhārata*? When, where, and how was it composed? And how did it come down to us today? That's a whole story in itself.

The *Mahā-bhārata* is the largest of a genre of literature known as *itihāsa*, which is generally translated as "history." It is actually formed of three distinct words—*iti, ha, asa*: "thus," "it happened," "in the past." So the *Mahā-bhārata* is considered an actual history, but there's *also* a history of the epic itself, since it originated prior to the time of the written word *(despite some very popular Hindu tales to the contrary)*.

In any case, we *do* know that the text has an untraceably

---

[3] *Bhāgavata Purāṇa* is another name for *Śrīmad-Bhāgavatam*.

certain point it was written down, wildly popular. In fact, to this day, lars about South Asia and mention diately know you mean the *Mahā-* of important scholars have made nificance of this work.

nt University of Chicago Indologist, J.A.B. van Buitenen, who rendered a highly respected, if incomplete, translation of the Great Epic, describes its influence as follows:

> More than any other text in Indian civilization, the Great Epic has been the storehouse of ancient lore ... Countless are the single references to epic material in the lyric literature ... Such casual references show how familiar the Indian was with the events and the heroes of the epic, so familiar that they in effect became proverbial.[4]

Indeed, the *Mahā-bhārata* is so celebrated that the various Indian arts as well as books on grammar, poetry, astronomy, and so on, all assume common knowledge of its content. To take birth anywhere in that part of the world is to know this story and its characters practically from infancy. The Great Epic is a pillar of Indian civilization and its cultural influence has been all-pervading.

In the mid-20th century, a major project was undertaken to collect and organize all the surviving manuscripts of the *Mahā-bhārata,* with the aim of discovering an "original" version of the text. The world's greatest Sanskritists—from India to Europe to North America—participated in this decades-long project, finally

---

[4] J.A.B. van Buitenen, vol. 1, book 1 of *The Mahābhārata: The Book of the Beginning*. (London: The University of Chicago Press, Ltd., 1973), xxvi.

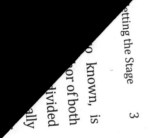

producing what they called a *Critical Edition*. The project's chief editor was the eminent scholar V.S. Sukthankar. Here's what he had to say about the stature of the *Mahā-bhārata*:

> The pre-eminent importance of the epic is universally acknowledged. Next to the Vedas, it is the most valuable product of the entire literature of ancient India, so rich in notable works. Venerable for its very antiquity, it is one of the most inspiring monuments of the world, and an inexhaustible mine for the investigation of religion, ... philosophy, law, custom and political and social institutions of ancient India.[5]

In other words, the cultural and spiritual influence of this ancient text cannot be overstated. And at its pinnacle stands the *Bhagavad-gītā,* a brief section of seven hundred verses that appears in the *Bhīṣma-parva,* the epic's sixth book. The *Gītā* is far and away the single most important text to come out of Indian civilization, essentially serving as that civilization's universal spiritual book.

So what is the *Mahā-bhārata*? First of all, it's an extremely large work, perhaps the largest epic text in the world. Of course, there is also the huge Tibetan narrative called the *Gesar,* which contains similar stories of kings and so on. However, it is comprised of a series of disparate oral traditions, leaving the *Mahā-bhārata* to retain its title as the longest single coherent text ever composed. It contains around 100,000 verses, almost two million words, and (depending on your source) is somewhere between seven and ten times larger than the *Iliad* and the *Odyssey* combined! Bottom line: it's a very large work.

---

[5] V.S. Sukthankar, vol. 1 of *Critical Studies in the Mahābhārata* (Bombay: Karnatak Publishing House, 1944), 12-13.

As to where the events of the *Mahā-bhārata* take place, although the story's core happenings occur in Northern India, as I previously mentioned, they stretch as far afield as Afghanistan in one direction and possibly Burma in the other. Gāndhārī,[6] for example, came from the Afghani city of Gāndhāra, today called Kandahar.

A more difficult question concerns whether we can date the events of the Great Epic and determine whether or not they actually took place. As to establishing *when* these events occurred, attempts have been made to date the *Mahā-bhārata* through archaeology (including metallurgy), philology (searching for references in texts that correlate to known history), and other such means. The results thus far have been inconclusive, with the most recent attempts setting the text's antiquity at around 3,000 years, based upon these modern academic methods. Suffice it to say, however, that the dates derived by such methods are highly speculative, and thus fundamentally unreliable.

Perhaps the most accurate indication of this ancient text's age comes by way of a gentleman named Aryabhata. Aryabhata lived in India some 1,500 years ago and is considered one of the greatest astronomers of all time. He's also one of the creators of trigonometry. Anyone familiar with this branch of mathematics has likely heard of the terms sine and cosine. What they may not know is that these terms are

---

[6] Gāndhārī, one of the *Mahā-bhārata's* primary figures, is the wife of the blind king Dhṛtarāṣṭra and the mother of one hundred sons. Gāndhārī is regarded as the emblem of virtue and wifely devotion; she is among the most esteemed moral forces of the Great Epic. Having married a blind person, she resolved at the time of her wedding to also spend the rest of her life blind, so as to share in her husband's fate. Thus she tied a cloth around her eyes, depriving herself of the power to see. Gāndhārī never wavered in her adherence to *dharma,* and, at certain critical points in the narrative, gave impeccable moral advice to her husband.

actually mis-transcriptions of the Saṅskrit terms *jyā* and *koti-jyā,* which come from Aryabhata.

As for his astronomical calculations, tracking the movements of the planets and so on, these were so precise that they were used during the golden age of Islam, and eventually translated into Latin as the Toledo Tables—the most accurate tools employed by European astronomy for many centuries. His groundbreaking discoveries followed the typical path of ancient knowledge: from India to the Islamic world to Europe. In other words, we're talking about a very bright guy! But how does all this relate to the dating of the *Mahā-bhārata*?

In Aryabhata's time, astrology was a very big thing. And one of the main motivations for studying astronomy was to obtain better data for astrology. Interestingly, this was also true of Europe, where the greatest astronomers—people like Copernicus and even Galileo —were trying to do the same thing.

(This embarrassing little detail, of course, is conveniently left out of Western astronomy courses.)

Getting back to Aryabhata, the core of his dating method lies in the fact that many of the *Mahā-bhārata's* key events come along with specific astronomical descriptions. The description of Kṛṣṇa's birth, for instance, contains details about the alignment of the stars at that time, as do many other occurrences, such as the battle of Kuru-kṣetra. Using astronomical calculations to fix dates was a common approach in ancient times; it wasn't only astrology, it was astronomy. They would explain when things happened by determining the month in which they occurred, the position of the stars, which asterism was in which lunar mansion, and so on.

So, about fifteen hundred years ago, Aryabhata went through the *Mahā-bhārata's* various astronomical descriptions, making calculations based upon his own highly accurate and respected methodologies. And, by so doing, he was able to determine that, all told, the events mentioned in the Great Epic took place approximately 5,100 years ago.

Now, for various self-interested reasons, different generations of Western scholars didn't want to admit that this and other Sanskrit texts had been around that long. The question is, "Why?"

During the colonial period, the first generations of British and other European Orientalists, Indologists, and South Asian scholars were proselytizing Christians. Their mission was to basically ridicule and debunk Vedic culture while convincing the Indian population to convert to the "only real religion."

Europeans at that time believed that world history began with the events of the Garden of Eden, which they dated back to so many thousands of years. Then, they traveled to India and suddenly discovered this very ancient civilization and body of texts that threatened to overturn all their Biblical dates. To uphold their speculations about the Garden of Eden, they had no choice but to proclaim that the entirety of the Sanskrit literature was more recent than the Bible.

After the Christians, the next generations of Western scholars were more agnostic in their outlook, yet they also were motivated to maintain that the *Mahā-bhārata* was a more recent work. To them, the existence of a 5,000 year old Sanskrit text gave India far too much prestige, almost implying that India was the cradle of human civilization. There was just no way they would allow for that.

If we had the time, we could hold a month-long seminar on the Indo-European issue alone. For now, suffice it to say that Aryabhata's findings about the antiquity of the *Mahā-bhārata* have never gone down well in the West. Thus you'll find various datings in Western scholarly literature that run counter to those findings.

Turning now to the *Mahā-bhārata*'s content, it can be said to take place on three different levels. On one level, it is the earthly struggle between cousin-brothers within the great Kuru dynasty, representing the forces of good on one side and evil on the other. On another level, the text references a wider battle between godly *avatāras*, like Kṛṣṇa and Vyāsa, and very powerful demonic beings, who also descended to this world for reasons that we'll discuss later. For now, suffice it to say that when the events of the *Mahā-bhārata* took place, both virtuous and villainous beings descended to Earth and played significant roles in all that transpired. Thus the Great Epic tells the story of an earthly dynastic struggle as well as a struggle between good and evil forces in the universe—*a battle of cosmic proportions!*

Finally, largely due to the presence of the *Gītā*, the *Mahā-bhārata* transcends both Earth and Cosmos, pointing us toward an eternal spiritual reality beyond the temporary world. The *Mahā-bhārata* takes place on all these levels, and we'll talk more about that in the days to come.

To comprehend the actors and actions of the *Mahā-bhārata,* we must first be able to understand the universe as portrayed in this work. The *Mahā-bhārata* and other Sanskrit texts contain vivid descriptions of the universe, including the workings of time, space, and so on. They also explain the universe's demography: who lives where within various spheres, and the relations between these diverse groups.

In comparing the *Mahā-bhārata's* perspective with that of other ancient texts—from Judeo-Christian to Egyptian to Greco-Roman—it can be said that the *Mahā-bhārata* provides the most sophisticated, broad, and exhaustive depiction of them all. And since the Great Epic's narrative operates within the framework of this depiction, exploring its various dimensions should help us to approach the text. We can begin with time.

Observing the movements of Earth, we see it turning on its axis and rotating around the sun, which also goes around in its own orbit; the seasons go in cycles, the moon goes in cycles, as do many other cosmic and natural phenomena. These observations led Vedic, Indo-European, and most Greco-Roman philosophers to conclude that the cycle is the essential cosmic motion and to conceive of time as moving in cycles.

In the Middle East, on the other hand, Hebrew, Christian, and Islamic theologians believed time to be linear, to extend sequentially along a straight line—meaning that at one point there's nothing, then there's something, and it just keeps going in one direction. By the early 19th century, this religiously-based Middle Eastern concept had become the established view of most Western academics. This includes the modern sciences, which, for all their anti-religious fervor, have basically embraced the notion of linear time—an embrace that may be somewhat loosening at the cutting edges of 21st century cosmology.

In any case, for ancient Indian civilization, as reflected in the *Mahā-bhārata* and other Sanskrit works, time is cyclical, and there are great planetary, and even universal seasons (or ages) known as *yugas*. This idea, by the way, can be found not only in Vedic literature, but also in the poems of Hesiod, who, after Homer, was the most important of the ancient Greek writers.

According to the Sanskrit texts, the first age is known as Satya-yuga, the golden age of truth—the longest of the four *yugas*. Then follow Tretā-yuga, Dvāpara-yuga, and Kali-yuga, the dark age of discord, contention, and strife. *(In other words, the "amazing" age we live in today!).*

The duration of each age is said to decline by a quarter, along with virtue, honesty, morality, and other positive features. The events of the *Mahābhārata* take place at the end of Dvāpara-yuga, the third age. In fact, the Great Epic repeatedly tells that Kali-yuga began at the precise moment that Kṛṣṇa left this world. In other words, Kṛṣṇa's leaving is the demarcation—the dividing line—between the previous Dvāpara-yuga and the present age of Kali.

In this connection, the *Mahā-bhārata* and other Vedic texts describe the duration of the *yuga* cycles, and the entire universe itself, in extremely vast terms, ultimately amounting to trillions and trillions of years. It's a gigantic, sweeping picture, which includes descriptions of different time systems in different worlds and talk of time relativity long before Einstein. The Sanskrit literature explains, for example, that one year of time in the celestial world can amount to many years of time on Earth. So there's a notion of the relativity of time.

And, ultimately, there's the notion that the soul—the eternal self—exists beyond the reach of time. In other words, the soul is not merely eternal in the sense of existing for endless material time, but actually exists in a system (or on a plane) that entirely transcends material time.

Moreover, just as in most countries there are upper, middle, and lower class neighborhoods, with different living conditions and facilities, the Sanskrit literature similarly mentions three divisions of worlds: upper, middle, and lower. Our planet, by the way, is considered a lower-middle world (*but with aspirations, and sometimes putting on airs, like geocentricism).*

Then there are the notions of *saṃsāra* and *karma*—regular features of almost all Indian systems, including Buddhism and Jainism. *Saṃsāra* is the understanding that souls are *not* their bodies; the body is simply a covering for the soul, its vehicle. Or, to use Kṛṣṇa's *Gītā* term, the body is *vāsāṁsi*, "simply clothes"—something you wear, like a wardrobe. The soul changes bodies just as we change clothes. We take on different *forms of dress.* That's *saṃsāra*!

And *karma* indicates that the process of transmigration is governed by a moral law. In other words, the transition from one body to another doesn't just happen whimsically or by chance. There is actually an ethical or moral law that directs the process, and *that* is the law of *karma*—another integral feature of this ancient civilization.

Ultimately, however, the *Mahā-bhārata* stresses one particular feature of Vedic civilization more that any other: the notion of *dharma,* perhaps the most important concept of the whole text. And because *dharma* is such a core concept, not only in Vedic but also in Buddhist culture, I'd like to spend the remainder of today's time talking about it. We can begin by defining the term.

The Sanskrit language was conceived by ancient grammarians like the great Pāṇini, whose work basically created the modern discipline of linguistics. Pāṇini, and all his colleagues and predecessors, viewed Sanskrit as an organic language, containing various verbal roots—roots of action that grow into words by adding stems, and thereby flowering in various semantic ways.

The dynamic root of *dharma* is *dhṛ* (*dh* combined with the vowel *ṛ*), which means "to hold, to sustain." For example, Kṛṣṇa is famously named Giridhari because He held up Govardhana Hill as a child. Here the suffix *dhara* (holder) comes from the same root as the word *dharma*, which means, among other things, "that which is established or firm."[7] This is a dictionary meaning, coming from the verbal root *dhṛ*, and from that, "a practice, a customary observance, prescribed conduct, law."[8]

Here the word "law" is not to be taken in a mundane sense—because, in a mundane sense, there can be an *unjust* law. *Dharma*, however, cannot be unjust, since the Sanskrit word for "unjust" is *adharma*, literally "not-*dharma*." So *dharma* must be just, and thus it actually refers to *the sacred law governing the universe*. The Greek word *logos* has some connection to the word *dharma*. And George Lucas is known to have studied this idea before creating *Star Wars*. In the iconic phrase, "may the Force be with you," the Force, in a sense, is *dharma*. So *dharma* is this force within the universe; or, again, the law that governs the universe.

For example, early in the *Mahā-bhārata* there is a powerful section in which Indra is talking to King Uparichara, who wants to ascend to heaven; and Indra is having some *"job-security angst,"* believing that the king is doing severe austerities to usurp his post.

Here it's interesting to note that Sanskrit actually contains wonderful humor. People sometimes think that sacred texts must be stuffy old tomes, but there's actually incredible humor in the *Mahā-bhārata*'s language. Here, for example, the king's name is given as Uparichara Vasu, which literally means "Upwardly Mobile Vasu"—*upari* means "upward" and *chara* means "mobile," so "upwardly mobile!" And Indra is trying to convince King Uparichara, "Just stay in your own position, and I'll stay in mine; let's not compete."

---

[7] See *Monier Williams Sanskrit-English Dictionary* (2008 revision), definition of *dharma*, http://www.sanskrit-lexicon.uni-koeln.de/monier/
[8] *Ibid.*

Indra wants the king to remain on earth to protect and sustain *dharma,* telling him, *dharmo rakṣati rakṣitaḥ hiṃsata hiṃsate*: "When *dharma* is protected, it protects; when *dharma* is injured, it injures." By the way, the word for "injured" in this verse is *hiṃsate*—like *himsa* (violence), *ahimsa* (non-violence), and so on.

The meaning of the above passage is clear. *Dharma* is this force within the universe, this divine law governing all things. And if you align yourself with that divine law, you will basically live an anxiety-free life and be protected by that system. It's similar in a good state: if you follow the law, the law will protect you; if you injure the law, the law will injure you.

This can be understood in even broader terms. If you follow the law, you not only protect yourself both legally and socially, you also contribute, more generally, to a civil society. You contribute to the general peace by doing your duty, not speeding with your car, not cheating, and so on. That's the basic idea: *dharma* is the divine law, and by observing that divine law, we contribute not only to our own wellbeing, but also to the peace and prosperity of the universe.

So this is *dharma*. And there are different types of *dharma* as well. For example, there is *yuga-dharma*: a particular duty for each particular age that is especially effective and powerful in terms of bringing people to enlightenment. Concerning the *yuga-dharma* for our age of Kali, it's something we all just did: coming together and singing the holy names of God, accompanied by beautiful music and dance—or, in Sanskrit, *saṅkīrtana*.[9]

---

[9] The *Śrīmad-Bhāgavatam* addresses this in the eleventh canto: *kṛṣṇa-varṇaṁ tviṣākṛṣṇaṁ sāṅgopāṅgāstra-pārṣadam; yajñaiḥ saṅkīrtana-prāyair yajanti hi su-medhasaḥ*: "In the Age of Kali, intelligent persons perform

There is also, for example, *raja-dharma* (royal *dharma* or *dharma* for leaders), *strī-dharma* (special duties for women), and *dhana-dharma* (rules governing the giving and receiving of charity). And, perhaps most significantly, there is *varṇāśrama-dharma*, which applies to the entire society. Indeed, unless one understands *varṇāśrama-dharma,* it will be difficult to understand what's going on in the *Mahā-bhārata.*

So what is *varṇāśrama-dharma*? Briefly, it's the division of human society into four *varṇas* (social divisions) and four *āśramas* (stages of life), each of which has its own specific *dharma*. We can start with the four *varṇas*, which are as follows: *brāhmaṇas* (teachers); *kṣatriyas* (governors and warriors); *vaiśyas* (merchants and farmers); and, *śūdras* (workers and artisans).

Interestingly, in the *Bhagavad-gītā,* one's *varṇa* is said to be determined not by birth, but rather by one's own qualifications and nature. That, of course, was the earlier system, which later became completely rigidified, and thus somewhat oppressive, leading to non-violent social revolutions, as in the case of Buddhism (but that's another story). Unfortunately, over time, the system of *varṇāśrama-dharma* gradually morphed into the hereditary caste system we all know *and loathe* today.

In any case, that's the *varṇa* part of the ancient system, as reflected in the *Mahā-bhārata*. And then there are the four *āśramas* (or stages of life): *brahmacārī* (young celibate students); *gṛhastha* (married, with children and various

---

congregational chanting to worship the incarnation of Godhead who constantly sings the names of Kṛṣṇa. Although His complexion is not blackish, He is Kṛṣṇa Himself. He is accompanied by His associates, servants, weapons and confidential companions." The Disciples of A.C. Bhaktivedanta Swami Prabhupada, canto 11, ch. 5, v. 32 of *Śrīmad-Bhāgavatam* (Los Angeles: Bhaktivedanta Book Trust, 1987), 489.

household duties); *vānaprastha* (literally, "departing for the forest," meaning that once the kids are grown and all the duties of family life have wound down, the parents retire and dedicate their lives to the spiritual practices of their youth, with the aim of ultimate enlightenment); and finally, *sannyāsa* (complete renunciation, for those that are more spiritually advanced). And again, each *varṇa* and each *āśrama* has its own *dharma* (prescribed duties, regulations, and rules). For example, there is *brāhmaṇa-dharma, kṣatriya-dharma, sannyāsa-dharma, gṛhastha-dharma,* and so on.

But ultimately, we not only have *dharmas* that guide behavior according to body type, be it male, female, king, poet, farmer, scholar, married, renounced, and so on. There is also a *dharma* of the soul. When we completely transcend the body and fully understand ourselves as eternal spiritual beings, then there is our eternal *dharma*, often referred to as *sanātana-dharma. Sanātana* means "eternal" or "everlasting." In the *Bhagavad-gītā,* when discussing eternal *dharma,* Kṛṣṇa uses the synonym *śāśvata* instead.

The *Bhagavad-gītā* is the spiritual heart, or essence, of the *Mahā-bhārata*, and the very first word spoken by Dhṛtarāṣṭra in the first verse of the first chapter is *dharma*: *dharma-kṣetre kuru-kṣetre samavetā yuyutsavaḥ*.

Dharma-kṣetre ("on the *dharma* field [this very poignant, pregnant utterance starts the narrative]"); and then, *kuru-kṣetre* ("on the field of the Kurus [this great dynasty]"); *samavetā* ("having assembled"); *yuyutsavaḥ* ("and desiring to fight"). So Dhṛtarāṣṭra is asking, "Having assembled there, and being eager to fight," *māmakāḥ* ("my own sons"), *pāṇḍavāś caiva* ("and the Pāṇḍava brothers"), *kim akurvata sañjaya* ("what did they do, Sanjaya?").[10]

(One interesting aside: the Sanskrit word *yuyutsu*, "one who is eager to fight," went to the East as jujitsu—the name of a martial art.)

In any case, after this opening verse, the narrative of the *Gītā* begins. Arjuna, a great warrior, gazes out over the "*dharma* field" and decides he doesn't want to fight, even though he's one of the greatest warriors in the world and his cause is just. Once we begin describing the events of the *Mahābhārata*, you'll understand that the rulers Arjuna faced on the battlefield—his own cousin-brothers—were actually up to a lot of very nasty things, including usurpation, thievery, rape, and murder. Still, facing his own kin on the battlefield, Arjuna became overwhelmed by sentiment and didn't want to fight.

And while the other chapters of the *Gītā* feature Bhagavān, Lord Kṛṣṇa, as the speaker, this first chapter can be thought of as Arjuna's *gītā*, because Arjuna does most of the talking—and he uses the word *dharma* a lot. In fact, Arjuna's basic argument is that the upcoming battle on the *dharma* field will actually be *bad* for *dharma*: "If we fight, we'll kill these warriors, and they all have wives and children. Who's going to take care of all these families? Everyone's going to fall into *adharma*; the world will go to hell." So Arjuna's stance in the first chapter is framed in terms of *dharma*: the war isn't good for *dharma* and thus should not be fought. Of course, Kṛṣṇa will counter Arjuna's argument by saying: "*Hello!* This is actually a *dharma-yuddha* (a righteous battle); this is *all about dharma*!"[11]

Finally, in the second chapter, after presenting all his

---

[10] H.D. Goswami, ch. 1, v. 1 of *A Comprehensive Guide to Bhagavad-Gītā with Literal Translation* (Gainesville: Krishna West, Inc., 2015), 151.
[11] *Ibid.*, ch. 2, v. 32, 157.

arguments about *dharma,* and right before Kṛṣṇa begins His teachings, amazingly, Arjuna says: *kārpaṇya-doṣopahata-svabhāvaḥ pṛcchāmi tvāṁ dharma-sammūḍha-cetāḥ*: "Right now, I haven't got the slightest idea about my *dharma*, because, *cetāḥ*, my mind, my consciousness, is *dharma-sammūḍha*, completely baffled about duty."[12]

So the first spoken word of the *Gītā* is *dharma*, and Arjuna frames his arguments against the battle in terms of *dharma*. And then, after all that, Arjuna says, "I really don't know what I'm talking about; I'm actually bewildered about *dharma*." So Kṛṣṇa will explain Arjuna's *dharma*—what he's really supposed to do.

Then, in Chapter Four, Kṛṣṇa explains why He has descended to this world, and in so doing, speaks one of the most famous verses in Hinduism. Anyone that has ever spoken to an Indian audience knows that as soon as this Sanskrit verse is recited, everyone joins in, because they all know it by heart: *yadā yadā hi dharmasya glānir bhavati bhārata; abhyutthānam adharmasya tadātmānaṁ sṛijāmyaham*: Whenever there is a *dharmasya glāniḥ* ("a collapse, a deterioration of *dharma*"), and *abhyutthānam* (literally, "an aggressive rise of *adharma*"), *tadātmānaṁ sṛijāmyaham* ("then I [Kṛṣṇa] manifest Myself").[13] So Kṛṣṇa tells that it's the waning or collapsing of *dharma,* and the rising of *adharma,* that brings Him to this world.

The next verse, in which Kṛṣṇa explains His earthly mission, is also extremely famous: *paritrāṇāya sādhūnāṁ vināśāya ca duṣkṛtām; dharma-saṁsthāpanārthāya sambhavāmi yuge yuge*: "To deliver the righteous, destroy the wicked, and

---

[12] *Ibid.,* ch. 2, v. 7, 155.
[13] *Ibid.,* ch. 4, v. 7, 165.

restore *dharma,* I appear in every age."[14] As you can see, *dharma* is a key concept in all of this.

But not all *dharmas* are created equal. For example, in Chapter Nine, Kṛṣṇa criticizes what He calls *trayī-dharma,* literally, "the triad" or "the three"—a common way of referring to the three Vedas.[15] Actually, there are four Vedas, but one is a little "voodoo-esque," with directions for the casting of spells and other such things. So, even back in ancient Vedic days, it was held somewhat at a distance, "Oh, the *Atharva* Veda. You keep the fourth, I'll just stick with the three."

Don't get me wrong. The *Atharva* Veda *is* one of the Vedas, and it is respected and held to be sacred. But higher-class *brāhmaṇas* tend to emphasize only the *Ṛg, Sāma,* and *Yajur* Vedas. And in the *Gītā,* Kṛṣṇa also refers to the Vedas as *trayī,* the three, and talks of *trayī-dharma*.

Kṛṣṇa's strong critique of the Vedas in the *Gītā* is a whole other, very interesting, topic. His criticism, in this case, focuses on the *karma-kāṇḍa,* the materialistic part of the culture, where the perspective essentially is, "I prayed to God and got a beautiful new house, a fantastic promotion," and so on. Within Vedic culture, there were materialists that used the power of the Vedas to advance themselves materially. And Kṛṣṇa, from the highest spiritual platform, is speaking of the folly of this approach, explaining that the real point of *dharma* is not to obtain material reward—that's not what it's about at all.

Kṛṣṇa says that those who take shelter of *trayī-dharma*—the *dharma* of the materialistic Vedas—earn only a round trip ticket: they go up to higher material planets and come right

---

14 *Ibid.,* ch. 4, v. 8, 165.
15 *Ibid.,* ch. 9, vv. 21-22, 182.

back down again. It's what Kṛṣṇa calls *gatāgataṁ*, literally, "going and coming." So there are materialistic *dharmas* that enable one to obtain certain material rewards—and they really do work. But they cannot help us to advance in spiritual life.

In Chapter Eleven, Arjuna praises Kṛṣṇa as *śāśvata-dharma-goptā*, "the protector of eternal *dharma*."[16] So here Arjuna declares that that there is a *dharma* of the pure soul, and that Kṛṣṇa protects that *dharma*. Then, in Chapter Fourteen, Kṛṣṇa Himself declares, *brahmaṇo hi pratiṣṭhāham* and *śāśvatasya ca dharmasya*: "I am the basis, the foundation, not only of the Brahman, but also of the eternal *dharma*."[17] So Kṛṣṇa says He is the *pratiṣṭhā,* the foundation of *sanātana-dharma,* eternal *dharma*.

Finally, in a dramatic concluding verse of the *Bhagavad-gītā*—not *the* final verse, but really, the *climactic* verse—Kṛṣṇa says, *sarva-dharmān parityajya,* "Giving up all *dharmas,*" *mām ekaṁ śaraṇaṁ vraja,* "go to Me alone for shelter."[18]

But what could He mean by this statement? Kṛṣṇa's whole point in speaking the *Bhagavad-gītā* is to convince Arjuna to do his *dharma* as a warrior, and yet, at the very end, Kṛṣṇa tells Arjuna to *give up all dharmas* and simply take shelter of Him. While these two commands may seem paradoxical, they are not contradictory since Kṛṣṇa (God) is the be-all and end-all of existence. There's a nice verse in the first canto, second chapter of the *Śrīmad-Bhāgavatam* that speaks to this point:

---

16 *Ibid.,* ch. 11, v. 18, 188.
17 *Ibid.,* ch. 14, v. 27, 199.
18 *Ibid.,* ch. 18, v. 66, 211.

vāsudeva-parā vedā
vāsudeva-parā makhāḥ
vāsudeva-parā yogā
vāsudeva-parāḥ kriyāḥ

vāsudeva-paraṁ jñānaṁ
vāsudeva-paraṁ tapaḥ
vāsudeva-paro dharmo
vāsudeva-parā gatiḥ

> "In the revealed scriptures, the ultimate object of knowledge is Śrī Kṛṣṇa, the Personality of Godhead. The purpose of performing sacrifice is to please Him. Yoga is for realizing Him. All fruitive activities are ultimately rewarded by Him only. He is supreme knowledge, and all severe austerities are performed to know Him. Religion [*dharma*] is rendering loving service unto Him. He is the supreme goal of life."[19]

Paradoxes, by the way, are a common theme in the Sanskrit literature and they have a very specific purpose when they arise. In the *Śrīmad-Bhāgavatam,* for example, with reference to Kṛṣṇa's descent, there is a recurring, apparently paradoxical theme: *ajo jāyate,* "the unborn has taken birth." Then there is *akartur karma,* "the actions of those who do not act." We'll talk more about paradoxes later in the week. *(You see ... it's a theological cliffhanger!)*

I've spent a good deal of time talking about *dharma* because it's so central to the *Mahā-bhārata*. Without understanding the

---

[19] Online Bhaktivedanta VedaBase, *Śrīmad-Bhāgavatam,* canto 1, ch. 2, vv. 28-29; http://www.vedabase.com/en/sb.

utter seriousness with which the figures in the *Mahā-bhārata* regarded *dharma*, one cannot properly grasp the whys and wherefores of their thoughts, feelings and actions, as represented in the text. For them, *dharma*, the universal cosmic force, the divine law governing all life, was a tangible, undisputable reality.

The *Mahā-bhārata* is essentially the tale of how a faction of powerful *Asuras* (villains) tried to use *dharma* to gain control of the worlds, beginning with the Earth, and how they were ultimately stopped in the culminating battle of Kuru-kṣetra.

Bhīṣma: the Terrible Vow

Think, for a moment, of the life of a small child, blessed with the fortune of good parents. The child goes about its days playing and thinking of its own needs, unaware of how the parents are working or worrying or struggling to protect the child.

In a similar way, from the perspective of the *Mahā-bhārata,* we are not aware of all that is being done on our behalf within the universe—things we take for granted each day that are not merely due to earthly circumstances: the fruits, vegetables, grains, and water that sustain all life; the regularity of sunrise and sunset; the remnant of moral order that enables us to pursue our own spiritual vision, and so on. Nor do we realize that powerful celestial beings manage such large affairs and work for the world's welfare, sometimes contending with powerful forces that oppose the good.

Even the Old Testament recognizes that within the universe there are various powerful beings. The commandment to have "no other gods before Me," for example, is not a claim that there *are* no other gods, but only that one has to get them in the right order. Other parts of the Old Testament actually list different deities, but always while insisting that one must give oneself only to the Supreme God.

So the notion exists not only in Vedic culture, but also in Biblical culture, that the universe beyond our Earth is not an uninhabited desert, but rather populated in various ways.

There are "celestial demographics," one might say: living beings up there, *and out there*, who are fundamentally beyond our reach.

The eighth canto of *Śrīmad-Bhāgavatam* describes a great battle that is basically the preface to the events of the *Mahā-bhārata*.[20] Often there are tensions in this world between those who would do good and those who would pursue their own selfish ends, regardless of the cost to others. And sometimes, despite our best efforts to avoid it, those tensions break out into violent conflict.

Long ago, in the higher spheres of the universe, something of this sort occurred between the *Suras* and the *Asuras* (Sanskrit for "the godly and the ungodly"). Interestingly, the leaders of these opposing forces were actually related as cousins, with the leading *Suras* being sons of Aditi and the leading *Asuras* being sons of Diti.[21]

In this case, the *Asuras*, the bad guys, were beginning to dominate the field, and had a serious chance of prevailing—that is, until Viṣṇu appeared on the scene. So who is Viṣṇu? For one thing, the whole *Mahā-bhārata* assumes we all know that Kṛṣṇa is Viṣṇu.[22] But apart from this, what do the Vedic literatures tell us about Viṣṇu?

We can begin with a word about linguistic analysis and the

---

[20] See canto 8, ch. 10, vv. 1-57 of *Śrīmad-Bhāgavatam*.

[21] Diti and Aditi were two rival daughters of the great cosmic progenitor, Prajāpati Dakṣa, and eventually two of the thirteen sister wives of Lord Brahmā's grandson, Kaśyapa Muni. Diti became the matriarch and champion of the *Asuras* while Aditi gave birth to the leaders of the *Suras*.

[22] "Vaiṣṇavism acknowledges a form of polymorphic monotheism. That is to say, it holds that there is one God who appears in numerous manifestations, each distinct and unique. These manifestations, moreover, are considered equal and yet hierarchical as well. They are one, and yet different." Satyaraj das, *Back to Godhead Magazine*, June 2013

dating of texts. It's fairly simple. If we study the English in, say, Chaucer, it's obviously older than the English in Shakespeare, which is obviously older than the English in the latest edition of the New York Times. So there are different detectable levels in the evolution of a language, and this can be seen in Sanskrit as well.

The four Vedas—Ṛg, Sāma, Yajur and Atharva—are considered the earliest Sanskrit texts, and among these, the Ṛg-Veda is the oldest, according to linguistic analysis. Without going over the whole history, suffice it to say that each of the four Vedas was entrusted to a very competent "extended family" of sages, who would carefully preserve these texts, handing them down from generation to generation, which is why we have them today. Apart from preserving the original Vedas themselves, these communities of sages also produced works that explained the meaning of their respective Veda. These explanatory texts, which are also very ancient, are called the *Brāhmaṇas*.

So the Ṛg-Veda is the oldest of the four Vedas, and among its *Brāhmaṇas*, the oldest is the *Aitareya Brāhmaṇa*,[23] which is thousands of years older than, for example, the commentary by Sāyaṇa.[24] What interests us here is the fact that the very first passage of the *Aitareya Brāhmaṇa* — this ancient in-house

---

[23] The *Aitareya Brāhmaṇa* is commonly attributed to one author, Mahidasa Aitareya, and is dated anywhere from 1000 BCE to 500 BCE. Broken into forty chapters (*adhyāyas*) grouped into eight *pañcikās* (Sanskrit for "group of five"), the work covers topics like animal and other forms of sacrifice, anointing practices of kings, and other religious holidays and observances. Some scholars also argue that it contains early references to a heliocentric (sun-centered) solar system.

[24] Sāyana Āchārya (1315-1387 CE) was a renowned Medieval scholar who produced more than 100 commentaries, including commentaries on nearly the entirety of the Vedas. His central work is t*he Vedārtha Prak*āśa ("The Meaning of the Vedas Made Manifest"). He is also the one who identified Mahidasa Aitareya as the author of t*he Aitareya Brāhmaṇa*

commentary on the Ṛg-Veda—refers to Viṣṇu as the highest god, Agni as the lowest, and all others as in between.[25] Agni is listed as the lowest because he lives within our house: the fire that keeps us warm, cooks our food, and so on. Interestingly, from this Sanskrit word for fire comes the English word "ignite"—Agni, ignite.

In any case, the *Aitareya Brāhmaṇa*'s reference to Viṣṇu is confirmed by statements in other Vedas as well. For example, in the Yajur-Veda (*yajur* means the way one does sacrifice, *yajña*) we find the statement, *yajño vai viṣṇuḥ,* "sacrifice is Viṣṇu." The idea is that the sacrifice creates a channel to the divine, meaning that somehow, by performing the Vedic sacrifice, one directly comes into Viṣṇu's presence. Statements similar to this are scattered throughout the earliest Sanskrit texts. Thus, traditionally, historically—in very ancient times—Viṣṇu was considered the *puruṣa* (creator of the universe), the *sāttva devata* (superintending deity of goodness), the *paramam* (supreme), and so on.

Now let's get back to that battle between the *Suras* and the *Asuras*...

Śrīmad-Bhāgavatam tells how, at a certain point in the battle, the *Suras* (the good guys) were almost defeated. Feeling discouraged, they began to earnestly meditate on Viṣṇu, who immediately came on the scene, seated on the back of Garuḍa.[26] Of course, Viṣṇu's arrival signaled a reversal and

---

[25] Martin Haug, trans., *The Aitareya Brāhmana of the Rigveda: Translation, with Notes* (London: Government Central Book Depot, 1863), 1.

[26] Garuḍa is the great eagle carrier of Lord Viṣṇu. Offspring of Kaśyapa Muni (with his eighth wife, Vinata), Garuḍa is said to be an invincible incarnation of the Brahman feature of the Lord. The flapping of Garuḍa's wings vibrates the hymns of the Sāma-Veda, of which the *Hare Kṛṣṇa Mahā Mantra* is the essence. See canto 8, ch. 10, vv. 52-57 of *Śrīmad-Bhāgavatam*.

ultimate turning point in the battle, and to make a long story short, the *Suras* went on to become victorious.

This, however, is not the end of the story. The *Asuras* (the bad guys) had no intention of giving up. Wanting to seize control of the universe for their own selfish purposes, they devised a strategy by which to proceed—a strategy that resulted in the events of the *Mahā-bhārata*.

(*It was like* Star Wars, *when the "Darth Vader gang" tried to use the Dark Side of the Force to dominate the universe.*)

If you make a study of insurgency movements throughout the world, you'll find that they all follow a similar pattern. There's some political or military force that attempts but fails to seize control of a state or country (be it Chechnya, Colombia, or Nigeria). After failing, they generally withdraw to a remote geographical location where the government forces can't reach them (like the mountains, desert, or jungle). The aim is to retreat to a place that is both topographically and geographically inaccessible—a secluded spot where they can hide out, regroup, and gain strength for their march upon the capital. According to the *Mahā-bhārata,* this is exactly what happened in ancient times.

After Viṣṇu's battlefield appearance and their ultimate defeat, the *Asuras* divided into two camps: one camp, led by Bali, respected Viṣṇu, and so wanted nothing to do with a so-called insurgency; the other camp wanted to continue the fight, being determined to impose their will.

Within the Vedic tradition, by the way, Bali is considered a very great soul due to his relation to Viṣṇu, who he eventually meets face-to-face. This is described in *Śrīmad-Bhāgavatam,*

Canto Eight: the story of Vāmana, the dwarf incarnation.[27]

Now the *Asuras*, even though on the "dark side," also had their *guru*, because a *guru* is simply an empowered teacher, with some *gurus* assisting the godly and others assisting their opposites. In this case, the *guru* of the *Asuras* was Śukrācārya, whose name literally translates as "Professor White," and who possessed a particular *śakti* (a *sañjīvanī mantra*), which worked like this: if the bodies of the *Asuras* had not been completely destroyed in battle, reciting this *mantra* would revive them—literally, bring the soul back into the body. This, of course, is exactly what Śukrācārya did, after which the reanimated *Asuras* formed their insurgency to take over the universe.

Their plan was to go to a remote, out-of-the-way planet—*on the other side of the cosmic tracks*—and to take control by manipulating the power of *dharma,* which even the *Asuras* recognized and respected. By their superior powers, and without violating *dharma*, they would take birth in the families of that planet's ruling dynasties, and eventually rule simply by growing up. But their plans didn't stop there. They would even take birth as carnivorous animals in all the great forests,

---

[27] After the great *Asura* king, Bali Mahārāja, had succeeded in conquering Indra and the *Suras*, he was approached by Vāmanadeva, the disguised child-dwarf incarnation of Viṣṇu. Appearing as a *brāhmaṇa*, Vāmanadeva requested a small boon. Because Bali discerned that the boy was some higher being, he was prepared to offer Him anything He requested. The child asked to be granted three steps of land, to which Bali readily agreed. With His first step, Lord Vāmanadeva strode across the entire upper planetary system; and with His second step, He traversed the entirety of the remaining universe. When King Bali realized that the dwarf was none other than the Supreme Lord Viṣṇu, he humbly requested Vāmanadeva to place His third step on his head. Being pleased with this devotional gesture, Lord Vāmanadeva awarded Bali Mahārāja his own planet, agreeing to become his personal gatekeeper. He also returned control of universal affairs to the *Suras*. See canto 8, ch. 18-23 of *Śrīmad-Bhāgavatam.*

jungles, and mountains that filled ancient India, with the aim of attacking and killing the sages that meditated there for the good of the world. Here, again, the idea was to cleverly destroy these communities without violating *dharma,* since killing human beings is in the nature of carnivorous beasts. It is *paśu* (the animal's) *dharma,* and thus does not incur bad reactions. This was the idea.

Now, it just so happens that the sleepy, little, out-of-the-way planet that the *Asuras* chose to occupy was none other than good ol' planet Earth, and that's the background of the *Mahā-bhārata.* The Earth was chosen. And if you know your *Star Wars,* the *Asuras* wanted to transform Earth into a type of "Death Star": to take over the planet and use it as a launching pad for further operations.

According to the *Vedas,* a particular goddess is responsible for this planet. Indeed, practically all the Sanskrit words for Earth are feminine: *bhū, bhūmi, vasundhara,* and so on. Realizing what was going on, and being unable to deal with the situation, Bhūmi, the goddess of Earth, went to Brahmā,[28] the creator, for help.

I remember back in the 50s when the Hell's Angels first became a cultural force in America, bursting on the scene by invading little towns in the California desert and literally taking them over. Those little towns usually had a sheriff and maybe one or two deputies—like Andy Griffith's Mayberry—

---

[28] Lord Brahmā is considered to be the architect and engineer of the material creation. He is self-born from the body of Viṣṇu, who, in the beginning, supplies him with all the elements, resources, and intelligence to design and generate the entire cosmos. Brahmā is a temporary post with a lifetime term limit, like the post of emperor or king. Brahmā's lifespan, corresponding with the duration of the universe, is calculated as 311 trillion, 40 billion human years, after which a new universe with a new Brahmā comes into being from Lord Viṣṇu.

and suddenly there are 20, 30 or 40 of these tough Hell's Angels roaring through town on their Harleys, and the sheriff can't begin to cope. So what does he do? He gets on the phone and calls the state government for help. The situation in the *Mahā-bhārata* was similar to this.

Bhūmi, like our sheriff, was unable to handle the invasion because the *Asuras* were from the universe's higher sectors, and thus had great material power. Her going to Brahmā for help is a well-known Vedic tale, told not only in the *Mahā-bhārata*, but in other Sanskrit works as well. Brahmā understood the situation to be serious since these were the same *Asuras* that had almost defeated the *Suras* in the celestial battle that I mentioned before. Only Viṣṇu's intervention had saved the day, tipping the balance in the *Suras'* favor. Right now, however, Viṣṇu was not present, so Brahmā went to the "Ocean of Milk" to summon Him by offering prayers.

Here it would be good to mention that the Vedas offer all types of extravagant, fantastical descriptions, and we should avoid being geocentric in our approach. Materialistic scientists, of course, never tire of reminding us that it is they who saved the world from the notion that the Earth is the center of the universe. Yet, when it comes to these extraordinary depictions, many scientists have retained a geocentric view. In other words, they assume that the way things currently happen on Earth are the way they've always happened and the way they happen everywhere else in the universe. But there is no logical reason to make this assumption. There is no logical reason to deny the possibility of things going on in the distant past or the greater universe that are outside our present experience, our awareness, and even our imagination. In the words of Shakespeare, "there are more things in heaven and earth than are dreamt of in your philosophy [or *conceived of* in your *science*]."[29]

Think, for a minute, of an ant crawling on your arm. Although the ant, in one sense, knows more about the topography of that arm than you do, because of its limited consciousness, it cannot comprehend that it crawls on an "arm," which is attached to a "human being," who is part of an entire "civilization." The ant is wholly unaware of the world we inhabit, even though it lives in the same location. Similarly, there's a real sense in which we human beings, with an awareness that barely stretches beyond our surroundings, will never be able to wholly comprehend where we are, what the Earth is, what occurs in other spheres, and so on.

In any case, Brahmā went to the shore of this great ocean and meditated, praying to Viṣṇu. Viṣṇu then telepathically informed Brahmā that He Himself would descend to restore *dharma* and make things right, and that the *Suras* should also take birth to join in the great earthly struggle to come. Viṣṇu also indicated that He would specifically take birth in the Yadu dynasty, one of the world's great dynasties at that time. That, of course, was the birth, the descent, of Kṛṣṇa. Therefore, two popular names of Kṛṣṇa are Yadava and Yadupati,[30] because He appeared in that dynasty.

Meanwhile, back on earth, the *Asuras* were taking birth and beginning the first wave of their insurgency. And while Kṛṣṇa's appearance was yet to come, another *avatāra* came down to assist Him; that *avatāra,* as mentioned earlier, was Vyāsa (or

---

29 From William Shakespeare's *Hamlet* (act 1, scene 5, lines 167-8). Hamlet speaks to Horatio, apprising him of the appearance of the ghost of Hamlet's father, the murdered king.

30 The Sanskrit names Yadava and Yadupati mean, "descendent of Yadu" and "lord of the Yadus," respectively.

Veda Vyāsa), who would participate in the events, recount them, and help to move the action along.

Imagine you are on Earth many, many thousands of years ago, and unsettling things are happening because the *Asuras*, the bad guys, have come. There are unprecedented attacks on *yogīs* and sages in the forests, and people are starting to notice that strange characters are taking birth as princes in important royal families. Of course, the godly people are still there, and they're still the majority on Earth; but things are starting to change, and there's great concern.

So, at this point, I'd like to go directly to some of the *Mahābhārata*'s stories. I'll start by talking about the events surrounding the union of King Śāntanu and the goddess Gaṅgā, and how these events are linked to the story of Satyavatī and her extraordinary relationship with Parāśara, the celebrated sage. It is the story of two couples, each of which came together only to be separated, and how the two remaining partners eventually found each other and fell in love. All this, of course, is of great relevance to subsequent events.

(So prepare yourselves ... For the next few minutes, it'll be getting a little romantic.)

If you look at a world map, apart from the Americas (which are somewhat removed from the rest), what you find is one gigantic land mass consisting of Africa, Europe, and Asia. We can divide it into different continents if we like, but it's actually one mass, comprising most of the world, with India practically at its center. And interestingly, up to around 250 years ago, over a quarter of the world's wealth could be found in India. Even the Roman Empire had severe economic problems because they were importing many items from India, and paying in gold, having nothing else that India wanted in return.

(I guess the Indians back then weren't into Roman statues.)

So anyway, you have this land, this India, which was practically the geographic center of most of the world, and by far the world's richest country *(something that Marco Polo happened to notice)*. Also, according to Megasthenes, an ambassador to India some 2,300 years ago, India was the one place in the world where there was no slavery, and in which there were not only human and animal rights, but also freedom and other types of advantages. India was the civilization that originated *yoga*, and even discovered that the real object of consciousness is *consciousness itself*. And, according to this ancient literature, India also was the place where the *avatāras* appeared.

(It was sort of like their private landing strip ... the "Airport of the Avatars.")

Now, in this highly sophisticated, ancient land, the greatest dynasty was that of the Kurus. In fact, that's why the *Bhagavad-gītā* begins with *dharma-kṣetre kuru-kṣetre*, "on the *dharma* field, on the field of the Kurus." So the Kurus were the great royal family of the time and their king was Śāntanu. It is said that Śāntanu was so virtuous that he had the power to heal by touch; this is mentioned both in the *Bhāgavatam* and in the *Mahā-bhārata*. In fact, that's the etymology of his name: he could bring healing to bodies simply by touching them.

In any case, through various circumstances, this great king Śāntanu one day encountered Gaṅgā, the goddess of the Ganges River, who happened to be visiting Earth at the time. She's not literally Ganges water *(you know, melting Himalayan snow)*; rather, she's the person that is the goddess of the Ganges, and so infuses her own pure nature into the Ganges' waters.

Here the idea is that behind every phenomenon there is a person. For example, here we see that the lights are on and the microphone is working, but this didn't just happen automatically; some *person* saw to these arrangements. The sound system may be mechanical, but there's a person behind its operation. Or let's say that all goes well and there's a nice morning breakfast waiting for us when we rise. This didn't just happen by itself; someone worked very sincerely to prepare this meal. The idea is that personal consciousness is behind everything; nothing is "automatic."

In the same way, there is Gaṅgā, the goddess of the Ganges river, who somehow met King Śāntanu while visiting the Earth. This was not as uncommon as one might think. Indeed, according to this picture of the ancient world, there used to be a great deal of interplanetary intercourse and travel. Nowadays we talk of a "global" village, but the *Mahā-bhārata* gives us the far broader picture of a "cosmic" village. And within that cosmic village, with higher beings trafficking back and forth, somehow King Śāntanu and Gaṅgā met, fell in love, and got married, even though she was a celestial being and he was an earthly man *(in that sense, it was what you might call a "mixed marriage")*.

There's a lot more to their story that I'll have to skip, since we're running out of time. For now, suffice it to say that they eventually have this very powerful child named Devavrata, who will become one of the main figures of the *Mahā-bhārata.* Upon his birth, however, Gaṅgā, for various reasons, could not stay on Earth, and returned to her celestial community, taking her newborn child with her. Śāntanu, of course, was heartbroken, and fell into a deep depression. Eventually, after training Devavrata in the human art of war and endowing him with various superhuman powers, Gaṅgā returned the son to the father, and again went back to the celestial realm. So even though Śāntanu was ecstatic at having his son back, he was still depressed at having lost Gaṅgā for a second time.

Shattered and dejected, Śāntanu was no longer able to govern *(let's face it ... this king really wasn't the bachelor type)*. So he left his ministers in charge of Hastināpur, the Kuru capital, and just started wandering, incognito and alone. And so he wandered, living in forests and so on, traveling hundreds of miles from his capital *(you can actually plot the geography on a map)*, until one day he met a very beautiful young maiden. And although this maiden appeared to come from an unbefitting, lower-class family, things are not always as they seem, and there is a story of how this truly remarkable girl came to be in her present circumstance.

Her name was Satyavatī. *Vatī* in Sanskrit is just the feminine form of *vān*, as in *bhagavān*[31] so the name Satyavatī means "one who possesses" (*vatī*) "truth" (*satya*). She was actually the daughter of King Uparichara Vasu. Remember him? Mr. "Upwardly Mobile Vasu"? Well Satyavatī was his daughter, but he decided not to raise her. Instead, he arranged for his *princess* to be raised by a family of fishing folk. Back then in India, fishing was not considered the most aristocratic occupation; so, relatively speaking, this was basically a lower-class family. Why, then, did Uparichara Vasu do such a thing?

There are different versions of "why" in different *Mahābhāratas*, but my personal view is that Satyavatī was actually

---

[31] *Parāśara* Muni, a great sage and the father of Vyāsadeva (the compiler of the Vedic literatures), offers a definition of God in the *Viṣṇu Purana*, explaining that God is *bhagavān*, one who possesses (*vān*) an unlimited quantity of the following six opulences: wealth, strength, fame, beauty, knowledge, and renunciation (see *Viṣṇu Purana*, book 6, ch. 5, v. 47).

destined to become the mother of an *avatāra* who would start the ball rolling in terms of counteracting the invasion of the Earth. Somehow, Uparichara Vasu knew this, and fearing for his daughter's safety, he sent her to grow up incognito in a fishing village, where even she did not know she was actually a princess.

As you can imagine, back then there was a very conscious, rigorous system of "genetic engineering." Of course, in those times, it was not done artificially, in laboratories, but rather naturally, through very precise marriages. The idea was to create, from these genetic pools, superior classes of human beings—great sages and kings. And since Satyavatī, the descendent of a long line of kings, was herself the product of careful "engineering," she was naturally endowed with all the superlative qualities of a princess: courage, intelligence, extraordinary beauty, and so on. Yet she grew up in this very simple, highly traditional fishing community, expecting to marry a fisherman and spend the rest of her days rowing or catching fish. With all these exceptional attributes blossoming inside, however, Satyavatī often felt restless and out of place, without understanding why.

(Later we'll tell the story of a young boy who also came from an extraordinary background, but who grew up in a lower-class family, never knowing why he felt so frustrated with his lot in life. That boy, of course, was Karna.)

Now Satyavatī's family lived on the Yamunā, and as a young girl, she would row a little boat across that river to earn extra income for her folks. One day, a very unusual person came, wanting to cross the river. It was the great sage Parāśara, who was about to play an important role in the plan to save the Earth—and, ultimately, the universe. For as soon as he saw Satyavatī, Parāśara knew that she was the one who would bring an *avatāra* into this world.

At the time, Satyavatī was an innocent girl in her early teens, growing up in an extremely conservative community. Suddenly, some man she's never seen, steps inside her boat, and literally makes an "indecent" proposal: "Can we just row over to that little island and make a baby?" Yet, as bizarre as this request must have seemed, somehow, Parāśara was able to convince Satyavatī to follow his lead. So they made their way to the island and, together, begot the renowned *avatāra* Vyāsa. And because Vyāsa was born on an island (in Sanskrit, *dvīpa*), he was called Dvaipāyana. Afterwards, Parāśara told Satyavatī that he could no longer stay on Earth, and left.

As for Vyāsa, it is said that, being an *avatāra,* he took birth and immediately grew into a young boy—which surprised Satyavatī even further. The boy then informed his mother that he was immediately leaving home for the Himalayan Mountains, where he would enter a deep trance to acquire the powers needed to perform his mission.

Of course, before leaving, Parāśara had mystically restored Satyavatī's virginity (*a consolation prize?).* But after all that had transpired, one can only imagine the emotional state of this young princess. On the one hand, she thinks she's the daughter of a fisherman, and on the other, she doesn't understand why she can't accept her lot in life. Then, suddenly, her life changes. She meets the great sage Parāśara, and is now dealing not with the lowest but with the highest rung on the social ladder. And this very exalted sage makes a shockingly risqué proposal, gives her a divine child, and leaves; then the child leaves, and again, she's back in her boat. *(And it's like, "Did this really happen?" Because she's back in her boat ... and everybody's gone ... and there she is ... alone.)*

So that's Satyavatī, the beautiful young princess.

Now let's get back to Śāntanu, who's wandering around depressed, with no desire to do anything more in life. Then, as fate would have it, Śāntanu and Satyavatī meet, and they fall in love—and then he explains that, *actually,* he's the emperor of the world.

Naturally, Śāntanu wants to marry Satyavatī, who's still in her teens. And in what happens next, we see an excellent example of the commitment of these ancient people to *dharma*. Even with falling deeply in love, even with the chance of going from rags to riches, they are nonetheless determined to follow *dharma,* regardless of the cost. Being a dutiful young girl, Satyavatī tells Śāntanu, "I must first get my father's blessings." And she's fully prepared to follow whatever decision he makes.

So the two go to Satyavatī's father, who is the king of the fishing folk in this little village. Of course, the father's first reaction is one of astonishment that, suddenly, the great Śāntanu, the Kuru monarch, is standing in his cottage. And the idea that this great king wants to marry his daughter also amazes him. Obviously, he wants the marriage, but being somewhat shrewd by nature, he says:

"I'd like to give my blessings, but I have a problem. You have a son, Devavrata, who is famous throughout the world, not only as the greatest warrior, but also as someone with superhuman powers. And it is he that is destined to inherit the Kuru throne. This means that the son of my daughter, my grandson, will never rule the kingdom. More than that, he must always live in fear, because who knows what Devavrata might do to him? I can't approve this marriage because I fear for my future grandson's life."

At this point, Śāntanu, who had indeed already promised the kingdom to Devavrata, wouldn't do or say anything due to his strict adherence to *dharma*.

It's interesting to compare this reaction to what we know about the European monarchy, or monarchies in other parts of the world, where such "impudence" would have been dealt with quite differently: "Would you like to keep your head on your shoulders? Give me your daughter! You can give me your daughter with your head *on* or your head *off*. It's up to you!"

In contrast, because Śāntanu was so devoted to *dharma*, he would not dare violate the relationship between a father and a daughter. Think of it! Here's this Emperor, this great king, and here's this fisherman, who's an absolute nobody on the social ladder. Yet the Emperor honors the relationship between the father and the daughter, even at the cost of his own desire and happiness, because that's *dharma*. And very reluctantly, practically more depressed than ever, Śāntanu returns to the city of Hastināpur, unwilling to discuss the matter with anyone.

Of course, it doesn't take long for anyone that actually knows the king to notice that he's more miserable, more depressed, more listless than ever. Eventually, Śāntanu tells his ministers everything. Still, the king could not bring himself to tell Devavrata, "my misery stems from promising the kingdom to you."

For his part, however, Devavrata wasn't blind. Seeing his father moping around, looking pale and withdrawn, he directly questioned the king about the cause of his suffering. Yet even then, Śāntanu would only answer with vague, roundabout sayings like: "We *kṣatriyas* (warriors) have a very dangerous family business," "For a *kṣatriya*, having one son is like having no son," "The life expectancy of a *kṣatriya* is not very long," and so on. Śāntanu insisted that his anxiety over the dynasty was the sole cause of his sadness, and left it at that.

Devavrata, however, could sense that there was something

more. As a last resort, he went to Śāntanu's ministers to find out if his father had told *them* the truth. After a while, and perhaps with some hesitancy, they finally explained his father's predicament: wandering to distant lands, meeting Satyavatī, again falling in love, wanting to marry, the fisher king's demands, and so on.

Understanding everything, Devavrata immediately set out for Satyavatī's village, went to the fisher king and said: "I want to bring your daughter to my father, and if the problem is the throne, let me assure you that, number one, I renounce all claims, and number two, I will never fight for another kingdom against the rightful heir."

Satyavatī's father was amazed that this highly qualified prince had so much love for Śāntanu that he would abandon his claim to the greatest throne on Earth, just to make him happy. There was no doubt in his mind that Devarata meant every word and would strictly keep his vow. But he had one more concern: Devavrata's sons, if he should have any. How could he be sure that one of them wouldn't act against his grandson in the future?

If we study the history of monarchies throughout the world, we'll find that the fisher king's anxiety was well placed. In the history of both the Roman and the Mogul empires, for example, there were sometimes century-long periods in which not one of their rulers died peacefully in bed *(and not because of being killed in battle, if you know what I mean)*. The history of the monarchy is checkered, to say the least!

And so to ease this final doubt, Devavrata made a vow that has become famous throughout India—and, to some degree, beyond. It even has a name, *bhīṣma pratigya*, "the terrible oath": never to marry, never to have children, but to remain celibate for the rest of his life. But why "terrible," or "awful" (in the original Old English sense of "awe-full," meaning awesome or awe-inspiring)?

It was because Devavrata wasn't some *yogī* or *svāmī*, who takes vows of celibacy as a matter of course. He was this young scion of the Kuru dynasty, this virile, passionate warrior, with royal blood burning in his veins. Thus his particular renunciation of wife, children, and so on was considered almost frightening. In fact, as soon as Devavrata made that vow, flower petals floated down from the celestial worlds, and the sound *"bhīṣma"* could be heard echoing from the sky. It seems that Devavrata's vow was so "terrible" that even the gods were filled with awe. And from then on Devavrata became known as Bhīṣma. In a sense, the gods changed Devavrata's name to Bhīṣma because of that vow—which, by the way, finally satisfied the fisher king, who happily approved the union of Śāntanu and Satyavatī.

Bhīṣma carried Satyavatī back to the Kuru capital and presented her to his father, letting him know that all barriers to their wedding had been removed. The marriage took place, and everyone was happy, at least for some time.

Eventually, however, things took a turn for the worse ...

Ambā: The Lady Scorned

Devavrata had renounced his claim to the Kuru kingdom, taken a lifelong vow of celibacy, and received the name Bhīṣma for his "terrible vow." Satyavatī's father had finally approved the marriage, and she and King Śāntanu soon tied the knot. After a while (and this is where we pick things up today), they had two sons: Citrāṅgada, their first born, and Vicitravīrya.

While all these events were taking place in and around the Kuru capital, the *Asuras (remember them?)* had been infiltrating the Earth in greater and greater numbers, and it was only because of Śāntanu's powerful presence that they were still unable to act. The king had extraordinary influence, and so, in a sense, the world was still relatively safe.

Of course, time catches up with even the greatest king, and an aging Śāntanu eventually retires, enters the forest, and passes away. After the death of the king, his eldest son Citrāṅgada inherits the Kuru throne, but meets an untimely death at the hands of a Gandharva.

If you know your *Lord of the Rings*, Gandharvas are something like the elves of that story: this liminal species that tends to come in and out of earthly affairs, causing frequent tensions between themselves and human beings. In the case of Citrāṅgada, he is challenged by a powerful Gandharva who also happens to be named Citrāṅgada. Basically, the Gandharva tells the Kuru king that he'd better change his name—or else! *(It was like, "this town ain't big enough for two Citrāṅgadas." I guess he had a little too much "Gandharva testosterone" or something ...)*

Of course, the Kuru king was himself a proud young warrior who obviously had no intention of yielding to such an absurd demand. So the two Citrāṅgadas do battle, fighting for a very long time. In the end, the Gandharva makes use of a supernatural weapon to kill the king—which, of course, is a disaster not only for Satyavatī, but for the entire Kuru kingdom. The only remaining heir is the younger brother, who next assumes the throne. But Vicitravīrya is still only a boy, unable to govern on his own. So Bhīṣma is asked to serve as regent, with Vicitravīrya as his ward.

All monarchies require the reigning king to produce a male heir, and the ancient Kuru kingdom was no different. Therefore, as soon as Vicitravīrya came of age, he was naturally called upon to marry, produce children, and keep the dynasty going.

Now, Bhīṣma had heard that the king of Kāśī[32] had three beautiful daughters named Ambā, Ambikā and Ambālikā ...

(... which, in Sanskrit, means, "Ambā," "little Ambā," and "little bitty Ambā." I mentioned, didn't I, that Sanskrit can sometimes make you laugh!? In Spanish, by the way, their names would be Amba, Ambita, and Ambititta.)

Bhīṣma also had heard that these princesses were just about to have their *svayaṁvara* ceremony—a prevalent

---

[32] Kāśī is the ancient name for modern day Banāras also known as Vārāṇaṣī. Often called the spiritual center of India, this North Indian city has welcomed pilgrims to its sacred Ganges shores and its over 2,000 temples for several millenia. Mark Twain said of this great center of learning and civilization, "Banāras is older than history, older than tradition, older even than legend and looks twice as old as all of them put together" (from Mark Twain, *Following the Equator: A journey around the world*. (Hartford: American Pub. Co, 1897), 480).

ceremony among this ancient culture's *kṣatriya* (warrior) class. *Svayaṁvara* literally means "personal choice," *svayaṁ* (personal), *vara* (choice), and this is how it works:

The princess, in consultation with her father, would design a particular challenge (some difficult feat of valor or weapons competition). They would then set a time and place, and spread the word to all the qualified princes of the world. On the day of the challenge, the princes would come from all directions, and the one that outdid the rest would win the maiden's hand. Generally, of course, the princess and her father would not exactly rig, but very much tilt, the outcome by creating a task that favored the prince they wanted to win. The victorious prince would then be garlanded by the princess, indicating that she would give her heart to him.

Now, for Ambā, Ambikā and Ambālikā, their father had arranged a major event: a triple *svayaṁvara*! And many princes, and even kings, traveled to Kāśī to compete—with the exception of Vicitravīrya.

Being the Kuru king, the leading monarch of the realm, Vicitravīrya certainly was expected to compete in the *svayaṁvara*. Yet, at the insistence of both Bhīṣma and Satyavatī, the still young king remained at home, and Bhīṣma went in his stead, pledging to bring the girls back to him. But why this decision?

Perhaps it was because Bhīṣma had become extremely protective of Vicitravīrya, having experienced the untimely death of Citrāṅgada. Certainly, he would have been aware of the dire consequences should this last remaining heir be killed. With both Citrāṅgada and Vicitravīrya dead, there would be no Kuru king. And so Bhīṣma personally went to compete, leaving his young stepbrother safely at home.

One important note: The Kuru king was considered the leading monarch (or emperor), but not in the way "emperor" was understood in the later Roman Empire, where there's one person on top who governs all. The ancient Vedic model was more like the European model at the time of the Magna Carta, where the leading monarch was known in Latin as *primus inter pares,* which translates as "first among equals." There's absolutely no record in any Vedic text of an emperor interferring with or taking charge of the internal affairs of any other kingdom. Instead, the Kuru monarch would lead an alliance of kings that would provide for the security of everyone. In return, the other kingdoms would offer some form of tribute to this leading king. The political history of these ancient cultures is another fascinating topic, but for now we'd better rejoin Bhīṣma on his way to the *svayaṁvara*.

What's interesting here is that when Bhīṣma rode into the arena, representing the imperial crown, it wasn't like one of those typical Hollywood movies about Rome, where the emperor rides in on his chariot bearing the Roman Eagle, and all others bow and scrape while he does or takes what he likes. Even though Bhīṣma was the regent of the Kuru empire, he still had to compete like everyone else.

In fact, when Bhīṣma showed up, there was quite a bit of murmuring from the crowd. Remembering his "terrible vow," they turned to each other and said something like, "What in the world is Bhīṣma, of all people, doing at a *svayaṁvara*?" And, as one might expect, there were more than a few chuckles and unkind jests going around at Bhīṣma's expense.

(Let's face it! Here was this person who had become famous throughout the world for his vow of lifelong celibacy. And then he shows up at a wedding *competition? What's* that *about?)*

So there was all this joking and many sarcastic remarks. Bhīṣma, however, being the most powerful warrior in the world, would soon be laughing last.

Without waiting to compete in the contest or asking anyone's permission, Bhīṣma simply thundered up to the three girls, swooped them into his arms, and placed them in his chariot—stunning the entire crowd. He then turned to all the princes and said, "I've just taken these three prizes by force. Now you can destroy me or be destroyed as you like. I'm ready to fight." And with that, Bhīṣma sped away!

Of course, all the fierce, young, out of control warriors went into hyper-drive. Taking up their weapons, they began to attack Bhīṣma with all their might. And Bhīṣma, who Gaṅgā had endowed with special training and powers, was thinking, "Oh! This is gonna be fun!" Then, without even breaking a sweat, he easily defeated all comers, with the exception of one. It was Śālva, who fought ferociously, presenting Bhīṣma with his most sporting challenge. In the end, of course, Śālva was defeated as well. It was a humiliating public thrashing for these proud *kṣatriya* warriors, after which Bhīṣma rode to Hastināpura with the maidens in tow.

(I always wondered what happened to those three girls during that fight. Apparently, they were in the chariot with Bhīṣma, but the text doesn't mention what they were doing. I guess they just had to keep ducking. In any case, somehow or other the girls survived without getting theirs heads lopped off, and Bhīṣma brought them back to Hastināpura.)

Now, in general, the opportunity to marry into the Kuru dynasty, the seat of world power at that time, would have been extremely prestigious for any princess—almost like a dream come true. But on the way back, the oldest girl, Ambā, told

Bhīṣma of a major problem: she had already given her heart to Śālva, the *kṣatriya* that had just given Bhīṣma his greatest challenge. Ambā explained that things were pre-arranged for Śālva to win the day, and all was going well until Bhīṣma ruined everything. "What will you do now," she asked, "since I've already given my heart to another king?"

Soon they reached the palace, and Bhīṣma immediately went to Vicitravīrya to discuss the matter of Ambā. They reasoned that because Ambā had already given her heart to Śālva, and he had given his to her, the best thing would be to simply send her back. Ambikā and Ambālikā were a different matter. With no prior commitments, they were delighted to marry into the world's greatest dynasty. For them, it was not a problem at all.

After Ambā had rested and refreshed herself for a couple of days, Bhīṣma arranged for a proper escort to Śālva's kingdom. Ambā set out with a happy heart and high hopes for the future.

And here begins one of the great, yet tragic, stories of the *Mahā-bhārata*.

When Ambā reaches the palace, she can't wait to see Śālva. The last time he saw her, Ambā and her sisters had been taken by Bhīṣma, who drove off after humiliating all the princes. But now, things have changed. Ambā is free. She has renounced the queenship of the greatest dynasty on Earth, all for love of Śālva. In all innocence and with a very pure heart, Ambā goes to tell Śālva the good news. But their so-called reunion is not to be—and that's putting it mildly. It is almost as if Ambā has become a total stranger.

(Not the first time in history that a girl discovers, too late, that her boyfriend's a jerk.)

To be fair, Śālva had been publicly humiliated by Bhīṣma,

who had forcefully taken Ambā for himself (or Vicitravīrya). For Śālva, taking Ambā back after Bhīṣma had sent her away was like taking Bhīṣma's remnants—his discarded leftovers—in charity. *Brāhmaṇas* could receive charity, but warriors were forbidden. That was their culture. To take Ambā back is more than Śālva can bear—it is almost worse than death. His rejection is firm and harsh: there would be no reunion, nor even an exchange of words. He wants absolutely nothing to do with her—*finito!*

There was another thing at play here as well. People of those times had a very strict moral code, which sometimes led to unreasonable moral choices and very bad consequences (as we'll soon see). In Ambā's case, according to the *dharma-śāstras,* the fact that she had spent a few unescorted days and nights at the Kuru palace—another man's "home"—basically took her off the marriage market.[33] But good moral judgement also requires the ability to distinguish between rule and exception—something that Śālva sorely lacked.

When the Kurus decided to deliver Ambā to Śālva, she didn't go at once. It had been a long, grueling trip from Kāśī, so Ambā was allowed to rest for a few days at the Kuru palace, which is all that she did. But to Śālva, who was a bit of blunt instrument, the fact that Ambā had spent even one unchaperoned night in another king's palace was enough. This, coupled with his public thrashing and loss of face, disqualified Ambā for all time: "Who are you? I don't even know you. What are you doing here? Are you trying to rub salt in my wounds?"

---

33 *Dharma-śāstras* are Vedic society's lawbooks regarding the morality, ethics, duties, and rights that pertain to specific social classes. The ancient *Manu-smṛiti*, originally enunciated by Brahmā's son, Svāyambhuva Manu, contains the most comprehensive treatment of such codes of conduct and is still regarded by many in modern India as an ideal canon of order.

And Ambā kept pleading, "You don't understand, I did this for you!"

And if I had to guess, I'd say that for Śālva it was more about pride than morality. Like I said, he really was kind of a royal jerk. His pride was more important than anything, including Ambā's love. So he just turned his back and turned her out.

To really get a feel for the heart-wrenching nature of this drama, it's important to understand that Ambā had been raised from birth as an honored princess. She had the perfect life. Nothing ever went wrong. Then, at her *svayaṁvara*, the happiest moment of her life, when she's just about to choose her husband and become a queen, everything suddenly goes wrong—and keeps on going wrong after that.

Ambā made her way back to the Kuru kingdom and told Bhīṣma everything. "Now there is no alternative, she said, "I must marry Vicitravīrya." The light was dawning that her options were rapidly shrinking. But Bhīṣma's response was as shocking as Śālva's: "I'm sorry for what happened to you, but you can no longer marry Vicitravīrya. You shouldn't have spent the night in Śālva's house."

Sometimes in popular Hinduism it is thought that Amba's anger stemmed from Bhīṣma's refusing to marry her due to his vow. But what really enraged Ambā, and led to Bhīṣma's death, was his unjust conclusion that she was no longer fit to marry Vicitravīrya.

So you have this tragic situation of a princess who is truthful, virtuous, and impeccable in her conduct, who acted out of love and, even from a moral point of view, was completely pure and faultless. Yet she goes from one powerful warrior to the other, being disbelieved and rejected at every turn.

To spice things up a bit, some versions of the *Mahā-bhārata* depict Ambā shuttling back and forth between Bhīṣma and Śālva many times—pleading and being rejected again and again. But given the character of this young princess, I don't think that would have happened. It seems that at a certain point in its retelling, the story of Ambā, already a tragedy, became something of a farce.

The actual story is basically that Śālva rejected her, then Bhīṣma rejected her, and her whole life collapsed overnight. Why? Because even though she was telling the truth and her virtue remained intact, neither Bhīṣma nor Śālva would give her the benefit of the doubt. Ambā was now "damaged goods," and no *kṣatriya* would have her.

This is one of the more powerful and moving stories of the *Mahā-bhārata*.

Eventually, all of Ambā's heartbreak, shock, and sorrow gave way to a terrible, burning rage over what these *kṣatriyas* had done to her—a rage that would ultimately cost both Śālva and Bhīṣma their lives. But that's a long way off. At this point, Ambā is receiving the "standard" advice from everyone: "Go back to your father, go back to your family, because there's really nothing left for you to do."

To understand what happens next, we must remember that Ambā is a royal princess, with the blood of a female warrior flowing in her veins. And given the conservative nature of this ancient religious civilization, what Ambā decides to do is truly amazing and unique. This is a civilization in which women are meant to be under a man's protection at every stage of life. But Ambā goes in an entirely different direction—the path almost never traveled by a woman of those times. Rather than going back to her family, she will strike out on her own, and with only one purpose in mind: *Revenge!*

Alone, Ambā enters the forest, seeking her grandfather, who has retired and become part of a community of sages and ascetics. When they hear her story, these austere men feel so badly for Ambā that they actually begin to weep out of pity, and her grandfather, crying, takes her on his lap. Still, at the end of the day, these sages echo the advice of the others: "What else can you do? Where else can you go? You must go back to your family!"

(It wasn't like modern times, you know, where a "scorned girl" can just say, "The heck with it! I'll move to New York, manage a hedge fund, and get a new boyfriend." It wasn't that kind of culture at all.)

But Ambā will not hear of it. She will have her revenge at all costs, regardless of what it takes. She sits down and starts to reflect on all that has happened, thinking about callous Bhīṣma and pitiless Śālva. And while she's extremely angry at both, she settles on Bhīṣma as the primary architect of her misfortune. Sure, Śālva turned out to be a real "blankety-blank," but Bhīṣma—*Bhīṣma!*—was the one she really wanted to suffer. But to take on someone like Bhīṣma, you need a lot of empowerment. And to obtain that power, Amba remains deep within the forest, by the bank of the Yamunā, and begins practicing a rigorous, almost frightening form of *tapasya*, thinking only of her revenge.

Within this *yoga* culture there's always the idea that *tapasya*—austerity, self-abnegation, self-denial—leads to power. In the case of Ambā, even the other *yogīs* are frightened by her determination. Finally, Śiva himself comes before Ambā and grants her the power to kill Bhīṣma. Having achieved all that she requires, Ambā is ready for the next life. She throws herself into the sacrificial fire, crying, "*bhīṣma-vadhāyeti,*" "to the killing of Bhīṣma!"[34] As "Ambā," she's limited. Her ultimate revenge requires a new body.

There's obviously far more to be told about Ambā, and we'll learn all about her new birth and ultimate revenge in the days to come.

Meanwhile, back at the Kuru ranch, another sad story unfolds. Vicitravīrya marries Ambā's younger sisters, Ambikā and Ambālikā. As a youth, Vicitravīrya was totally dedicated to *dharma*. But after his marriage, something changed. Now, all he seems to care about is prolonging his honeymoon. Bascially, he goes into the royal bedchambers and never comes out—at least for some time.

The text explains that Vicitravīrya so over-indulged in personal gratification that he contracted the disease *yakṣma*, known in English as consumption, and later, as tuberculosis. The disease eventually kills the young king, who leaves behind two beautiful widows, but not a single heir. This, of course, throws the Kuru dynasty into a full-blown crisis.

The Kuru dynasty, as described in the *Mahā-bhārata,* had existed for century upon century, always upholding *dharma,* always giving shelter to all living beings. And although people were not aware of it at the time, it was the Kuru dynasty that would protect the world from the attempted takeover of the *Asura* insurrectionists.

But suddenly, everything is thrown into jeopardy! Vicitravīrya, the last legitimate Kuru king, dies without leaving an heir. Bhīṣma, of course, is still there. But his renunciation of the throne and his vow of celibacy make it impossible for him to rule

---

[34] V.S. Sukthankar, et al, bk. 5 (Udyogaparvan), sect. 188 of *Critical Edition of the Mahābhārata.* (Poona, India: Bhandarkar Oriental Research Institute, 1966), 18a.

or produce heirs. The crisis was unprecedented!

Satyavatī was younger than Bhīṣma, who had actually brought her back to his father. Still, being the widow of Śāntanu, she was by law the Queen Mother and, by marriage, Bhīṣma's stepmother. She was now an integral part of the historic Kuru dynasty, and with the kingdom on the verge of collapse, she felt the burden of doing something about it. In her legitimate role as stepmother, she had a private talk with Bhīṣma about his vow. She said that while she admired his resolve, this was a time to think first of the dynasty and the protection of *dharma*. Bhīṣma would have to accept his stepbrother's widows and produce heirs. There was no other way.

At this point, Bhīṣma gives a very famous speech in which he flatly declines this extraordinary opportunity. To sum it up, he basically says, "Let the whole planet explode! Let the universe descend into chaos! I will not break my vow!"

Bhīṣma's reaction is interesting, since by analyzing the actions of various characters in the *Mahā-bhārata*—Bhīṣma's, and later, Kṛṣṇa's and others—we can easily discern different moral philosophies. Western philosophers, for example, would identify Bhīṣma's current moral outlook as "act-based" or "deontological" ethics: the idea that the act itself is moral or immoral, and that any possible, or even probable, consequences must be disregarded. This is a good description of Bhīṣma's stance: "The consequences don't matter. I gave my word, and I'll keep it! That's my morality! And if that causes the ruin of the Kuru dynasty, the destruction of *dharma*, the *Asuras'* takeover of the Earth, *so be it!* It is the act of keeping my vow that matters most." *(Amazingly, Immanuel Kant actually held this position as well.)*

Fortunately, as we will see later in the *Mahā-bhārata*,

Kṛṣṇa's moral teaching is far removed from Bhīṣma's "act-based" perspective. In fact, it is Kṛṣṇa's strong view that "an act's consequences are very much a part of the act." In other words, when you do something and you know there will be certain consequences, the moral quality of your decision (or conduct) is based not on the act alone, but rather on the act *and* its consequences.

Actually, much later in the *Mahā-bhārata,* Kṛṣṇa will tell "Grandfather Bhīṣma" the story of a sage who was proud of always telling the truth. Anyone asking him a question would always receive an *entirely honest* answer. One time, a group of innocent people ran in terror through his *āśrama* and hid in the forest, being pursued from town by murderous thieves. Knowing of the sage's reputation for honesty, the thieves went to him and asked if he knew where those innocents were hiding.

"Yes," he replied.

"Well, where are they?"

"They're right over there, behind those trees."

Thanks to the blind honesty of this sage, the criminals easily found, robbed, and killed their victims. Kṛṣṇa reveals the sage's fate: because he told the truth, he went to hell. Why? He knowingly caused the death of innocent people—that was the *consequence* of his so-called *act* of truth.

Bhīṣma will eventually come around and become one of Kṛṣṇa's greatest devotees. But in terms of this crisis, and Satyavatī pressing him to produce an heir, for Bhīṣma, it is the act of keeping his vow that is most important—nothing else matters. He refuses to marry; he refuses to beget heirs to the Kuru throne. Satyavatī is now desperate, seeing no way forward—until Bhīṣma himself comes up with another solution.

And with that cliffhanger, we'll end for today!

The Sages: Secrets Kept, Secrets Revealed

When we stopped yesterday, Satyavatī was desperately trying to persuade Bhīṣma to accept Vicitravīrya's childless widows. But Bhīṣma had taken a lifetime vow of celibacy and simply wouldn't hear of it. He adamantly refused! He did, however, offer another way forward, upheld by *dharma*.

It's interesting that whenever problems like this arise in the *Mahā-bhārata*, people always refer to *dharma*. When something must be done, it must be done according to *dharma*. Nowadays, when trying to deal with some issue, say, a problem in the community, one generally looks for a solution that doesn't violate the law. If someone proposes a particular solution, for example, someone else might say: "Sounds good, but is that legal? Can we really do that?"

But it's very different when the law is actually sacred—when it's more than something we follow just to avoid getting into trouble or something like that. There's a famous line in a central verse of the *Śrīmad-Bhāgavatam* that nicely explains the way Vedic culture views *dharma*: *dharmaṁ tu sākṣād bhagavat-praṇītaṁ*,[35] which literally means, "*dharma* is that which is personally brought forth by the Lord." Thus, *dharma* is the law of the universe, the law of God—something more

---

[35] See canto 6, ch.3, v.19 of *Śrīmad Bhāgavatam.*

serious than just avoiding legal troubles, staying out of jail, or dodging a fine.

So Bhīṣma explains to Satyavatī that there is a *dharma* for situations in which a dynasty has no heir, and no way of begetting one. In such extreme cases, with a dynasty at stake, *dharma* allows for a *ksatriyā* (the feminine form of *kṣatriya*) to beget a child with a pure-hearted *brāhmaṇa* who is free from lust; further, the child that is produced through such a union belongs entirely to the mother and the *deceased* father (the king).

Nowadays, of course, we have artificial insemination, whereby a childless couple can have a child that is legally theirs with the help of a biological donor. And, just as in ancient times, the donor has no legal claim upon the child that's produced. Thus in both Vedic and modern times there have been similar solutions to these types of problems. And this was just one of many practical problems in Vedic civilization that were handled by applying different *dharmas*.

In the texts, for example, we find mention of something called *āpad-dharma* (*āpad* means "emergency" or "crisis"). Let's say you look out your window one night and notice your neighbor's house on fire, with the parents gone and the children sleeping in bed. So you run to their house, break windows, kick down doors, and do whatever it takes to grab those kids and take them to safety. Everyone applauds, and you even get your "fifteen-minutes" on the nightly news. But now let's say there is no fire in your neighbor's house, yet you run over, kick down doors, grab their kids, and bring them to your house. This time you've got some serious criminal problems! We can all see the difference.

So this special category called *āpad-dharma* was meant for

just such emergencies. There are Sanskrit statements, for example, directing that such things should never be done *anāpadi*, "unless there is an actual emergency." This is a very typical statement in the literature.

So here, Bhīṣma suggests the *dharma* that allows Ambikā and Ambālikā to beget a legitimate Kuru heir by coupling with a pure-hearted *brāhmaṇa*. At this point, Satyavatī, with great embarrassment, takes Bhīṣma to the side and tells him something very private and confidential: the secret of the child that she and the sage Parāśara begot prior to her marriage to Śāntanu. One can imagine that this was one tough conversation, especially given the conservative nature of that civilization. Surprisingly, however, Bhīṣma took the news quite well, particularly when he discovered that his newfound "brother" was a highly exalted *brāhmaṇa*—indeed the greatest of all the *brāhmaṇas* on Earth. What better choice to perpetuate the Kuru dynasty?

Now, when the *avātara* Vyāsa took birth, grew to boyhood, and abruptly left for the Himālayas, he was not completely insensitive to the fact that Satyavatī was his mother. Thus, before departing, he told her, "If you ever need me, just meditate, remembering me, and I'll appear."

And so this is exactly what Satyavatī does: she sits down in meditation, remembering her remarkable son, and, true to his word, Vyāsa immediately appears before her. She then explains the problem, as well as Bhīṣma's proposed solution, asking her son if he will kindly be that *brāhmaṇa*.

While Vyāsa agrees to his mother's proposal, he explains something very significant and suggests a way forward that will produce the best results. First he explains the obvious: the consciousness of the father and mother at the moment of conception will determine the quality of the child.

(That's why it's best not to be staggeringly drunk on the dance floor when conceiving. You never know who you're letting into your life.)

In any case, with this consideration in mind, Vyāsa suggests that since Ambikā and Ambālikā had just experienced the trauma of losing a young husband, it would be wise to allow the girls a year to recover. During that year, he explains, they should accept a *vrata* (a vow) to engage in *yoga* (meditation); this would raise their consciousness to the highest possible level, thus guaranteeing a glorious Kuru heir. Taking that year would also give them time to prepare for their awkward role and adjust to Vyāsa's singular appearance.

Now don't get me wrong. It's not that Vyāsa was ugly or something like that. It's just that he was a sage, an ascetic, who'd been living in the mountains for quite some time. If you've ever seen photos of India's Kumbh Mela festival, which always includes some very unusual characters, you probably know what I mean. I don't know if Vyāsa had dreadlocks or anything like that, but he was definitely fresh from the mountains, and the text talks about that. Also, being an *avatāra*, Vyāsa had large, piercing eyes, which, at first sight, might have startled the girls and disturbed their consciousness. They were, after all, girls that had always been surrounded by the opulence, beauty, and refinement of palace life.

For all these reasons, Vyāsa advised a waiting period of one year before the girls actually conceived—and this really was sagacious advice, coming, as it did, from the world's greatest sage! Unfortunately, Satyavatī rejected his approach, reasoning that any delay would only further prolong the problem of a Kuru dynasty without a king—a problem that was already starting to affect the kingdom.

The *Mahā-bhārata* mentions that during this period, other kingdoms had been taking advantage of the Kuru dynasty's lapse of leadership. Some began stealing Kuru land and violating Kuru borders. And, even more ominously, certain evil kings were making moves and threatening the kingdom. It's really not that different from today, where we have certain world leaders that are extremely threatening and oppressive, and everybody knows their names. Back then, similar types were starting to oppress their neighbors, taking advantage of the fact that for the first time in history there was no Kuru monarch to ensure world peace. And Satyavatī, as the Queen Mother, felt the burden of this decline and the pressure to do something about it.

Vyāsa countered that one more year wouldn't make much difference in terms of dealing with these problems, but could make an enormous difference when it came to the quality of the Kuru heirs. Vyāsa could easily account for himself as the father, but he had no control over the consciousness of the mothers at the time of conception. Again, he strongly advised Satyavatī to wait. But Satyavatī was unwilling to heed Vyāsa's warning. She insisted that it must be done now—a decision that would cause a great deal of trouble in the future.

There's a scene in the *Mahā-bhārata* where Satyavatī goes to her daughters-in-law one-by-one and tries to persuade them to conceive a child with Vyāsa, who was a great sage, it's true, *but probably not the guy of their dreams*. So Satyavatī talks to them convincingly of the gravity of the situation, and the queens gradually understand. Feeling it their duty to ensure the preservation of the dynasty, they agree, but not without a good deal of trepidation and anxiety. Satyavatī decides to begin with Ambikā, the oldest.

As I talk, I can't help wondering about the psychological impact of all these challenging events on these young women: first they have to witness the humiliation of Ambā; then their young husband dies of a debilitating disease; then there are all these problems of succession and dynastic collapse; and finally, they've got to be intimate with this "most peculiar" personage. One can only imagine their anxious state of consciousness as the time for conception neared.

When Vyāsa came to Ambikā, she was immediately taken aback by his appearance. Vyāsa was a powerful, luminous sage, but he also had this long, matted hair. And, let's face it, *it's not like he donned a tuxedo just for her*. To the contrary, he wore what he always wore—the typical "forest dress" of an ancient sage: deerskin, acquired not by killing a live deer, but by removing the skin of a dead one. (Among sages, it was commonly supposed that the skin of a deer kept carnivorous beasts away.)

Vyāsa's unconventional appearance, coupled with the fact that she was still mourning her dead husband, was far more than Ambikā could bear. She was so startled and overwhelmed by the situation that when Vyāsa entered her bed, she submitted, but closed her eyes during the act. She just didn't want to see what was going on.

When Vyāsa emerged from Ambikā's room, Satyavatī anxiously asked about the outcome—because, as an *avātara* sage, Vyāsa could envisage the future. Soberly, he told his mother, "During conception, Ambikā closed her eyes and would not look at me. Thus, although she will have a son, he will be blind from birth." That son, of course, was Dhṛtarāṣṭra, the eldest of the new generation of Kuru *kṣatriyas* conceived by Vyāsa.

Satyavatī, of course, was devastated because she knew that a blind king could not rule, leaving the problem of succession unresolved. But *why not* a blind king? It's really quite understandable. Ancient Vedic civilization wasn't like today's, where a president or prime minister declares war and then sits nine stories down in a secure bunker, watching the action via live feed.

In the Kurus' time, if a ruler declared war, he had to be first in the field, first to risk his life, and so on. Vedic kings had to personally patrol their kingdoms to make sure everything was in order. And if difficulties arose, they had to personally don their armor, strap on their weapons, and lead their troops into battle. This approach, of course, turned out to be a natural restraint on warfare, since, as in chess, you want to avoid endangering your king!

In any case, because of these standard obligations, there was no way that a blind heir could step into the role of king; it wasn't a feasible option. Therefore, Satyavatī asked Vyāsa to try again, this time with the youngest, Ambālikā.

Now, Ambālikā was aware of what had happened to her sister, so this girl was gonna keep her eyes open no matter what! But when Vyāsa entered her bed, although her eyes were open and she did the needful, Ambālikā was so unnerved by the situation that she literally turned pale with shock and disbelief. Afterward, Vyāsa had to tell his mother, "Ambālikā kept her eyes open, but turned white with anxiety during conception. Therefore, although her child will be highly qualified, he will be very pale."

It's interesting how the reaction of each queen (her

consciousness) had a direct bearing on the child. Sure enough, just as Vyāsa had predicted, Ambālikā's newborn was very light-skinned; so they named him Pāṇḍu, which means "pale." After a few years, however, Satyavatī was thinking: "First a blind child, then a pale one; why not try a third time to see if we can produce a truly perfect heir?"

So Satyavatī again approached the elder sister Ambikā and suggested that she try once more, this time calmly and with open eyes. Ambikā considered this a truly dreadful prospect, but at this stage, she was too emotionally drained to argue with her mother-in-law. Instead, she summoned a very beautiful maidservant to take her place in bed.

As soon as Vyāsa entered the room, he immediately understood that the person waiting for him was not Ambikā, but rather a maidservant. This particular maidservant, however, felt great respect and appreciation for Vyāsa, and thus treated him with all the consideration he deserved. And because this girl was so wise in appreciating this great sage, her son, Vidura, was the wisest of them all. In fact, the *"vid"* in the name Vidura is also found in the word *veda,* which means "knowledge." Vidura, however, was also disqualified from taking the throne, having been born of a maidservant.

A quick comment: It is quite a common theme in much of world literature that someone in a so-called lower position actually has the best character—like this maidservant, who remains unnamed in the text.

After the birth of Vidura (which also contained some anomaly), Vyāsa said, "I think we should just call it a season," and returned to the mountains. So now there were three Kuru offspring, but only one with the qualification to assume the Kuru throne: Pāṇḍu. Thus, despite his "complexion issue" (which was not a major thing), Pāṇḍu became king, and there was great rejoicing in the kingdom.

At this juncture, a question arises that's worth exploring. Bhīṣma, as we know, was a great warrior. We know that he was part-human, part-god, and that he received military training in the celestial worlds, where he was given extraordinary powers and weapons. We also saw how handily he crushed the princes that battled with him at Ambā and her sisters' *svayaṁvara*. And, in the future, we will see how his military prowess remained undiminished, making "Grandfather Bhīṣma" the greatest, most respected general of the Kuru-kṣetra war.

Given all this, one could legitimately ask why there was a crisis at all? Why were Kuru lands being stolen? Why was there aggression and turmoil? What was the problem, since Bhīṣma was there? Why didn't *he* protect the realm till the next king came along?

Logically speaking, the answer must lie in the fine print of Bhīṣma's vow never to become king. Absent a Kuru heir, Bhīṣma's involvement in temporarily overseeing dynastic affairs would have amounted to an independent exercise of power, thus technically violating his vow. And remember, Bhīṣma's moral philosophy was that the act of keeping his vow is everything! Once a genuine Kuru heir was there, however, even as a baby, Bhīṣma could legitimately take action on his behalf, as a servant to the throne. In other words, the birth of the Kuru heirs freed Bhīṣma to act without violating his vow. Once they were born, Bhīṣma could take charge, and the Kurus could begin reasserting their authority. And there are descriptions of how the entire kingdom rejoiced to know that the Kuru dynasty had been saved.

Here we can also mention a very important point about the

relationship between Pāṇḍu and Dhṛtarāṣṭra, which will really determine the rest of the story. Pāṇḍu, as we will see, was deeply devoted to his older brother, and whatever he would gain in riches and treasure, he would immediately offer to him. Dhṛtarāṣṭra, however, never got over the fact that he was unable to rule; his resentment was always simmering below. He didn't blame Pāṇḍu, but he definitely had *serious issues* with his own blindness—issues that would eventually surface in very malicious, even villainous, ways.

So we have Dhṛtarāṣṭra, who was physically very powerful, but couldn't rule because he was blind, and we have Pāṇḍu, who was also an extremely powerful warrior, despite the fact that he was pale (paleness is often associated with weakness, anaemia, and so on). There's one particular incident that, to me, really showcases Pāṇḍu's *kṣatriya* power.

Like all kings, Pāṇḍu was obliged to marry and produce heirs, and the Kurus had heard that a great and very beautiful princess from a neighboring dynasty was about to hold her *svayaṁvara,* where she would select the husband of her choice. Her name was Kuntī, and we'll tell more about her in a few minutes. (Recall that we already learned about the *svayaṁvara* ceremony in the story of Ambā.)

If you know your geography, modern India is roughly like a diamond, with Delhi in the north central region. The ancient Kuru capital, Hastināpura, was located on the Ganges, approximately 80 miles northeast of Delhi. And if one traveled south from Hastināpura along the Ganges, one would eventually come to the next kingdom down river, known as Pañchāla— the kingdom of Draupadī and Drupada (two prominent figures in the events to come). So these were two great kingdoms located along the Ganges.

Roughly parallel to the Ganges, and running west of it, was the sacred Yamunā river. Both rivers originate in the Himālayan mountains; and, as with the Ganges, the northern part of the Yamunā belonged to the Kurus. If one traveled south from the Kuru lands along the Yamunā, one would eventually come to a third kingdom: the traditional land of the Yadus, the dynasty in which Kṛṣṇa appeared. Mathurā, on the banks of the Yamunā, was the Yadu capital and the birthplace of Kṛṣṇa. It is close to Vṛndāvana, where Kṛṣṇa lived in His childhood and youth. And that's our geography lesson for today!

Now let's rejoin Pāṇḍu traveling south to the kingdom of Kuntī-bhoja to compete in Kuntī's *svayaṁvara*. As we saw with the *svayaṁvara* of Ambā and her sisters, when these sort of events take place, tremendous battles can break out among rival princes, who are all very proud, passionate young warriors. Even when someone wins the princess in competition, he often must fight his way out of the arena to secure his prize. And this is what makes the princes' reaction to Pāṇḍu so singular—and revealing of his stature.

When Pāṇḍu arrived, he immediately rode into the arena like a charging bull, and all the other princes simply stepped aside. His physical appearance and obvious strength intimidated all who witnessed him. And the text actually says that he seemed almost like a second Indra (the powerful god of the celestial worlds). To put it simply, he was just head and shoulders above the rest in every way—and they knew it. In the midst of everyone, he rode straight to Kuntī, who chose him at once by placing the symbolic garland around his neck. Meanwhile, all the other princes were, like, "Great choice," because nobody wanted to tangle with Pāṇḍu, nobody wanted to challenge him. They simply made their way to their chariots and left for their respective kingdoms. It was truly a remarkable and very unusual outcome for such an event. And so, after the wedding ceremony, Pāṇḍu took Kuntī and began the journey north to Hastināpura.

One aside: Apart from reading through the *Mahā-bhārata* in the original language, I've tried to think about the text's narrative like a historian. If we plot the points on a map, we find that in journeying down to the kingdom of Kuntī-bhoja, Pāṇḍu would have passed through Mathurā.

At that time, there would have been a particular prince living there named Kaṁsa, who features very prominently in this narrative. Like Kuntī, Kaṁsa was part of the Yadu dynasty, and he and Pāṇḍu were actually contemporaries. (In the future, when Kṛṣṇa appears in the Yadu dynasty, Kuntī and Kaṁsa will be related to Him as aunt and uncle, respectively.)

Later in the narrative, when Pāṇḍu leaves this world, Kaṁsa (a major *Asura*) usurps the throne, imprisons his father, and persecutes his own dynasty. In the history of world power, there are many unfortunate examples (as in the Mogul dynasty) of rulers taking power and then basically getting rid of anyone that stands in their way, including members of their own family. For the sake of a throne, such persons have been known to kill all their brothers, all their cousins—and you can throw in a few sisters for good measure—all on the chance that they might cause trouble in the future.

Kaṁsa was actually Kālanemi, the first to attack Viṣṇu when He arrived at that celestial battle I mentioned the other day (the one that took place *after* the milk ocean had been churned). If you recall, the *Suras* and the *Asuras* were fighting, and the *Asuras* (I call them "the bad guys") were gaining the upper hand. Then, being prayed for, Viṣṇu showed up to help the *Suras*. What's interesting here is that when Viṣṇu appeared in the midst of this titanic battle, it was not to attack anyone, but rather to bring peace. That, of course, didn't stop the *Asuras*—who, true to form, attacked Viṣṇu without provocation. And the first to attack—the one who hated Viṣṇu most—was none other than Kālanemi, who had now taken birth in the Yadu dynasty as Kaṁsa. Living in Mathurā under his father Ugrasena, he is not yet able to act because Pāṇḍu is too powerful.

In any case, from a historical point of view, it's interesting to imagine that Pāṇḍu must have met Kaṁsa when passing through Mathurā on the way to Kuntī-bhoja. After all, they were both kings and there were even family ties between them.

Earlier I mentioned that I would tell a little bit about Kuntī, a very prominent figure in the *Mahā-bhārata*, who plays a crucial role in the narrative's later events.

Kuntī's story begins with her biological father King Śūrasena, who was blessed with many children. Śūrasena's most dear friend was another king named Kunti, who happened to be childless. Thus, as an act of love for a dear friend, Śūrasena gave the king his next newborn, who grew up in the kingdom of Kuntī-bhoja as the daughter of King Kunti.[36] As you can imagine, this child was so deeply loved and cared for by the formerly childless king that she was actually called Kuntī, after her father (Kuntī is the feminine form of Kunti).

When Kuntī was a young girl, around 12 or 13 years of age, something happened in her life that was not too dissimilar from what had happened to Satyavatī in her youth. Thus, like

---

[36] The full name of the king was Kunti-bhoja (like his kingdom), "bhoja" being a sub-branch of the Yadu dynasty.

Satyavatī, Kuntī had a secret, something she kept hidden from everyone.

It all started when the sage Durvāsā visited Kuntī-bhoja. In Sanskrit, Durvāsā essentially means "hardly dressed," so it seems he may have been wandering around wearing scant clothes—although his name *can* mean other things as well.

Now this Durvāsā had a reputation for being an extremely irritable sage, who was quick on the draw if ever he wasn't pleased. They say that doing a lot of austerities can sometimes give you a bad temper, and Durvāsā was known for this.[37] So everyone, everywhere wanted to avoid upsetting the irascible sage and receiving one of his infamous curses. Blessings and cursings, by the way, feature very prominently in these texts, and Durvāsā was notorious for cursing at the drop of a hat, even for the smallest offense *(like, if they brought his lunch ten seconds late, or burned the rice, or ... whatever!)*.

So when King Kunti heard that Durvāsā was coming to town, his immediate reaction was, "Wonderful, a great sage is coming," and his next, more thoughtful, reaction was, "Oh my God, not him, not Durvāsā!"

At the time, Kuntī was a very beautiful, sweet tempered girl of around thirteen years, who was famous for her devotion to her elders, taking great pleasure in serving their needs. Therefore, the king asked Kuntī if she would mind taking care of Durvāsā during his stay. Kuntī agreed, and ended up serving this frightening *yogī* so nicely that he was really touched by her devotion. When, by his own *yoga* power, he perceived that this

---

[37] Durvāsā was instrumental in precipitating a great heavenly war with the *Asuras* by cursing Indra for a trivial insult that had been innocently committed by Indra's elephant. The curse weakened the *Suras*, providing an opportunity for the *Asuras* to prevail.

girl would have some difficulty in the future, he gave her a special *mantra*, a powerful technique, whereby she could summon the presence of any god. What he either left out or kept very vague in his explanation was that once the god was summoned, he would be compelled to give Kuntī a child.

Now Durvāsā was a renounced sage, so perhaps he felt awkward about spelling this out; or perhaps he thought the point was so obvious that it didn't need mentioning. Whatever the reason, Durvāsā just gave Kuntī this *mantra* and left.

So now Kuntī, this youthful teen, had this powerful *mantra*, and she was naturally curious about how (or even if) it worked. One day, while standing on the balcony of her quarters and gazing up at the sun, she thought, "I wonder how this actually works." And, of course, everyone knew that the sun god was an extremely handsome, luminous figure.

So, almost as a test, Kuntī recited the *mantra* while thinking of the sun god Sūrya, who immediately descended from the sky to her room—something she didn't really expect. On one level, she knew she could call the sun god, but on another level, she didn't believe that she could actually *call the sun god!* She didn't think that Sūrya actually would come. But he *had* come, he was standing right before her, and he had some very shocking news: the one little item that Durvāsā left out—the thing that must happen next!

(And Kuntī was, like, "Wait a minute! I just dialed your number; I didn't bargain for this!")

As sympathetic as Sūrya may have been, he had to tell the teenage princess that even he could not check the power of the *mantra* that was now compelling him to act. There was simply no way out. The inevitable took place. And afterwards, Sūrya restored Kuntī's physiological virginity (a common occurence in such cases). This, however, was little comfort to this unmarried girl, who now had a baby to explain and contend with. Given the highly conservative nature of ancient Vedic culture, for Kuntī, this was an unmitigated disaster—a catastrophe of monumental proportions. And so she panicked!

(I mean, what was she gonna tell her father? "Well dad, I have a kid; but, hey, don't worry: I'm still a virgin, so it's all good!")

As a highly protected, extremely innocent young girl, Kuntī was not emotionally capable of handling the situation. She could see no other alternative but to give the child up. Thus, in a story reminiscent of the Old Testament, she put the infant in a basket and set the basket floating down the river.

In the Biblical story, if you remember, Moses was floating down the Nile, and his sister, Miriam, was following along the bank to make sure her brother survived and found a good home. Here we can assume that Kuntī made a similar arrangement after placing her child in the river, and thus was aware that the baby had been taken in by a very pious, goodhearted couple, Adhirath and Rādhā, who lovingly raised the boy from infancy.

And no one ever knew that he was actually Kuntī's son—a son who would later return to become one of the main figures in the *Mahā-bhārata*. So that's a little bit about Kuntī, the mother of the Pāṇḍavas, the aunt of the *avatārī* Kṛṣṇa, and one of the most beloved personalities of the *Mahā-bhārata*. And now, that selfsame Kuntī was traveling with Pāṇḍu to Hastināpura to assume her role as wife of the emperor and queen of the entire Kuru dynasty.

One day, after coming to Hastināpura and settling in with his new bride, Pāṇḍu was approached by Bhīṣma, who requested him to take a second wife. As always, the main reason was to further guarantee a qualified heir to the Kuru throne; because, as we've seen with Vicitravīrya's untimely death, the absence of a ruling king can actually threaten the political and social stability of the world.

In consideration of Bhīṣma's suggestion about a co-wife, we can end today with some thoughts on the institution of polygamy, which never has been that successful (and there's both historical and linguistic evidence that confirms this claim).

Let's begin with the linguistic evidence. The word for "co-wife" in Sanskrit is *sapatnī—sa* for "co-," and *patnī* for "wife." The masculine form of this word requires a change of only one letter, from *sapatnī* to *sapatna.* And here's where it gets interesting. The Sanskrit word *sapatna* translates as "enemy" or "rival," which is what co-wives often end up becoming. Indeed, history is full of all kinds of disastrous co-wife stories.

If you know your *Rāmāyaṇa*, you'll remember that the entire disaster of this epic springs from the jealousy of the co-wife Kaikeyī, who caused a mountain of chaos. And there are many such stories in the ancient texts, where polygamy leads to all kinds of troubles, including even infanticide. This we can find in the Sixth Canto of *Śrīmad-Bhāgavatam* (in the history of King Citraketu), where a co-wife went so far as to poison her rival's child simply because she couldn't have one of her own.[38]

This leads our discussion to the strategic problem of what

---

[38] See canto 6, ch.14, v.44 of the *Śrīmad Bhāgavatam*. The childless co-wives of King Citraketu's primary queen were extremely envious of the fact that she had borne the king a son. Thus, one night, they poisoned the infant child to death. King Citraketu and his wife were completely devastated by this loss, but they soon received instruction from the great sage, Narada, who momentarily brought the child back to life to impart transcendental knowledge to his parents. Thus hearing about the emphemeral nature of all material relationships and the eternal nature of the soul, their pain at the loss of their son was relieved.

things should be made legal and illegal in society, and what things should simply be left to custom. The Greeks talked about the conflict between *physis* and *nomos* (nature and law). In other words, what things should actually be legislated from a practical or realistic point of view?

For example, in the early part of the 20th century, the American government tried to outlaw the production and consumption of liquor, an attempt that proved totally—almost comically—disastrous *(except, perhaps, for Al Capone)*. More recently, the government again has tried to apply the very same strategy, this time with the so-called "War on Drugs." And, again, it has proved an utter failure: more drug availability and usage than ever, the rise of violent drug cartels, and so on.

The Vedic approach, on the other hand, was often more realistic. The idea was that certain people in society will engage in certain undesirable activities no matter what. So instead of trying to abolish these activities through strict legislation, try to at least manage them by keeping them within the law. In other words, don't create laws that no one's going to follow and that actually end up weakening the rule of law—giving rise to the "El Chapos" of the world.

So, after all this negative talk about co-wives, we'll begin tomorrow by telling how Bhīṣma chose a co-wife *(don't laugh)* for Pāṇḍu.

Pāṇḍu: Deadly Curses, Heavenly Boons

So the three Kuru brothers were Dhṛtarāṣṭra, Pāṇḍu, and Vidura; and of these, Pāṇḍu became the Kuru king, married Kuntī, and returned to Hastināpura. Not long thereafter, Bhīṣma told Pāṇḍu to take a second wife in order to secure the future of the throne. It was around this time that word came from the Madra kingdom that a beautiful, highly acomplished princess named Mādrī would soon be selecting her husband.[39] This time it was decided that none other than Bhīṣma would travel to Madra on Pāṇḍu's behalf to obtain and return with the princess.

(You could call this an odd choice after Bhīṣma's "great success" with Ambā's svayaṁvara. *You know, the one that will eventually cost Bhīṣma his life. In any case, this time he tried a different approach: doing it the old-fashioned way*—with money!*)*

You probably know that not only in India, but in many places throughout the world, including Europe, the dowry was a longstanding custom, where the bride's family would give some substantial gift to the family of the groom. Well, when Bhīṣma arrived in Madra, he found that Mādrī was being protected not by her father, but rather by her brother Śalya,

[39] The kingdom of Madra was in Northwest India, near Pakistan, and is not to be confused with old Madras.

who will feature later in the story. Apparently, Mādrī's father was no longer there, so Śalya himself spoke on Mādrī's behalf: "In our family," the young king said, "we're quite proud, and thus we don't *give* dowries, we *receive* them." The statement in itself is interesting because it indicates a variety of customs in ancient Vedic culture—there wasn't just one way of doing things.

Bhīṣma evidently had come prepared. He gave Śalya the dowry, brought Mādrī home, and now Pāṇḍu had two great queens. After only a brief honeymoon, Pāṇḍu set about taking care of dynastic business. Here we can note that Pāṇḍu (perhaps consciously) avoided going down the disastrous path of his dharmic father Vicitravīrya, who (if you remember) became endlessly caught up in the indulgences of his honeymoon until illness and death overtook him.

I mentioned earlier that in the interregnum—the period in which there was no king—all kinds of bad things were happening in the world: neighbors violating borders and stealing Kuru lands, certain world leaders bullying other kingdoms, oppressing innocent people, and so on. Pāṇḍu, let's not forget, was this extraordinarily powerful king. His father was Vyāsa, the great sage and *avatāra,* and his mother was Ambālikā, a princess.

So, after a brief "getting to know you" period with his wives, Pāṇḍu immediately went forth to secure Kuru lands, eliminate the oppressors of innocent people, and set the world aright! The text describes his triumphant return to Hastināpura bearing an amazing amount of tribute (treasure) in a long train of wagons. People would pay tribute to the Kuru king, and this wealth would be used to maintain a type of central government, not in the sense of managing other kingdoms, but rather in the sense of leading and sustaining an alliance that protected all. But Pāṇḍu also received many personal gifts, and being of a detached and generous nature, he gave these valuable items to his wives, his brothers, and everyone else, keeping very little for himself.

He especially lavished gifts upon his blind older brother Dhṛtarāṣṭra. I mention this because, as I said, Dhṛtarāṣṭra clearly had issues: he was the firstborn, the legitimate heir, yet he had a disability that prevented him from ruling as a warrior king. And even though Pāṇḍu was an ideal younger brother (something that Dhṛtarāṣṭra genuinely appreciated), he could never forget that his blindness had deprived him of the throne.

In any case, Pāṇḍu eventually returned the realm to order, and having done so, he wanted to take his wives and go off to the forest. This is something of a common theme in ancient literature. At a certain point, great kings would leave behind the opulences and headaches of their somewhat overdone lives in the palace, and go to the woods, to nature, where they would enjoy camping at the side of a river, and so on.

For example, there's a point in the *Rāmāyaṇa*, where Rāma had been banished to the forest, and all the citizens of Ayodhyā were weeping and lamenting, "Poor boy, you had such a great life in the palace, with soft pillows, sheets as white as foam, and whatnot." But Rāma responded, "Actually, I like it out here. It's more natural."

This was the case with Pāṇḍu as well. He and his wives retreated for a bit of "eco-tourism," living in the forest and enjoying the beauty of nature. And while there, Pāṇḍu would hunt (which is something of an issue in its own right).

In ancient Vedic culture, kings were permitted to hunt because, again, it was their job to personally protect their kingdom. To do so, they obviously had to become proficient with their weapons, and this required practice. But, although it wasn't officially illegal for kings to hunt, there are many stories in the Sanskrit literature about kings who ruined their lives by hunting. It's similar to the situation with polygamy, which I mentioned earlier. Although this practice wasn't forbidden, there are many stories in the texts about polygamy causing a great deal of havoc. So what does this mean?

Vedic civilization was an extremely old civilization with a tremendous amount of real-world experience. Over time, a system developed in which certain undesirable activities weren't necessarily criminalized or made illegal, but were rather culturally discouraged. These were activities that people would do regardless. To criminalize them could engender a disrespect for the rule of law, since great kings themselves were doing them. And so, instead of being banned, such activities were culturally discouraged—for instance, by emphasizing historical examples in which those activities led to disaster.

There's actually a long list of great kings—some of the greatest, in fact—who basically destroyed their lives through hunting accidents. One of them, of course, is Daśaratha, the father of Rāma, who destroyed his life and ultimately died because of a hunting accident.[40] Then there's the famous Parīkṣit, the last great king of the Kuru dynasty, the great-grandson of the Pāṇḍavas, who was personally saved by Kṛṣṇa while still in his mother's womb—his life was also upended

---

40 While hunting, then crown prince Daśaratha killed a young boy in the forest, mistaking him for a deer. The boy's blind parents transferred their grief of separation to the future king via a curse, planting the seed for prince Rama's eventual exile. C. Rajagopalachari, *Valmiki's Ramayan* (London: Bharatiya Vidya Bhavan, 2000), 56.

while hunting.[41] And then, of course, there's the tragedy of Pāṇḍu, which we'll talk about now.

It began one day when Pāṇḍu was hunting in the forest, tracking a stag and a doe. Coming within range of the deer, who happened to be mating at the time, the king aimed his arrows and shot. Then, to his horror, he heard the male deer shriek in what sounded like a human voice.

(Now something like that can really ruin your day, and even your whole "eco-tour!")

As it turned out, this deer couple were not deer at all, but rather two very powerful *yogīs*. It seems they had done so many austerities for such a long time that they had become physically frigid—and thus unable to produce a child. To overcome this passionless state, they used their *yogīc* power to transform themselves into deer *(because deer have absolutely no problem with that kind of activity; they're quite procreative)*. When Pāṇḍu came upon, shot, and mortally wounded them, the two *yogīs* were literally in the act of begetting their child.

Realizing what he had done to this young *brāhmaṇa* couple, Pāṇḍu was mortified. He had dedicated his entire life to serving and protecting the *brāhmaṇa* class, and now *this*?! He humbly explained that he was hunting deer and had no idea that the two were human *yogīs*. With his last few breaths, the dying *brāhmaṇa* (a *yogī* named Kindama) turned toward Pāṇḍu and declared that because Pāṇḍu didn't know, he wouldn't have to suffer for the sin of killing *brāhmaṇas*. He would, however, have to suffer for the

---

[41] Becoming fatigued while hunting, King Parīkṣit came upon the hermitage of the sage Śamīka Ṛṣi, who was deep in meditation and unresponsive to the king's request for water. The king, feeling insulted, garlanded the sage with a dead serpent and left. When the sage's *brāhmaṇa* son returned home and saw this "offense," he cursed the king to die within seven days. See canto 1, ch. 18, v. 24-25 of *Śrīmad-Bhāgavatam*.

sin of killing creatures that were in the act of begetting a child.

Kindama avowed, "The act of begetting is sacred in any form of life, and because you killed us in that act, you will have to pay in kind. Whenever, in the future, you attempt to beget a child, you also will die in the act."

This, of course, was a devastating, life-changing event for Pāṇḍu, to say the least. Once again we have a royal life that had been almost charmed. He was born a Kuru prince, became a Kuru king, married two beautiful princesses, and basically dominated the world. He was generous, he was kind, he followed *dharma,* he served the *brāhmaṇas*—he had a completely fortunate life.

Now, due to one fatal error, everything had changed, and Pāṇḍu had two terrible agonies to contend with. First, he had killed exalted *yogīs* in the prime of their lives, which was extremely traumatic—particularly for him. And second, he was now basically unable to beget children—sons who could continue the noble Kuru line into the future. He had killed those he had sworn to protect and gravely jeopardized his own life, all within the blinking of an eye. Pāṇḍu was the Kuru king; yet Pāṇḍu would never be able to produce a Kuru heir.

Faced with these drastic disappointments, Pāṇḍu decided to retreat high into the mountains rather than return home. His worldly life had failed despite all efforts, so now he would pursue the spiritual. With love, he requested Kuntī and Mādrī to go back to the comforts of Hastināpura, as he intended to perform severe austerities high in the mountains. They, however, wouldn't hear of it. They had no interest in such things and only wanted to be with him. Kuntī and Mādrī would follow Pāṇḍu and take up whatever austerities he performed. Pāṇḍu relented and let them stay with him.

There's a key point that must be mentioned here because it's so pivotal to the *Mahā-bhārata*'s central story. In deciding to practice austerities in the mountains, Pāṇḍu *never renounced* the Kuru throne, nor the *right* of his eventual children to *inherit* that throne. He simply decided not to return to Hastināpura, and requested Dhṛtarāṣṭra to care for the kingdom until his return.

When Dhṛtarāṣṭra got word that Pāṇḍu would not be coming back, and that *he* was to rule in Pāṇḍu's stead, it was as if destiny had fulfilled his heart's long-festering desire—the desire for the Kuru throne. Despite his younger brother's undoubted devotion, and despite his own genuine sympathy for Pāṇḍu's plight, Dhṛtarāṣṭra must have had mixed feelings about the situation on two grounds.

First of all, it appeared that Pāṇḍu wasn't coming back any time soon, and thus, for all intents and purposes, Dhṛtarāṣṭra would be calling the shots as the stand-in king. And secondly, if Pāṇḍu actually could never have children, there was a chance that his own firstborn would take the throne, giving him, by proxy, the power he had always sought. To say that Dhṛtarāṣṭra was not free of personal ambition would be putting it mildly; this is something that comes out again and again as the narrative progresses.

In any case, Pāṇḍu and his wives went up the mountain heights to a place called Śataśṛṅga, which means "Hundred Peaks." There they lived in a community of *yogīs* and performed almost frightening austerities. Being an extraordinary *kṣatriya* king, Pāṇḍu had incredible strength, power, resilience, and determination, all of which he now focused on the path of self-realization.

Meanwhile in the south, there was another who was happy

about Pāṇḍu's retreat to the mountains—someone we've already met, who had no need to conceal his joy: Kṛṣṇa's uncle Kaṁsa, who was actually the *Asura* Kālanemi. If you remember, Kālanemi had taken birth on Earth, along with many cohorts, to gain control of the planet.

The *Asuras'* program, however, had been basically put on hold because of Pāṇḍu's near-supernatural strength. His current indefinite absence, of course, was the green light the *Asuras* had been waiting for, and they intended to take full advantage by more boldly pursuing their ends. This is confirmed by looking at the dates and chronologies of the *Mahā-bhārata* from a historiographical perspective—in this case, as it relates to Kaṁsa.

Kaṁsa made his move at around the same time that Pāṇḍu was cursed and decided to remain in the wilderness. It almost seems as if Kaṁsa was waiting for an opening, since he was unable to act so long as Pāṇḍu ruled. Kaṁsa basically took the opportunity offered by Pāṇḍu's withdrawal to seize power, imprison his father, usurp the throne, and persecute members of his own dynasty. These accounts are found in the *Śrīmad-Bhāgavatam* and alluded to in the *Mahā-bhārata*. There's a lot of overlap.[42]

While all this is taking place in Yadu territory, up in the mountains, Pāṇḍu achieves success in self-realization, and also hears of Kaṁsa's aggressions from members of the Yadu dynasty. Learning of such goings-on in the world he is sworn to protect causes Pāṇḍu tremendous distress, and he becomes almost obsessed with the urgent need for sons to protect the Earth—even if he dies in the process.

---

42 From *Śrīmad-Bhāgavatam*, canto10, ch.1, v. 64-69.

Pāṇḍu decides to speak to Kuntī about using the *āpad-dharma* that Bhīṣma used in the case of Ambikā and Ambālikā: when there's an emergency relating to dynastic succession and the begetting of heirs, a pure-hearted *brāhmaṇa* can beget a son in the womb of a *ksatriyā* (warrior lady). By *dharma*, the child then becomes the legitimate heir to the throne. This is Pāṇḍu's solution, and he begs Kuntī to accept it.

At first Kuntī protests. She's repulsed by the idea of intimacy with anyone other than her husband. But Pāṇḍu continues to plead, reminding Kuntī of how much is at stake. Of course, *we* know that Kuntī has a solution, wrapped in a mystery, inside an enigma that no one knows but her: the powerful *mantra* given by Durvāsā whereby she can summon any god to beget a child. And while she's unprepared to tell Pāṇḍu of her teenage trial run, and the child that was *"sent down the Nile,"* she does tell him about Durvāsā's boon.

Pāṇḍu, of course, is astonished and overjoyed. He immediately agrees. However, since news of Pāṇḍu's curse has spread far and wide, the next question becomes, "What will people think and what are we going to tell them?" Here it's important to understand how seriously Vedic civilization's kings regarded public opinion, as in the *Rāmāyaṇa*'s narrative of Rāma.[43]

After carefully considering this point, Pāṇḍu and Kuntī

---

[43] Upon being freed from ten months of captivity under the power of Ravana, Rāma's wife, Sita, publicly exonerated herself of all suspected impropriety by surviving a "trial by fire." Nevertheless, some foolish people still doubted her chastity, citing Vedic custom that a woman must never spend a night out of the house. Thus, for the sake of His kingdom, Lord Rāma, being bound to redress even the slightest rumor of *adharma*, was forced to banish his exalted wife from Ayodya. Keerthanacharya Sreenivasa Ayyangar, *The Rāmāyaṇa of Vālmīki, Part 2.* (Madras: The Little Flower Co., 1962), 1586-1587.

decide that she should summon the god of justice, Dharma, because if the child is born of Dharma himself, no one can say that the act of begetting him is against religious principles (*adharma*). "Clever!"

So Kuntī sat in meditation, thinking of Dharma, who immediately appeared and begot a son who would become famous as Dharmarāja (the king of *dharma*) for his unimpeachable virtue and justice. That, of course, was Yudhiṣṭira. And Pāṇḍu was thrilled to have such a worthy heir.

As you can imagine, when word of Yudhiṣṭira's birth got back to Hastināpura, Dhṛtarāṣṭra was not at all pleased. He was the eldest, he was extremely ambitious, and he was fully capable of ruling as king—except, of course, for one fateful flaw: the blindness that deprived him of it all. With Pāṇḍu's curse and withdrawal to the mountains, he had assumed that his path was finally cleared, and that his heirs would one day sit on the Kuru throne.

At the time of Yudhiṣṭira's birth, Dhṛtarāṣṭra's wife, Gāndhārī, was also supposed to give birth, but the delivery had been delayed again and again—the child simply wasn't coming out. It was during this wait that Dhṛtarāṣṭra received news about the birth of Pāṇḍu's son—for him, the worst possible news imaginable. It wasn't that Dhṛtarāṣṭra had no love for his younger brother. To the contrary, he greatly loved and respected him. It was just that his ambition tended to get the better of him, and he knew what the birth of Pāṇḍu's son meant. By *dharma*, he was the legitimate heir to the throne, being born prior to Dhṛtarāṣṭra's son (who would turn out to be part of the *Asura* invasion)!

When Gāndhārī finally gave birth, they named the child Duryodhana, which can mean "someone who's difficult to fight" *(or simply, "a dirty fighter")*. And Duryodhana definitely lived up to his name! As was the custom following a royal birth, Duryodhana's parents asked the *Jyotish Kovidas* (expert astrologers) to draw up a chart and make a reading. What they found horrified them to the core, and they pleaded with the parents to neither raise this son as their own, nor make him heir to the Kuru throne. "If you do," they warned, "this child will destroy the entire Kuru dynasty."

But, out of deep parental attachment, Dhṛtarāṣṭra was thinking, "This is my boy!" And he just couldn't do it; he just couldn't abandon his child.

(I guess he was one of those parents who hope for the best. You know, "I'll send him to the best schools, *there's nothing that a lot of TLC can't* fix." *TLC, tender loving care.)*

In any case, this is what's going on: Yudhiṣṭira is born first and Pāṇḍu never renounced his claim to the throne. He just doesn't return to Hastināpura. Because the *Mahā-bhārata* says again and again that, for Yudhiṣṭira, the kingdom was the *pitṛ-paitāmahaṁ rājyam*, "the kingdom of his fathers and forefathers."[44]

Afer the birth of Yudhiṣṭira, Pāṇḍu didn't want to stop there; he wanted more sons to ensure the dynasty and the safety of the people. He again spoke to Kuntī, and they decided, "*dharma* is great, but sometimes you need real firepower; virtue is great, but sometimes you need strength." So they summoned Vāyu, the god of wind, the most powerful of all the gods, who came and begot Bhīma, the strongest of all the Pāṇḍavas.

(These children, by the way, are all called Pāṇḍavas, from the

---

[44] From book 12 (*Śāntiparva*), ch. 31, v. 47 of *Critical Edition of the Mahā-bhārata.*

word Pāṇḍu; the term Pāṇḍava is a patronym—a name derived from the father's name.)

Of course, with the birth of his second son, Pāṇḍu felt like he and Kuntī were really on a roll. Why stop there? Why not really go for the moon and summon Indra himself (the head of all the gods)? Once again, Kuntī chanted the *mantra,* this time while meditating on Indra. And, as expected, Indra came and begot the most spectacular son of all: Arjuna, the intimate friend of Kṛṣṇa, who heard *Bhagavad-gītā* directly from Kṛṣṇa's lips.

In the excitement of all these births, Mādrī, Kuntī's co-wife, had been more or less forgotten and was beginning to feel like a third wheel. With no *mantra* to offer, she felt as if she had become *nothing*, while Kuntī had become *everything*. She went to Kuntī pleading, "Use your power for me, let me also give the king sons." And Kuntī, being extremely generous and kind, allowed Mādrī to use the *mantra* to summon a god.

Mādrī sat down and chanted the *mantra*, calling the Aśvinīs, the *twin* gods *(so, in a sense, she "double dipped")*. The Aśvinīs are physicians to the gods, renowned throughout the celestial world for their extraordinary beauty. They aren't exactly *upadevas* (junior gods), but they're in a somewhat subordinate position relative to certain gods. In any case, they came and begot the most handsome of the Pāṇḍavas: the twins Nakula and Sahadeva.

When the twins were born, however, Kuntī became a little peeved, feeling that Mādrī had taken advantage of the situation: "I gave you this power, and you called not one, but two gods. If I allow you again, who knows what you'll do? So please be satisfied with your two twin boys." Pāṇḍu, of course, wanted to just keep going. Why stop now? But Kuntī basically put on the brakes.

("This is getting out of hand; I can't have a kid with every god in the universe!")

When you look closely at these texts, you realize that these were real people. For example, when Pāṇḍu was trying to induce Kuntī to bear another child, he couldn't just order, he had to convince. So he tried to persuade by presenting different arguments, one of which included a famous verse: "It is the *dharma* of a woman to follow her husband whether he's right or wrong."[45] But what's interesting here is that right after Pāṇḍu quotes this verse, Kuntī defeats him with her own argument. And then he says, "Okay dear, we'll do it your way." Despite the verse's implication that the wife is subordinate to the husband, in the real world, both husband and wife worked together as a team.

Kuntī basically told Pāṇḍu that if she continued to use Durvāsā's *mantra* to summon gods and produce more and more sons, the world would begin to think of the Kuru queen as a loose woman, and rightly so. "You have five extraordinary sons, and you should be grateful and leave it at that." Pāṇḍu submitted, and that was the end.

So the final count is five Pāṇḍava brothers, all one year apart: Yudhiṣṭira, Bhīma, Arjuna, and then the twins, Nakula and Sahadeva (with Nakula being the "older" of the two). Meanwhile, back in Hastināpura, Dhṛtarāṣṭra was also begetting sons, with Duryodhana, his firstborn, being roughly the same age as Bhīma.

One more highly significant point: at around the same time that Arjuna was born, the most important personality of the

---

[45] *"Asheela kamvrto va gunyar va parivarjita, upcharya sitrya sadhya ya sat tam dev vat pati."* From George Bühler, *The Laws of Manu.* (Charleston: BiblioBazaar, 2009), ch. 5, v. 154.

entire *Mahā-bhārata* also took birth: *Avatārī* Kṛṣṇa. Recall that the Sanskrit word *avatārī* means, "the source of all other *avatāras*." And now, I'll say a few words about Kṛṣṇa.

Kṛṣṇa was Arjuna's cousin—and, of course, a cousin to all the Pāṇḍavas. Here's the genealogy: Kuntī was the mother of Yudhiṣṭira, Bhīma, and Arjuna. Kuntī's brother, Vasudeva, was Kṛṣṇa's father. Indeed, the very first verse of the *Śrīmad-Bhāgavatam* begins: *oṁ namo bhagavate vāsudevāya.*[46] In this invocation, the Sanskrit word Vāsudeva refers to Kṛṣṇa. Vasudeva (with a short *a*) is Kṛṣṇa's father, and Vāsudeva (with a long *ā*) is Kṛṣṇa Himself. Vāsudeva means, "Kṛṣṇa, the son of Vasudeva."

Jesus, as we know, was born in a manger, in very humble circumstances. And Kṛṣṇa was also born very humbly, but in a prison house instead. Very briefly, here's how this came to pass.[47]

Kṛṣṇa's father and mother, Devakī and Vasudeva,[48] had just gotten married and were driving home on Vasudeva's chariot. At the reins was someone we've already had the displeasure of meeting: the great *Asura* Kaṁsa, Devakī's cousin-brother, who had volunteered to drive the newlyweds home. As they rode along, Kaṁsa was really trying hard to be a good *Asura—an oxymoron, if ever there was one*—when suddenly, *"No More Mr. Nice Guy!"* Kaṁsa had heard an unembodied voice echoing

---

[46] From *Śrīmad-Bhāgavatam,* canto 1, ch.1, v.1.

[47] For a very charming rendering of the entire story of Kṛṣṇa's birth, see A.C. Bhaktivedanta Swami Prabhupada, *Kṛṣṇa, the Supreme Personality of Godhead* (Los Angeles: Bhaktivedanta Book Trust, 1970), 24-30.

[48] Vasudeva is the son of King Śūrasena, the brother of Kuntī and father of Subhadrā (who married her cousin Arjuna—a system still prevalent in some parts of India). Vasudeva was appointed minister of King Ugrasena, and later married eight daughters of Ugrasena's brother Devaka, of which Devakī is one.

from the heavens (in Sanskrit, *vāk a-śarīra*): "Kaṁsa, you fool, you are driving the chariot of the woman whose eighth child will kill you."

Remember that cosmic battle from a previous epoch, the one I've already mentioned a few times? Back then, it was Kṛṣṇa, in the form of Viṣṇu, who had killed Kālanemi, now appearing as Kaṁsa. So when Kaṁsa heard it foretold that Devakī's eighth child would kill him, he thought, "Forget my sister, forget everything!" His true colors emerged! In an instant, he grabbed Devakī's hair, jerked her back, unsheathed his sword, and was about to take her head.

This is a classic example of a bona fide *Asura.* He didn't bother to think, "Well, the voice said this, but who knows for sure?" He immediately decided to kill! He didn't hesitate. He didn't think twice.

Vasudeva, of course, had to think fast if he was going to save his new wife. They hadn't even made it back home, and he was already on the verge of becoming a widower. At this point, *Śrīmad-Bhāgavatam* contains various interesting passages in which Vasudeva is attempting to reason with Kaṁsa, trying to convince him not to kill Devakī. Then he finally says, "Look, the voice said it would be the eighth son, right? So there's time, and here's what we can do. I'll give you my word as a *brāhmana* that whenever Devakī gives birth, I'll bring the newborn infant to you to deal with as you like." Here Vasudeva's object was to save his wife from imminent death, buy some time, and make a better plan in the future. And somehow his strategy worked. Kaṁsa changed his mind and let his sister go.

After some time, however, he received word from reliable sources that the *Suras* (the gods) knew of the *Asuras'* plan to take control of the Earth, and had already taken birth in the Yadu and other dynasties to stop them. Kaṁsa was warned to be careful since this could threaten all his recent gains. He also knew that if the *Suras* had already descended to Earth, then Viṣṇu would not be far behind: *Viṣṇu*, who had destroyed him once in the celestial realm. *Viṣṇu*, whom he feared and hated more than any other being!

His thoughts then turned to Devakī, Vasudeva, the warning in the sky, the eighth child (a god? worse?)—it was all too much! Kaṁsa was upset, to say the least. And neither logical arguments nor honorable pledges would do. He immediately had Vasudeva and Devakī arrested and thrown behind bars, hoping to bring things under control. Then, not taking any chances, he killed each of Devakī's children on the very day they were born—waiting to "take care" of number eight as well. That eighth child, of course, was Kṛṣṇa, who had something very different in mind for Mr. Kaṁsa—something more in line with what had happened to Kālanemi.

Tomorrow we'll talk more about Kṛṣṇa's birth and how this relates to Pāṇḍu and the Pāṇḍavas. We'll also find out about Pāṇḍu's ultimate fate.

Kṛṣṇa: Tipping the Scales

When we ended yesterday, Kaṁsa had imprisoned Vasudeva and Devakī, and then proceeded to kill Devaki's newborn babies one after another. The tally was six dead sons; then Devakī became pregnant with number seven: Kṛṣṇa's older brother Balarāma, who escaped prison by immediately transferring Himself to the womb of Rohiṇī, a Yadu princess.

(By the way, the *Rāma* in the chant *Hare Rāma*, refers to Balarāma, although it also can refer to Rāmachandra.)

In any case, Princess Rohiṇī was taking shelter in the rural community of Vṛndāvana, the place where Kṛṣṇa would grow up as a child. The residents of Vṛndāvana, including Nanda (who became Kṛṣṇa's foster father), were allied with and intimately connected to the Yadus. Thus, when Kaṁsa began terrorizing his own dynasty, some Yadus fled to the relative safety of Vṛndāvana. Rohiṇī was among these.

Now a word or two about the personality Yogamāyā. Generally, the term *māyā* simply means "mystic power." But for spiritual practitioners with a strong sense of God's illusory energy, *māyā* is that power of God which tests our sincerity, our devotion, and our commitment to reality, by offering various illusory alternatives. In the jargon of *Śrīmad-Bhāgavatam*, that illusory spiritual power is called *mahā-māyā*. And *yoga-māyā* is the spiritual power of God that does the opposite—frees us from illusion and brings us to enlightenment. The goddess Yogamāyā also manages *kṛṣṇa-līlā* (Kṛṣṇa's transcendental pastimes). In the case of Balarāma, for example, it was technically Yogamāyā who transferred Him from the womb of Devakī to the womb of Rohiṇī in Vṛndāvana.

Kaṁsa, of course, knew that Devakī was pregnant with her seventh child. But when he came with murderous intent, he was told that Devakī had miscarried.

(This made him think, "Even celestial voices can't be trusted these days; if you can't trust celestial voices, who can you trust?!")

We, of course, know that Devakī's seventh child is alive and well in Vṛndāvana. Just as Kṛṣṇa is famous as Yaśodānandana (the son of Yaśodā), Balarāma is famous as Rohiṇī-nandana (the son of Rohiṇī).

Kaṁsa's killing of all Devakī's children prior to Kṛṣṇa's birth was essentially just *Kaṁsa being Kaṁsa*—warming up for the big event. The "voice" clearly told him that the *eighth* child would kill him, but he wasn't taking any chances, even if it meant killing innocent infants. Soon, of course, Kaṁsa would come face-to-face with his true nemesis! Devakī had become pregnant with number eight: the child that would eventually end his life.

The story of Kṛṣṇa's birth is extremely well-known in India, and a favorite theme of Indian art. Kṛṣṇa took birth in Kaṁsa's prison, and to assure His parents that He wasn't a helpless infant, He first appeared in Vasudeva's mind, then entered Devakī's heart (and womb), and finally came out as almighty Nārāyaṇa—the same Nārāyaṇa that you chant this beautiful prayer to each day:

kāyena vācā manasendriyaiś ca
buddhyātmanā vānusṛtir-svabhāvā
karomi yad yat sakalaṁ parasma
nārāyaṇāyaiva samarpayām

"Whatever I do with my body, speech, mind and senses, or with my intellect and soul, following my own nature, I fully offer all that to Nārāyaṇa alone."[49]

From the Vaiṣṇava perspective, Nārāyaṇa is "God at the office" and Kṛṣṇa is "God at home." At home, people relax, kick off their shoes, and do whatever they want; but at work, they have to dress up and be a little more formal to make an impression. As "God at the office," or Nārāyaṇa, Kṛṣṇa has such formal responsibilities as taking care of the material universes and so on; and as "God at home," or Govinda, Kṛṣṇa simply relaxes, tends the cows, plays with his friends, and dances with the *gopīs*.

When Kṛṣṇa first appeared in Kaṁsa's prison, He did so as majestic, almighty Nārāyaṇa, just to "check in," so to speak, and let His parents know who He was. Then, right before their eyes, He transformed into a tiny, helpless baby. And that must have been a lot to process!

Vasudeva and Devakī had seen Kṛṣṇa (in the form of almighty Nārāyaṇa) transform into their infant son, so somewhere they knew that Kṛṣṇa was God Himself—that is, on one level, there was nothing to fear. At the moment, however, all they could see was this helpless infant lying before them, and their hearts filled

[49] This prayer is from the song *Sri Vallabheti Vara Deti,* from the book *Mukunda Mala Stotra* by Mahārāja *Kulaśekhara*. The translation is by the author himself, H.D. Goswami.

with fear and the overwhelming desire to protect their child.

In a sense, many who try to serve God in various ways share the same two moods: we know that God has a plan, and is the ultimate controller and doer; yet, we still worry about doing things right, what will happen in the future, and so on. So it's natural that in the service of God we still care about our own and others' decisions, actions, and reactions.

In this case, Vasudeva and Devakī understood the obvious: they couldn't simply wait with Kṛṣṇa in their prison cell for Kaṁsa to show up. They had to get the baby out—*and now!* At this point, Yogamāyā entered the scene, miraculously putting everyone in the palace to sleep, opening the prison doors, and freeing Vasudeva from his shackles.

Vasudeva picked up Kṛṣṇa and escaped, heading toward the Yamunā, which had to be crossed before getting to Vṛndāvana—where Kṛṣṇa would be safe. The night was stormy and the river was swollen and overflowing; making a crossing would be extremely dangerous. Again, Yogamāyā stepped in and simply parted the waters, opening a path for Vasudeva and his son. In this way, Vasudeva was able to take Kṛṣṇa across the river to Vṛndāvana.

(The image of Vasudeva holding baby Kṛṣṇa while walking between the parted waters of the Yamunā is a very popular scene, often depicted in Indian art.)

When Vasudeva arrived in Vṛndāvana, he went to the house of Yaśodā,[50] who herself had just given birth to a female child. It had been a difficult, exhausting birth, with the child coming out unexpectedly when no one was there. Vasudeva quietly

---

50 In their previous lives, the gentle and pious Nanda Mahārāja and Mother Yaśodā were highly exalted devotees of the Lord who ardently prayed to have Kṛṣṇa as their own son (*Śrīmad-Bhāgavatam*, canto 10, ch. 8, v. 41).

entered the residence. Yaśodā was lying there, totally unconscious, with her daughter at her side. He leaned down, quickly switched babies, and left Vṛndāvana with the female child.

At this point, we might ask, "Why didn't Vasudeva just run for it?" Well, for one thing, his wife would have been immediately killed; and for another, Kaṁsa had spies and agents everywhere, so there was really "nowhere to run to, nowhere to hide," as the saying goes. Vasudeva, in other words, had been dealt a bad hand. So he played the only card he could: he took the female child back to Kaṁsa's prison, placed her on Devakī's lap, fastened his shackles back on, and acted as if nothing had happened.

The next morning, Kaṁsa was informed that Devakī's eighth child had been born, so he rushed to the prison to kill the infant. But instead of finding his old nemesis Kṛṣṇa (or Viṣṇu), he found a baby girl. And he thought, "What's going on here? First a miscarriage and now this?! You just can't trust those celestial voices, can you! Anyway, boy, girl—what does it matter? The infant has to go." And here we come to one of the great scenes of the *Śrīmad-Bhāgavatam*, told in various places, but told best in this work.[51]

Kaṁsa moved toward Devakī and wrenched the infant from her arms, with Devakī crying and pleading to at least spare her female child. Kaṁsa wouldn't hear it. He lifted the newborn girl by her legs—his own blood niece!—and tried to smash her against the stone floor. But the child slipped from his grip and flew into the sky. Appearing with terrible weapons, she

---

[51] From *Śrīmad Bhāgavatam,* canto 10, ch. 3.

revealed herself as the goddess Durgā,[52] who is known by numerous names: Devī, Shakti, Yogamāyā, Bhadrakālī, and so on.

(Anyone that's seen her depicted in Indian art knows one thing: you don't mess around with Goddess Durgā.)

In any case, the goddess displayed her most terrifying form and spoke to Kaṁsa in ominous tones: "The child who will kill you is already alive on Earth. Stop being cruel to Vasudeva and Devakī or things will only get worse for you!" Then, she simply disappeared, leaving Kaṁsa stunned and shaken to the core. With the words of the goddess ringing in his ears, he immediately released Vasudeva and Devakī, sending them on their way. He really was *"shocked and awed"* by the whole experience.

Then again, Kaṁsa was quite a resilient *Asura,* and not one to succumb to virtue. Wasting no time, his ministers sat him down and gave him something of a demonic pep talk: "Relax, we can handle this. Sure the goddess has powers, but so do we. After all, we're not just run-of-the-mill human beings. We'll use all the powers at our command, and then let's see them stop us!"

Kaṁsa's ministers also warned that the *Suras,* who had come to stop their takeover of Earth, could be anywhere. They were spread all over the countryside just waiting for their chance—and, in a sense, they had Kaṁsa surrounded. Realizing that the child who would kill him was alive somewhere on Earth, Kaṁsa ordered the killing of every male

---

[52] Goddess Durgā is famous as Yoga-māyā, the superior, internal potency of the Supreme Lord. She is also understood to be Kṛṣṇa's sister, known also as Ekānaṃśā or Subhadrā. Goddess Durgā also acts as the Lord's inferior, external energy *mahā-māyā,* which covers and bewilders the souls that enter the material world.

child born within the last ten days. His henchmen then went everywhere, butchering innocent children!

(What can I say? That was Kaṁsa.)

Kṛṣṇa, of course, was safely enjoying His childhood *līlā,* or pastimes, in Vṛndāvana. The tales of Kṛṣṇa's childhood, boyhood and youth are, perhaps, the most popular group of stories in Indian history, having inspired countless productions in the visual arts, music, poetry, theater, books—everything! And among these, Kṛṣṇa 's playful dealings with the cowherd girls of Vraja (including the renowned *rāsa-līlā*) are probably the most famous of all.

In any case, Kaṁsa gradually understood that Kṛṣṇa was in Vṛndāvana, and thus became determined to kill Him. At this point, he didn't want to personally kill Kṛṣṇa, because he thought, "That might not be prudent." So he sent all these powerful—I don't know what you'd call them: "Monsters"? "Demons?" They were actually great *yogīs,* but *yogīs* that used the "dark side of the Force," to put it in modern cinematic terms. And they had this *yogīc* power called *kāma-rūpa* (literally, "desire form"), which enabled them to transform into any shape they desired.

To give one example, the first of these was this evil, left-handed witch named Pūtanā, whose natural form was truly hideous. Using *kāma-rūpa,* she transformed herself into an exquisitely beautiful young lady—on the level of a goddess!—and entered Vṛndāvana. Indeed, Pūtanā had become so goddess-like that none of the villagers even asked who she was or what she wanted. She just made her way through the village, entered the house of Kṛṣṇa, and began admiring the infant. She turned to Yaśodā and said: "Your child is so beautiful. May I nurse Him for a while?" And even Kṛṣṇa's own mother was so beguiled by Pūtanā's beauty that she gave her precious child to a total stranger!

Now Pūtanā had a plan. Before coming, she had smeared her nipple with a deadly poison, with the aim of killing Kṛṣṇa *(she was, after all, an agent of Kaṁsa)*. So she placed Kṛṣṇa on her lap and offered Him her breast. Yet even though Kṛṣṇa was an infant, He wasn't at all fooled; He fully understood the witch's evil intent. He accepted Pūtanā's breast, but gradually began sucking harder and harder; so hard, in fact, that he started to take her life along with her milk. Realizing that her life was being pulled right out of her, Pūtanā panicked and began screaming and shrieking, trying to free herself from the child: "Get him off! Someone please get him off!" But Kṛṣṇa just kept sucking and sucking until the witch was dead.

Of course, after she died, Pūtanā was unable to maintain her artificial form, and suddenly, before everyone's eyes, the "beautiful goddess" changed back into this gigantic ghastly thing. But Kṛṣṇa thought, "Well, I *did* drink her breast milk, so technically she was a mother." And on that basis, despite the fact that she had come to kill Him, Kṛṣṇa granted Pūtanā liberation. This is the spirit of *kṛṣṇa-līlā*! Kṛṣṇa's a *good sport* about these things, even with His would-be assassins.

This pastime also illustrates an important point about Kṛṣṇa. God doesn't *become* God by this or that practice. And He doesn't require "growing up" to reach His full potential. God is always God in all circumstances—even as a so-called baby: omniscient, omnipotent, and so on.

In any case, Kaṁsa sent many such superhuman agents to kill Kṛṣṇa, and all the different forms they took were truly astonishing: from a heron as big as a hill, to an eight-mile long serpent, to a gigantic donkey, and so on and so forth.

Essentially, Kṛṣṇa had this daily demon-killing festival, easily destroying all comers without even disturbing His play. He also danced with the *gopīs*, stole butter, lifted Govardhana Hill, and performed many other famous pastimes. Of course, we won't go into these today, but anyone interested can find them in the tenth canto of *Śrīmad-Bhāgavatam*.[53]

Meanwhile, back in the Himālaya Mountains, the Pāṇḍavas were also enjoying their childhood. Arjuna was the same age as Kṛṣṇa, Bhīma was one year older, Yudhiṣṭhira two years older, and the twins one year younger. By the way, *hima* in Sanskrit means "cold" or "snow," and *alaya* means "place." So Himālaya means, "the place of snow" or "the place of cold."

Now, to understand the *Mahā-bhārata* and things that will happen later, it's important to remember that the Pāṇḍavas grew up not as *kṣatriyas* (or warriors), but rather as *brāhmaṇas*, and more, as boy sages. I mean, they were these little kid *yogīs*, running around the hills with deerskin and dreadlocks *(you know, that matted hair you don't bother brushing three hours a day).* So these were the Pāṇḍavas. And this portrait will help explain some of their later behavior. Because even though the Pāṇḍavas were very powerful warriors, they were sometimes reluctant to use their own power.

The Pāṇḍavas had actually taken birth on Earth to assist Kṛṣṇa in His mission of saving the world from the *Asura* insurrectionists, mentioned several times in our talks. Recall that Kṛṣṇa originally told the creator, Brahmā, to instruct the *Suras* (the gods) to begin taking birth on Earth. The specific instruction was, *yaduṣūpajanyatām*: "You, along with your wives, should take birth in the Yadu Dynasty."[54]

---

[53] From *Śrīmad-Bhāgavatam* canto 10, parts 1-4.
[54] From *Śrīmad-Bhāgavatam,* canto 10, ch.1, v. 22.

Throughout the text of the *Mahā-bhārata*, the Pāṇḍavas are constantly called "the Bhāratas" because they were Pāṇḍu's sons by law, making them part of the Kuru Dynasty, also known as the Bhārata Dynasty, in honor of that ancient king. Genetically, however, their only earthly genes came from Kuntī, who was a Yadu princess. In this sense, they were truly Yadus, since their fathers were not of this world at all, but rather some of the universe's greatest gods. Apart from this, the Pāṇḍavas also had a very special connection with Kṛṣṇa.

Briefly, it is understood within the tradition that the Pāṇḍavas, Kuntī, Draupadī (who we'll soon meet), and other great personalities of the *Mahā-bhārata* are actually eternal associates of Kṛṣṇa. These associates travel with Kṛṣṇa from universe to universe, displaying wonderful, adventurous pastimes that people can then talk and sing about—and in this way practice *bhakti-yoga*. So there's a very special connection between Kṛṣṇa, the Pāṇḍavas, and the Yadus.

The Yadus, of course, knew that Kṛṣṇa was now on Earth. So they sent their personal priest into the mountains to inform Pāṇḍu and tell him that the *Asuras* were becoming more aggressive. Unfortunately, Pāṇḍu was not long for this world. At a certain point, the *brāhmaṇa yogī's* curse finally took effect.

The season was spring, a romantic time of year for those so inclined. High in the mountains, the wildflowers were blooming and the day was exceptionally warm. Pāṇḍu and Mādrī were still relatively young, and in this charming atmosphere, with Mādrī scantily dressed, she looked especially alluring—because it was just them, practicing *yoga* in the mountains, surrounded by *yogīs*. And somehow, noticing Mādrī's lovely appearance, Pāṇḍu was struck—*and struck hard!*—with this overwhelming attraction, this uncontrollable desire. He had become a perfect *yogī*, the master of his senses, a self-realized soul; but on that particular day, in that particular circumstance, because the curse was now acting, nothing mattered. Pāṇḍu approached Mādrī with only one thing in mind—*and it wasn't* yoga!

As soon as Mādrī saw the look in Pāṇḍu's eyes, she immediately understood his intention—and, of course, she was terrified, knowing that this would lead to her husband's death. First she tried reasoning with him, but it soon became apparent that Pāṇḍu had *lost* all reason! Then she tried physically keeping him away, but good luck with that! He was, after all, *"Pāṇḍu!"*—a king so strong that no prince dared challenge him at Kuntī's *svayaṁvara.* How could little Mādrī resist his embrace? She couldn't, of course, and at the moment of enjoyment, Pāṇḍu died.

There's a very moving scene where Mādrī lets out this terrible cry that's heard in all directions—because they're up in the mountains where everything echoes. And as soon as Kuntī hears that sound, she knows exactly what it means and exactly what has happened. She gathers the five Pāṇḍava boys together and tells them, "Stay here, don't move." Then, leaving her children, she sets off in the general direction of the cry to confirm what she already knows.

Pāṇḍu's death, of course, changes everything. The loss for themselves and the world is incalculable, and all of them—widows and fatherless sons—are overwhelmed with grief. Their lives will never be the same again, and now they must decide what to do.

In ancient Vedic civilization there was a practice known as *sati,* whereby a *kṣatriya* wife could voluntarily enter her husband's funeral pyre and thus follow him into the next world. I'll say just a few words about this practice before going on.

In later Indian history, *sati* became a type of murderous, forced practice, eventually outlawed by the British. Unlike ancient *sati*, this later version literally forced unwilling women to walk into their husband's funeral pyre to die along with him.

Of course, there are cases, even today, of couples who are so committed to each other that when one becomes afflicted with a terminal illness, the other chooses to die along with his or her mate. I remember reading about Arthur Koestler, the famous British author, who found out he had terminal cancer and decided to commit suicide. When the time came, Koestler's wife decided to join him, saying, "I cannot live without Arthur, despite certain inner resources. Double suicide has never appealed to me, but now Arthur's incurable diseases have reached a stage where there is nothing else to do."[55]

In any case, what we see in *ancient* Vedic civilization is that wives who were advanced in *yoga* actually had the power of *yogāgni*, or "*yoga*-fire"—a form of mystical self-immolation. This can be seen in the story of Satī, the wife of Śiva, which can be found in the fourth canto of *Śrīmad-Bhāgavatam*.[56] In fact, the practice known as *sati* was probably named after her.

As the story goes, Satī's father Dakṣa insulted Śiva during a great sacrifice, and Satī became so upset that she no longer wanted a body that had been received from such a great offender. So she simply sat down, went into *samādhi* (*yoga* trance), and created this *yogāgni*—this fire that emerged from

---

[55] Celia Goodman, ed., *Living with Koestler: Mamaine Koestler's Letters 1945–51.* (London: Weidenfeld & Nicolson, 1985), 78-79.
[56] From *Śrīmad-Bhāgavatam*, canto 4, ch. 4.

her own body to consume it. This is how she gave up the body connected to Dakṣa and came back as Pārvatī. In any case, very advanced souls could actually go through the fire into a higher realm.

(I mean, don't try this at home; this is definitely not something we should do! This was actually done in former ages when people had powers and levels of consciousness that we can't even imagine, let alone imitate.)

Returning to the aftermath of Pāṇḍu's death, both Kuntī and Mādrī had the power of *yogāgni,* and thus knew that wherever Pāṇḍu went they could join him—and both wanted to go. But Mādrī strongly argued against Kuntī's going. "Number one," she said, "at the exact moment of Pāṇḍu's death, his desire was to be with me, so I have to go with him to fulfill that desire. And secondly, let's face it, you're my spiritual superior; thus, you'll be able to raise all five sons as your own, without discrimination—something I may not be able to do." Mādrī had confidence that Kuntī was on such an exalted spiritual level that she would be able to view all five sons with equal vision. Those were Mādrī's arguments, and Kuntī reluctantly accepted them.

There are actually two different versions of Mādrī's death in the *Mahā-bhārata,* because there were different revelations, different stories coming down from different parts of India. And the tendency in Indian history was to be inclusive, meaning that instead of choosing between different versions of stories, it was common to keep them all.

In the first version, Pāṇḍu is cremated right there in the mountains, and Mādrī immediately enters the flames to join him. But it's the *second* version that personally interests me the most, because it develops into one of the most visually dramatic scenes of the entire *Mahā-bhārata.* It is this version that I'll try to describe now:

High in the Himālaya Mountains, after discussing with Kuntī, and entrusting the twins to her care, Mādrī simply gives up her life, having the power to leave her body at will. (Remember that both Kuntī and Mādrī have spent years practicing a very severe discipline of *yoga*, which has made them very powerful *yogīs* in their own right.)

Thus left behind, with the bodies of both Mādrī and Pāṇḍu before them, Kuntī and the Pāṇḍavas are overcome by a profound sense of loss, wondering what comes next. Soon, word comes from Dhṛtarāṣṭra that she and the children should return to Hastināpura.

Those familiar with the area's topography know that when walking down from the Himālaya heights, one gradually comes to foothills, and then to the Ganges valley, which is essentially the main population center. With this setting in mind, we can try to picture this royal funeral procession winding its way down the mountain, to the foothills, and then to the valley below, bearing the bodies of Pāṇḍu and Mādrī—the king and queen of the Kurus. Walking beside them are Kuntī, the surviving queen, and the five Pāṇḍavas—Yudhiṣṭhira, Bhīma, Arjuna, Nakula, and Sahadeva—who, at the time, are between nine and twelve years old.[57]

Coming down from the highest mountains in the world, they are accompanied by the great *brāhmaṇas* and *yogīs* that have lived with them in the wilderness for all these years. As the procession reaches the foothills and begins its journey

---

57 "The *Mahā-bhārata* Chronology," http://www.hindunet.org/hindu_history/ancient/mahabharat/mahab_patnaik.html.

down to the valley, we can imagine the crowds of people that have come to catch a glimpse of these legendary figures, unseen for so many years.

A few words, now, about the five Pāṇḍava princes, who had lived isolated lives high in the Himālaya hills, and had been raised in innocence by parents who were strict *yoga* practitioners. To this point in their lives, these children had never seen a horse, an elephant, a city, or an army, let alone a palace, and all the trappings and fineries of palace life. In fact, they had never even seen more than a few dozen people together in one place at one time. So when picturing the five Pāṇḍavas coming down from those hills, mingling with the procession's adult entourage, picture five child-*yogīs* with sun-tanned faces, long matted hair, deerskin clothes, and so on—*think little Vyāsas!*

From a psychological point of view, one can imagine the impact on these young boys of all the recent shocks in their lives. First, their father passes away, followed by the death of one of their mothers—because Mādrī was a mother to them all. So almost overnight, the twins have been orphaned and Kuntī's three sons have lost two-thirds of their parents. Add to this the fact that for the first time in their lives, the five Pāṇḍava princes are entering not just ordinary society, but *their own* imperial capital. They're going straight from this remote *yoga* retreat, ten thousand feet up in the Himālaya Mountains, to Hastināpura, the hustling, bustling capital of the Kuru dynasty! So we can just imagine what it must have been like for them.

Earlier, I mentioned the crowds watching from below as the funeral procession came closer and closer. This is another really moving scene, with everyone looking at the Pāṇḍavas and asking: "Are those little ascetics the sons of Pāṇḍu? Yes, they must be! Who else could they be?" And, of course, all the people remembered Pāṇḍu, their beloved king, and how he had saved the Kuru Dynasty and restored peace to the world. Pāṇḍu, their great hero, who had now passed away, leaving Kuntī and these marvelous little princes behind.

It is said that the people so loved Pāṇḍu that when they saw the procession coming from the foothills and approaching the capital, the entire population rushed past the city gates to receive their dead king. In fact, Pāṇḍu's death had left the people so overwhelmed with grief that for several days no one even bothered to return to Hastināpura. They literally slept on the ground, mourning the loss of Pāṇḍu, and waiting for the procession to arrive.

These descriptions, I think, make it crystal clear that the five Pāṇḍavas would soon become wildly popular in Hastināpura. Once seeing and getting to know them, the people absolutely adored them, and were waiting for the day that a Pāṇḍu heir would be crowned king.

This, of course, brings us back to Dhṛtarāṣṭra, for whom none of this was good news. By *dharma*, Dhṛtarāṣṭra had now become the legal father of the Pāṇḍavas—and what a dangerous father he was, with all that resentment and ambition burning inside! His nephews were innocent little boys who had just lost their dad and were looking to Dhṛtarāṣṭra for love, affection, and shelter. Indeed, this is what made Dhṛtarāṣṭra's later actions so despicable. Because, let's face it, his only real aim was to take the kingdom from the Pāṇḍavas and hand it over to his son. The only thing holding him back was the sense that he had to move with caution. He had to avoid going too far, too soon, and possibly provoking a popular uprising!

This brings up an amazing feature of ancient Vedic civilization that is worth mentioning here—the fact that there was freedom of speech. You can find many occasions in the *Mahā-bhārata* where people would go right into the town square and criticize or rebuke the king in very strong language. And there is not the slightest hint in the text that such actions were considered inappropriate or illegal. There were no punishments, repercussions, or reprisals for speech. People had the freedom to criticize the government in this civilization. Thus Dhṛtarāṣṭra's fear of public reaction was legitimate, and something that crops up here and there throughout the *Mahā-bhārata*.

In any case, it's not that Dhṛtarāṣṭra was himself an *Asura*; he was just blind—not only physically, but in other ways as well. Duryodhana, however, was another matter. *He* was a full-blown *Asura* insurrectionist, determined to take over the Earth by any means. Knowing that his father really wanted him to be king, yet seeing that he was hesitant when it came to drastic measures, Duryodhana decided to take matters into his own hands and get rid of the Pāṇḍavas once and for all.

Thus, only a few days after Kuntī and the Pāṇḍavas arrive in Hastināpura, Vidura, the wisest of the three brothers, calls them aside to warn that their lives are in danger—that a plot is underway to assassinate them. *"Assassinate?!"* First they lose a father and a mother, then they're thrust into this unknown world, and now—after everything that's happened—someone's trying to *kill* them?! What an introduction to life as a Kuru prince! And that's the state of the Pāṇḍavas.

Now let's return for a few minutes to Kṛṣṇa in Vṛndāvana, and catch up on events there. To go over the geography one more time, Hastināpura was situated in the north, on the

Ganges River. And perhaps a hundred or so miles southwest of Hastināpura was the village of Vṛndāvana, with Mathurā nearby.

Let's recall that Kaṁsa has been sending one demonic *yogī* after another to kill Kṛṣṇa, but that, so far, all have failed. Frustrated, Kaṁsa concludes that what he needs is a "home court advantage"—he needs to get Kṛṣṇa "on his own turf," so to speak. His plan is to lure Kṛṣṇa to Mathurā—the seat of Kaṁsa's military power—and kill Kṛṣṇa there. So he asks Akrūra to travel to Vṛndāvana to bring Kṛṣṇa back,[58] which leads to one of the most famous scenes in all of Indian literature: the *gopīs*, being heartbroken at Kṛṣṇa's leaving, throw themselves in front of Akrūra's chariot to physically prevent Him from going. Of course, Kṛṣṇa *does* leave and the *gopīs* aren't trampled—just devastated at their loss.

In any case, Kṛṣṇa travels to Mathurā with His older brother Balarāma,[59] where Kaṁsa has arranged a wrestling match that he is sure will end with Kṛṣṇa's death. This type of wrestling, by the way, wasn't like "WWE Wrestling," for instance, where combat is basically a choreographed affair. What they called wrestling back then was more like today's mixed martial arts, which is more or less "no holds barred": you can punch, you

---

58 Akrura (whose name derives from the Sanskrit *akrur*, meaning, "who is not cruel") was a minister to Kaṁsa and a chief of the Yadus. Unbeknownst to the *Asura* king, he was also a great devotee of Kṛṣṇa.

59 Balarāma is Kṛṣṇa's elder brother in Their earthly pastimes. Balarāma's eternal status is as the first plenary expansion of Kṛṣṇa that creates and maintains the spiritual and material worlds. "This child, son of Rohiṇī, will give all happiness to His relatives and friends by His transcendental qualities. Therefore he will be known as Rāma. And because He will manifest extraordinary bodily strength, He will also be known as Bala. Moreover, because he unites two families—Vasudeva's family and the family of Nanda Mahārāja—He will be known as Saṅkarṣaṇa." From *Śrīmad-Bhāgavatam*, canto 10, ch. 8, v. 12.

can kick, you can do almost anything to take down your opponent. And Kaṁsa had specifically selected his greatest wrestlers—two gigantic killing machines—to fight with Kṛṣṇa and Balarāma, two twelve-year-old farm boys. When the time came for the match, even the audience was shocked at the imbalance, and thought, "What's going on here?" Little did they know!

To make a long story short, even before the wrestling match, Kṛṣṇa and Balarāma took it upon Themselves to make all kinds of mischief in Mathurā, starting with taking the cloth that was meant for Kaṁsa, having it tailored, and wearing it Themselves! Next, in a scene reminiscent of the *Rāmayana*,[60] Kṛṣṇa went to some sacrificial arena, grabbed this gigantic bow, and pulled its string till the whole thing snapped like a twig. Then, at the gate of the wrestling arena, Kṛṣṇa and Balarāma confronted a large killer elephant purposely placed there to block Their way. When the elephant's caretaker ordered it to attack, Kṛṣṇa killed the beast with its own broken tusk.

Finally, in the wrestling arena, Kṛṣṇa and Balarāma easily killed not only these two great wrestlers, but many others as well, until all the rest simply ran away. Kaṁsa, of course, was just fuming with anger and frustration. He ordered the stadium band to stop playing *(kind of childish, don't ya think)*, and wanted Kṛṣṇa and Balarāma run out of town! Then, flying into a terrible rage, bordering on madness, he ordered the death of almost everyone in sight—from Nanda to Vasudeva to Ugrasena, his own father. At this point, Kṛṣṇa thought,

---

[60] At her *svayaṁvara* ceremony, Lord Rāma won the hand of Sītā, the daughter of King Janaka, by breaking the unstringable bow of Lord Śiva, which was so large that it required 5,000 men to lift and transport.

"Okay, that's it! I've had quite enough of Mr. Kaṁsa and his persecution of the Yadu Dynasty."

Now imagine one of those giant Super Bowl stadiums; and then imagine Kaṁsa all the way at the top, in one of those fancy owner's boxes, looking down over the field. (And remember, Kaṁsa is no ordinary human; he's a powerful *Asura* from another world—a person who would easily dominate and overwhelm even the greatest human fighter.) Then imagine Kṛṣṇa rushing all the way up to that box to finish Kaṁsa once and for all. Kaṁsa, of course, realizes that his time has come, and pulls his sword to kill Kṛṣṇa. But Kṛṣṇa just knocks off Kaṁsa's crown, grabs him by the hair, and throws him down several stories to the floor below, effectively ending Kaṁsa's life.

It's an amazing scene: this little child rushing to the top of the arena, grabbing this powerful *Asura*, and just tossing him out like a rag doll. And, of course, you can imagine the shock. I mean, this is going on right in front of the whole city! Then, just to show everyone that this great, fearful tyrant is really dead, Kṛṣṇa grabs his lifeless body and drags it across the ground, like a lion dragging dead prey. And that was the end of Kaṁsa.

So all this is going on in Mathurā at roughly the same time that the Pāṇḍavas come to live under the so-called "care" of their uncle, whose only real desire is to get his son on the Kuru throne.

The adventure continues tomorrow ...

The Kurus: Agent Provocateurs

So, a quick review. Pāṇḍu and Mādrī had departed this world, and their bodies had been taken by procession down the Himālaya mountains to Hastināpura, accompied by Queen Kuntī and the five Pāṇḍava princes—the heirs to the Kuru throne. With their father gone, Dhṛtarāṣṭra has become the Pāṇḍavas' "father" by *dharma*, but cares only about securing the throne for Duryodhana, his first-born son. The threat is extreme, and Vidura has warned the Pāṇḍavas that there are plots afoot in the capital to have them killed.

This brings us to Duryodhana, identified by expert astrologers as an extremely dangerous *Asura*—someone who would bring down the entire Kuru dynasty if allowed to flourish. At the time of Duryodhana's birth, these same astrologers advised Dhṛtarāṣṭra and Gāndhārī not to raise the child or let him anywhere near the throne. But the royal couple were too attached to their little son and refused to heed their warnings. The current danger to the Pāṇḍavas and their mother comes entirely from him.

Now Duryodhana, who is roughly the same age as Bhīma, is what you might call a precocious young *Asura*. Although he and the Pāṇḍavas are now only around thirteen years of age, he already bears his cousins terrible malice, bitterly resenting their popularity with the people. He's also already "up nights" thinking about that throne! Yudhiṣṭhira's claim is strongest because Pāṇḍu was the legitimate king and Yudhiṣṭhira is the first-born of the whole dynasty. These two factors undisputedly make him the rightful heir, apart from the fact that he's adored by the people, who really want him to be king. Duryodhana can't stand any of this and becomes determined to eliminate all five Pāṇḍavas, beginning with Bhīma.

Duryodhana and Bhīma, being the same age and being very competitive youths, had developed this "perfection" of sibling rivalries. Bhīma, if you recall, was the son of Vāyu, the wind god, so he was naturally the stronger of the two. When the Pāṇḍavas first came to Hastināpura, all the princes would come together for childhood sports, and Bhīma was always defeating Duryodhana—he was just too much to handle. This, of course, fueled Duryodhana's envy, which led to his first attempt on Bhīma's life: cake laced with a lethal dose of poison.

A popular name for Bhīma (found in the *Bhagavad-gītā*) is *vṛka-udaraḥ*, "wolf belly," indicating that he had a voracious appetite and could literally digest anything! *(I mean, he alone could have kept the entire food industry in business!)* Thus, although Bhīma ate the poisoned cake, he apparently digested it with such gusto that it had no effect. Not to be deterred, Duryodhana quickly hatched another plot.

One day, after a bit of sport, he and Bhīma were relaxing on the bank of a river, and Bhīma fell into a sound sleep, which he often did after a good meal. Having planned ahead for this chance, Duryodhana quietly tied Bhīma up with what were supposed to be special, unbreakable ropes, then rolled him into the river to drown. But when he hit the water, Bhīma woke up and snapped the ropes like cotton threads (as if they weren't even there). Another failed attempt!

Of course, Duryodhana was still only a budding young assassin, still hoping that practice would make perfect! But then something happened that postponed any further attempts on the Pāṇḍavas' lives: the arrival of one of the *Mahā-bhārata*'s most important characters—Drona, or Droṇācārya, as he came to be known. And because of Droṇācārya's prominence, I'll take a few minutes to tell you about his history.

Like so many others in the *Mahā-bhārata*, Droṇācārya had a very unusual and dramatic birth. Once, the renowned sage Bharadvāja went to the Ganges to perform his daily ablutions. When he arrived, it just so happened that a beautiful *apsara*[61] named Ghṛtachī was herself in the act of bathing. Seeing the beauty of this scantily dressed nymph, the sage became overwhelmed by desire and lost his semen, which he then preserved in an earthen pot (or *droṇa*). It was from this semen that the powerful *brāhmaṇa* Droṇācārya was born.

Brāhmaṇas, as you know, are the teachers—the professors of Indian civilization. And just as modern universities have specialized professors teaching different types of knowledge, the *brāhmaṇas* of ancient Vedic culture also had their areas of expertise, Droṇa's being the military sciences: martial arts, weapons skills, military strategy, and so on.

In the rendering of Drona's story, there's a popular Hindu misconception that I'd like to rectify by providing some additional information. While attending school *(gurukula)* as a child, Droṇa, a *brāhmaṇa,* became close friends with a young boy named Drupada, who was a *kṣatriya* by birth and heir to the throne of Pāñcāla —after the Kurus, one of ancient India's most prominent dynasties. Drupada and Droṇa were children

---

[61] *Apsaras* are heavenly maidens known for their exquisite beauty and dancing expertise. They visit the lower planets on occasion to seduce great sages and warriors at the behest of certain jealous demigods wishing to weaken those they deem threats to their position.

of the same age, and Drupada, feeling great affection for his friend, promised that when he grew up, he would share all that he had with Droṇa.

Years later, when the two actually *had* grown up, and Drupada was king of Pāñcāla, Droṇa went to Drupada's palace to remind the king of that childhood pledge and to request his share of the kingdom. Obviously taken aback by this sudden appearance and outrageous demand, Drupada barely acknowledged their old friendship, and basically told Droṇa, "I'm not really into splitting Pāñcāla in two right now, so that would be a 'no!'" Things went back and forth for a while, with Drupada even demeaning Droṇa, saying, "If you beg like a proper *brāhmaṇa*, I can arrange for a little something before you go." Droṇa, of course, refused and quickly left the palace, but not without harboring terrible thoughts of revenge!

Here we come to that correction I mentioned earlier. In the more colloquial versions of Droṇa's visit to Pāñcāla, Droṇa is portrayed as a penniless *brāhmaṇa* seeking a way out of poverty. In fact, if you look at the various renderings that have gradually crept into diverse *Mahā-bhārata* manuscripts, there's even one version in which Droṇa's little son is crying for milk that his father can't supply: "But all the other kids have milk!" "I know son, but we're poor; we just can't afford milk." Supposedly, it was this "milk-incident" that finally drove Droṇa to Drupada's palace. But when we consider certain facts found in the *Mahā-bhārata*, this woeful tale of poverty simply doesn't wash. It couldn't have been what happened, and here's why.

Droṇa married a wonderful lady named Kṛpī,[62] who had a twin brother named Kṛpā. These twins had a truly mystical birth, after which they were adopted by none other than the great Kuru emperor Śāntanu *(remember him?)*: husband of Satyavatī, father of Bhīṣma, grandfather of Pāṇḍu, and great grandfather of the five Pāṇḍavas themselves.

As the story goes, Sage Gautama's grandson Śaradvān was "born with arrows," meaning that he was born a great archer, after which, with maturity and practice, he became even greater. But when he performed *yoga* penance to become the greatest archer of all, Indra felt threatened and sent the celestial nymph Janapadī to divert the celibate youth. Distracted by the beautiful lady, Śaradvān lost control, abandoned his weapons, and retreated into the forest to undergo more penance. Before leaving, however, his semen fell on wayside weeds, dividing them in two. From these, boy and girl twins mystically took birth.

At around that time, Śāntanu was hunting in the forest and happened upon the infant twins. Realizing that they were born of a great sage, he named them Kṛpā and Kṛpī, took them back to his palace, and raised them as his own. The male twin, Kṛpā, eventually became the great Kṛpācārya, one of the supreme generals of the battle of Kuru-kṣetra, while his sister Kṛpī married Droṇa, which brings us back to my setting the record straight.

The important point is that in marrying Kṛpī, Droṇa actually married into the richest family in the world at that time. And there is another factor that weighs against the notion that Droṇa was an impoverished *brāhmaṇa*. The powerful martial *avatāra*

---

[62] In Sanskrit, *ṛ* is pronounced ri, as in "trip," and *ī* is pronounced like the double e in "sweet." So Kṛpī rhymes with "trippy"— a phonetic tip for those who insist on calling the honorable lady "Creepy."

Paraśurāma, upon retiring from further warrior-like activities, awarded Droṇa all his supernatural weapons.[63]

So here we have Droṇa, who not only marries into the fabulously wealthy Kuru dynasty, but also receives these extraordinary weapons from none other than Paraśurāma himself. Given this, does it really make sense that Droṇa would have difficulty paying for the ancient equivalent of a carton of milk? Not at all! At least, not to me!

In fact, when Drupada rebukes Droṇa, refusing to give him half of his kingdom, Droṇa immediately heads for Hastināpura, the great Kuru capital, where he is warmly received. With his deep family connections, his vast knowledge of martial arts, and the mystical weapons of an *avatāra*, all he has to do is basically show up and he's completely endowed.

The story of Droṇa's Hastināpura arrival is the stuff of old Hollywood swashbucklers—heroic, dashing, and wonderful!

As he enters the city, Droṇa sees the Kuru and Pāṇḍava princes puzzling over the retrieval of a ball, which had fallen into a well during play. They're all gathered around the well, when young Droṇa walks up, bows, and asks them to step aside. He withdraws an arrow, readies his bow, and shoots down into the well, piercing the ball. Then he shoots a second arrow, which hits exactly into the back of the first; and then another, and another, and another, each of which does the same in its respective order. In this way, Droṇa creates a literal chain of arrows to the top of the well, which he uses to easily extract the ball. Then, he casually turns to the wide-eyed princes and asks, "Anything else?"

---

[63] The Sanskrit word *paraśu* means "axe," and someone that has lots of fun wielding his axe is called "Paraśurāma." Of course, there's a whole story of how, in another time, Paraśurāma used his axe to save the world. But that's not for today.

The boys, of course, are astonished at this feat of archery, and ask, "Who are you?" Droṇa responds, "Go find Grandfather Bhīṣma and tell him what you have seen. He will tell you who I am." Since Pāṇḍu's death, Pitāmaha Bhīṣma has been overseeing the kingdom, acting as regent until the heir comes of age. So all the princes run to tell Bhīṣma what they saw, and he immediately says, "Oh, that's Droṇa."

Shortly after his arrival, Droṇa is made headmaster of the royal military academy and charged with training the Pāṇḍavas and Kurus in military science. *(He also got a nice little palace, and all the milk he could drink!)*

Here I can tell a wonderful story about Droṇa's teaching method and the exceptional attributes of Arjuna. To test his students, Droṇa created a small mechanical bird and placed it in a tree. He then called upon each of his students to shoot an arrow through the eye of the "bird," beginning with Yudhiṣṭhira.

"Yudhiṣṭhira, come forward. Do you see the tree containing that bird?"

"Yes, master."

"And do you see that bird?"

"Yes."

"How about me? Do you see me?"

"Yes, I see you."

"Thank you. You may sit down."

In this way, Droṇa summoned each and every prince, asked the same series of questions, got the same series of answers, and then told each to please sit down.

Finally, it was Arjuna's turn. He came forward and Droṇa asked, "Do you see the tree?"

To everyone's complete puzzlement (with the exception of Droṇa), Arjuna answered, "No."

"Well, do you see that bird?"

"Not at all." *(What, he doesn't see the bird?!)*

"How about me? Do you see me?"

"No sir, I do not." *(Has he gone mad?!)*

"Well, what *do* you see?"

"Only the *eye* of the bird!"

Immediately Droṇa commanded, "Shoot!"

Arjuna fired his arrow, piercing the eye of the mechanical bird.

This story is often used to exemplify the single-pointedness that is required for success in spiritual life. Arjuna, who was destined to become the greatest archer of his time, saw *only* the target and nothing else, just as the serious spiritual practitioner must see only the goal, without diversion to anything else.

So here we have just one example of the type of training these princes received. And it becomes even more interesting when you remember that none of them were ordinary human beings: neither the Pāṇḍavas, who were sons of the *Suras*, nor Duryodhana and some of his brothers, who were themselves *Asura* insurrectionists. All of them had incredible powers, Droṇa continued to train them, and, at a certain point, he deemed them fit and ready for graduation.

At this point, two highly significant events will occur that will have great bearing on the remainder of the *Mahā-bhārata*. The first involves the collection of Droṇa's *guru-dakṣiṇā*, a type of tuition or gift that is offered to the teacher when training is complete; the student must obtain the *dakṣiṇā* and the *guru* has the right to ask for whatever he wants. The second occurs at the princes' graduation ceremony. Naturally, after you send your kids to school, you want to go to their graduation. So there's going to be a graduation ceremony, and something very amazing will happen there.

Before graduation, however, comes the *dakṣiṇā*. And what a vengeful *dakṣiṇā* Drona has in mind! "Boys," he says, "I've awarded you these fantastic weapons, and I've endowed you with tremendous expertise in their use. Now I want you to invade the kingdom of Pāñcāla, defeat Drupada, and secure his kingdom for me! That is my *dakṣiṇā*!"

Drona's demand was particularly hard on the Pāṇḍavas because, as we learn from the text, Drupada was one of their father's dearest friends, practically a member of the Pāṇḍu family. Now they had to hand him a stinging, humiliating defeat, and for a *kṣatriya* to be so defeated was literally worse than death. Kṛṣṇa even mentions this in the *Gītā* [2.34]:

sambhāvitasya cākīrtir maraṇād atiricyate

"For the highly esteemed (*sambhāvitasya*), infamy (*akirti*) is worse than death (*maraṇād atiricyate*)."[64]

So, on the one hand, there was this old family friend, and on the other, there was the order of the *guru*, which was sacrosanct in ancient Vedic civilization. As conflicted as the Pāṇḍavas must have been, they had no choice; they had to follow their *guru*'s command. They attacked the kingdom of Pāñcāla, soundly defeating Drupada.

Now if we recall the last time Droṇa and Drupada met, we can just imagine the scene that's about to unfold. After getting the expected good news, Droṇa comes before a terribly humiliated Drupada, and says, "You know, I'm such a nice guy, that I'm going to do for you, what you wouldn't do for me. I'm going to give back half your kingdom." *(And he really meant it;*

---

[64] H.D. Goswami, ch. 2, v. 34 of *A Comprehensive Guide to Bhagavad-Gītā with Literal Translation* (Gainesville: Krishna West, Inc., 2015), 157.

he really thought he was being a nice guy.) Not having much of a choice, Drupada swallowed his pride, bit his tongue, and took back half of Pāñcāla, his ancient family dynasty. But from that day forward he had only one thought in mind: revenge, meaning the killing of Droṇa!

This incident highlights an unflattering aspect of Droṇa's character—a flaw that Bhīma himself would point out during the Battle of Kuru-kṣetra: Drona was a *brāhmaṇa*, receiving the honors of a *brāhmaṇa*, and yet he had *kṣatriya*-like political ambitions. In the Vedic system, there's supposed to be a clear separation between the two. The *brāhmaṇas* receive great honor and esteem in society precisely because they're in a higher state of consciousness, detached from worldly affairs. To accept such honors while simultaneously harboring political ambitions is hypocritical, problematic, and potentially compromising. In Droṇa's case, his own political aspirations will lead him to fight and kill for the wrong side in the battle between the Kurus and the Pāṇḍavas.

Be that as it may, Droṇa has exacted his revenge by humiliating Drupada and taking the kingdom of Pāñcāla, and Drupada is completely depressed at having lost family lands. He's not interested in half a kingdom; he wants the entirety of Pāñcāla restored to his rightful rule. But he's depressed because he realizes that neither he nor his sons will be able to defeat Droṇa's vast *brahminical* and military power. So Drupada makes a fateful decision: if his *kṣatriya* power is of so little value that he can lose his throne and be utterly humiliated by a so-called *brāhmaṇa*, he will leave for the forest to find some sage with the *yogīc* potency to deal with the problem of Droṇa.

For the time being, however, let's leave Drupada to his

search and return to Hastināpur, where the Pāṇḍavas have not yet heard of Drupada's decision.

Having paid their *guru-dakṣiṇā* by humiliating one of their father's dearest friends, all because of Droṇa's political ambitions, it was now time for the graduation ceremony. I guess everyone here has been to at least one of these milestone events. Whether in a modern or in an ancient context, it's a time of great joy, celebration, and family pride. Some things never change. Dhṛtarāṣṭra even built a special arena for the occasion.

Of course, during the ceremony, all the princes got the chance to show their families what they'd learned in school—exhibiting their different martial skills, using their various weapons, and so on. Arjuna, in particular, displayed amazing skills with all types of regular and mystical weapons. He could perform remarkable feats with arrows, release weapons with *mantras*, manipulate the physical elements, and so on. Indeed, all the princes could manipulate the physical elements: creating water, creating fire, moving earth, and so on—because, back then, there was a type of martial *yoga*. And under Droṇa's tutelage, the Pāṇḍava and Kuru princes had actually acquired these amazing weapon-*siddhis* (or perfections).

Let's digress for a couple of minutes to talk about how these mystical powers worked. It's an interesting topic. In the Sanskrit literature, for example, you frequently read about great sacrifices, where empowered *brāhmaṇas* are able to do almost anything with sacrificial fire. They can create things, they can destroy things, they have almost unlimited power.

A key to figuring out how these *yogīc* abilities worked is found in the Vedic notion that all things in existence are interconnected—an idea borrowed by James Cameron for his film *Avatar*. And to understand the notion of interconnectedness, we can turn to Kṛṣṇa's statements in the *Bhagavad-gītā*, specifically: *mayā tatam idaṁ sarvaṁ, jagad avyakta-mūrtinā*; and, *yo māṁ paśyati sarvatra, sarvaṁ ca mayi paśyati*. Together, their meanings reveal a certain sense of God that is applicable here.

In the first half-verse, Kṛṣṇa explains that God pervades the entire universe with his invisible feature,[65] and in the second half-verse, He explains that one who sees God everywhere and sees everything in God is a real *yogī*.[66] To add a bit more nuance to these explanations, we can also include *Gītā* verse 6.29:

sarva-bhūta-stham ātmānaṁ sarva-bhūtāni chātmani
īkṣhate yoga-yuktātmā sarvatra sama-darśhanaḥ

This basically means that the "*yoga*-linked self" sees God in all creatures and all creatures in God.[67] In other words, the *yogī* sees the same Supreme Self everywhere. And because God is everywhere and pervades all things, in a sense, every point in space connects to every other point in space.

When you study these ancient texts on Vedic sacrifice, you find that the *brāhmaṇas* were able to create different fires in the sacrificial arena: fires representing the earth, fires representing the heavenly world, fires representing the world of the forefathers, and so on; and the sacrificial arena was basically a microcosm of the universe. Think of your computer and the icons on your screen. By clicking on a particular icon you can activate all types of things connected to that icon. In

---

[65] *Ibid.* ch. 9, v. 4, 181.
[66] *Ibid.* ch. 6, v. 30, 174.
[67] *Ibid.* ch. 6, v. 29, 174.

the same way, the fires within that sacrificial microcosm were almost like icons, as were the various things offered in those fires. Together, these enabled the *brāhmaṇas* to connect with and access all varieties of powers.

For example, different *mantras* or different physical objects would actually become icons connected to cosmic elements like earth, water, fire, air, and ether. This, of course, is a whole other, extremely elaborate, topic, but this is the basic idea. So it's not just mythology. It was actually an extremely subtle and sophisticated science.

Perhaps now, we can better comprehend how highly trained and gifted *kṣatriyas* like Droṇa and his uncommon pupils were able to fight using mystic *mantras,* super-charged arrows, elemental weapons, and the like. And here's another interesting fact. In Indian culture, there's a procedure known as *ācamana*, in which one purifies oneself with drops of water before performing *pūjā* or serving deities. Well, a similar procedure was always used by *kṣatriyas* just before releasing their celestial weapons.

Two types of weapons are mentioned in the *Mahā-bhārata*: minutia weapons, which are your ordinary, run-of-the-mill human weapons; and *divya* (celestial) weapons, which are from higher dimensions. And especially when releasing these higher weapons, the text will always indicate that one must perform *ācamana* and chant certain *mantras*, which invoke them by connecting to powerful forces within the universe. There was even one skill (or method) for releasing a weapon, and another for withdrawing it—yes, one could actually pull back a weapon after it had been released. That's something you can't to with a cannonball or a bullet. The closest that modern technology has come to something like this is the ability to make missiles self-destruct or divert from an intended target into the sea. And with this, we can return to Dhṛtarāṣṭra's arena, where the graduation ceremony for the Pāṇḍava and Kuru princes is taking place.

As Arjuna continues exhibiting all these fantastic military abilities and powers, suddenly there's a commotion at the arena entrance, as a very passionate, hostile, and angry young stranger walks to the center of the grounds, points toward Arjuna, and boldly announces, "Whatever he can do, I can do as well." The entire crowd is stunned to silence at this shocking claim: "Is the guy deranged?" No, not at all.

The angry young man is none other than Karṇa, Kuntī's long-abandoned son, who we last saw floating down the Ganges in a basket. This means, of course, that Karṇa is actually a brother to the Pāṇḍavas, although neither he nor they know it. Indeed, there's only one person on Earth who knows the truth: Kuntī herself! And she's not about to disclose that fact to anyone. In any case, now would be a good time to say a few words about this singular young man.

In India, Karṇa is seen as every mother's son, in the sense that everyone feels sorry for the poor abandoned lad. And although I can also sympathize, if you actually read the *Mahā-bhāraṭa's* Sanskrit text, a somewhat different picture emerges. In other words, there are a few things we need to know about Karṇa in order to balance our understanding.

Recall that Karṇa was born due to Kuntī's teenage union with the sun god, and was then sent floating down river, where he was found and adopted by a very loving, childless couple. So the first point is that Karṇa was not unloved; to the contrary, he grew up in a tremendously loving environment.

The *Mahā-bhārata's* next mention of Karṇa is when he

barges into the graduation ceremony while these young princes are performing for their families. Remember that two of the Pāṇḍavas were complete orphans and the other three had lost their father and one of their mothers. Also, in Hastināpura, they've grown up in very difficult, even dangerous, circumstances. And now Karṇa, for no reason that's mentioned anywhere in the *Mahā-bhārata*, has singled out Arjuna as the object of his loathing and wrath. He can't stand the attention he's getting and wants to humiliate Arjuna in front of his whole family—on the very day of his graduation! So this is the "poor Karṇa" that causes Indian mothers to weep.

Now I'm not trying to destroy Karṇa's character, because he also has many good qualities and attributes. After all, he *is* born of the sun god and the exalted Queen Kuntī. To be fair, however, Karṇa does have some character flaws that are simply undeniable.

For instance, in his eagerness to gain power, Karṇa lied to the *avatāra* Paraśurāma, who we've mentioned several times before. Paraśurāma's mission in coming to Earth was to destroy certain *kṣatriya* elements that were violating *dharma*, after which he basically retired. Still, Paraśurāma had all these powerful "*avatāra*" weapons, and Karṇa wanted to become his student. The challenge was that Paraśurāma had a real problem with *kṣatriyas* and would only teach *brāhmaṇas*. At that point, Karṇa lied, telling Paraśurāma that he himself was a *brāhmaṇa*. Of course, as explained in the text, the truth eventually came out, and in a most clever way.

One day Paraśurāma was lying down with his head in the lap of his student when some kind of ferocious little bug began biting Karṇa. Not wanting to disturb his *guru*'s sleep, Karṇa just clenched his teeth, tolerated the pain, and didn't say a word. When Paraśurāma awoke and noticed what was going on, he immediately understood that only a *kṣatriya* could have this type of self-command and tolerance of pain. Obviously, then, Karṇa was really a *kṣatriya*! Paraśurāma was furious, cursed Karṇa in various ways, and so on.

The thing that Karṇa had going for him, of course, was that his birth was the most aristocratic of all Kuntī's children. In Vedic culture, it is understood that all the royal families in the world, all the *kṣatriyas*, come down from either the sun god or the moon god. So Karṇa, being the direct son of Sūrya and the Yadu princess Kuntī, was extremely aristocratic. And yet, like Satyavatī, he wound up in a social situation where he was unable to act according to his stature, qualities, and birth. He was frustrated, but tried to overcome his circumstances by lying and cheating.

At a later point in the *Mahā-bhārata*, something similar will happen to the Pāṇḍavas—a circumstance in which these great warriors lose everything, including the opportunity to act as *kṣatriyas*. And yet we see a very different response: they don't lie or cheat; they essentially go away and dedicate themselves to self-realization.

Returning to the graduation ceremony, as I already mentioned, there is not a hint anywhere in the *Mahā-bhārata* that Arjuna or any of the Pāṇḍavas had ever offended Karṇa. Yet he entered that arena with the absolute determination to humiliate, defeat, and even kill Arjuna, because ... Well, you almost want to use the *"e"* word: he's *envious*! He just can't stand Arjuna's success.

The thing is that Karṇa not only claims but actually begins to show that he can perform as well, if not better, than Arjuna. Finally, he challenges Arjuna to a duel: "Let's settle this here and now! A fight to the death!" And again, Arjuna has never laid eyes on the guy in his life. Where's all this malice, this vitriol coming from? Arjuna has no idea, but it's clear that Karṇa has some serious issues here.

Then, before things get too out of hand, Bhīma plays the caste card and says, "Hey buddy, what's your last name? What's your *ghotra*? Are you even a *kṣatriya*? Because *we've* never heard of you, and we know all the royal families in these parts." This leads to a very poignant moment in the *Mahābhārata* where Karṇa's aging father, the chariot maker Adhiratha, enters the scene—a respectable guy, but nowhere in the league of the princely class. And, at once, everyone realizes, "Oh my god, that's his father," answering the question of Karṇa's status.

Karṇa, of course, is deeply mortified by the revelation, but Duryodhana (observing everything with an *Asura*'s watchful eye) realizes, "Here's the man that can get me what I want; here's the man that can kill Arjuna." So he steps forward, with the most transparent of motives, suddenly becoming *Monsieur Liberté, Egalité*, and says, "Well, if he's not already a king, I'll make him one now!" And with that, Duryodhana immediately anoints him as king.

This is interesting because the Old Testament kings were also anointed—they were anointed with oil (*mashiach*); and the Vedic kings were anointed with water (*abhiṣiktaḥ*). So it appears that *abhiṣiktaḥ* is the Sanskrit equivalent to "messiah": "the one who's been anointed."

This story also illustrates that there was flexibility in the ancient Vedic caste system. Notice that when Duryodhana made Karṇa a king, no one stood in protest, saying, "Wait a second, you can't just make him a king." In fact, the Vedic *brāhmaṇa* literature explicitly states that despite one's birth, it is *qualification* that ultimately counts. And in the *Gītā*, Kṛṣṇa repeatedly maintains that one's position in the *varna* system is born of one's nature (*svabhāva-jā*) and depends on one's qualities (*guṇa-karma-vibhāgaśaḥ*).[68]

So Duryodhana, who had accumulated all kinds of lands under his father,[69] immediately anointed Karṇa and made him the king of Aṅga, some remote place out there in the Kuru boondocks. But what's interesting here is that Karṇa never once visited Aṅga, which is not entirely uncommon in these sorts of circumstances.

If you study the history of the Japanese monarchy, for example, you'll find that while certain rulers were technically in charge of this or that province, they never actually visited there. Instead, they hung out in the emperor's palace, the center of state affairs. Karṇa was like that. Indeed there's no mention anywhere in the *Mahā-bhārata* of Karṇa ever setting foot in Aṅga. He's rather always seen hanging around Duryodhana.

In any case, now that Karṇa has been made part of the kingly class, he can legitimately challenge Arjuna to a fight. Unfortunately, the fight is cancelled on account of rain. What happens is that Sūrya, the sun god, and Indra, the rain god, see that their sons are heading for conflict. So they create this major weather event that disperses the crowd and ends the ceremony. There will be no fight today, but the battle lines have been clearly drawn.

With Karṇa now on board for the Kurus, Duryodhana becomes more confident and emboldened, believing that he

---

[68] *Ibid.* ch. 4, v. 13, 165-166.
[69] Dhṛtarāṣṭra means "one who held on to the kingdom."

can now defeat the Pāṇḍavas. It's a brand new day, and he's ready to resume, and even intensify, the old assassination game. He comes up with what he thinks is a foolproof plan for getting rid of the Pāṇḍavas once and for all. And if it's discovered, or goes awry, there's always Karṇa, waiting in the wings to protect him.

Earlier, when Duryodhana was younger and first tried killing Bhīma, Dhṛtarāṣṭra had found out what his son was up to; and yet, there were no consquences or repercussions. It was more like, "Don't do that again; or, at least, don't get caught." Now, years later, Duryodhana again approaches his father with a more modest proposal: "If I had just one year without the presence of the Pāṇḍavas, one year with full authority over the Kuru treasury, one year with the power to grant awards and promotions, bribe generals, and secure alliances with other kingdoms, I could easily gain control of the entire Kuru kingdom." To this, Dhṛtarāṣṭra essentially replied, "Go for it!" In reality, though, Duryodhana has something far more sinister in mind.

One thing becomes apparent when reading ancient Indian political texts: they were really into espionage; theirs was a spy-intensive political culture. So Duryodhana instructs some of his agents to spread the rumor that somewhere toward the north of the Kuru kingdom, in the foothills, where it's cooler in the summer, there's this fabulous new resort called Vāraṇāvata. Soon all of Hastināpura is abuzz with the news: "Have you heard about Vāraṇāvata?" "Of course, we're planning on a trip this summer." "Well, we've just got to go! I hear it's really amazing!" In this way, gradually, everywhere in the kingdom, it's Vāraṇāvata this and Vāraṇāvata that. Vāraṇāvata, "the new destination of choice!"

Of course, the Pāṇḍavas also eventually hear that there's this great new location, "Vāraṇāvata." So one day, Dhṛtarāṣṭra, in consort with Duryodhana, calls the Pāṇḍavas into his chambers and says, "You know, everybody's talking about Vāraṇāvata. I think maybe you kids should go take a vacation there. *How does a year sound to you?*"

The Pāṇḍavas agree, and here it's important to remember that these five boys grew up as *yogīs*, as sages, and they were still extremely innocent and naive. Dhṛtarāṣṭra was their father by *dharma*, so the idea that he could desire their harm, or that they could refuse to obey him, was entirely inconceivable at this point in their lives. The culture back then was that strong. In fact, even a few years ago, when children in India would write letters to their father, they would begin, *Pujya Pitaji,* "Worshipable Father." It's still a very strong culture, even today; so imagine what it was like thousands of years ago.

Of course, once the Pāṇḍavas agree, Duryodhana puts the more sinister and secret aspect of his plot into motion. He instructs a cohort named Purochana, one of his darker agents, to go to Vāraṇāvata and build a special house for the Pāṇḍavas—a very nice house that, in reality, will be a deadly fire trap! He tells Purochana to build with every available flammable material so that the house will just burst into flames and consume everyone inside. And this is precisely what Purochana does. If anything, Purochana is worse than Duryodhana.

Fortunately for the Pāṇḍavas, their good uncle Vidura discovers the plot at the last minute, just as the princes are making their way out of the city, accompanied by crowds of people, who have come to see them off with great fanfare, celebration and pomp.

Vidura makes his way toward his nephews. He needs to pull them aside and tell them what he knows, but with caution, since half the people in the crowd are Duryodhana's spies—and Duryodhana himself is also lurking about. He can't tell it to them straight, since he might be overheard; and he can't send someone later, since he has no idea when the fire will occur. What if it's on "day one"? No. He has to tell them now, but how?

Vidura's solution is to deliver the message in a type of Vedic "jive talk" called *mleccha-vaca*, a language of the lower classes. He goes up to Yudhiṣṭhira and starts explaining things in this obscure language that almost no one understands. Yet even then, he fears that if he's too explicit someone in the crowd may figure it out. So he speaks to Yudhiṣṭhira in very indirect and cryptic terms: "One is not in danger who knows that fire cannot burn the soul; one can find his way who knows the stars." As oblique as these statements might seem, they were enough for Yudhiṣṭhira, who was very bright and thoroughly trained to be an extremely shrewd and clever warrior. From Vidura's *mleccha-vaca*, he immediately knew there'd be an assassination attempt by fire and they would have to escape at night.

With that, the Pāṇḍavas leave for Vāraṇāvata, where Purochana awaits: the assassin who will ignite their tinderbox house when they least expect it, killing them all in the process. To do the job, he has housed himself next door, in an armory where weapons are stored. And here's the tricky part: even though the Pāṇḍavas know of the plot to burn their house, they can't just pack up and leave, since this would alert Duryodhana, who would immediately come after them with the whole Kuru army (now under his full control).

The situation is very tense. The Pāṇḍavas know that an attempt will be made on their lives, but they don't know when. And they can't let Duryodhana know that they know, so leaving in plain sight isn't an option. They're effectively stuck in a fire trap, waiting for the trap to spring—or, in this case, ignite! Is it *checkmate* for the Pāṇḍavas, or only *check*? You'll have to wait till tomorrow to find out!

Bhīma: The Unstoppable Force

Yesterday, we left Queen Kuntī and the Pāṇḍavas in the "resort town" of Vāraṇāvata, living in this highly flammable house. To make sure that the house would "do its job," Duryodhana had instructed Porochana to use the most burnable materials available; he was then to wait for just the right time to set it all ablaze, with Kuntī and the Pāṇḍavas inside. Fortunately, just as they were about to leave Hastināpura, Vidura secretly warned them of the danger.

After arriving in Vāraṇāvata, the Pāṇḍavas introduced themselves to the community in a way that provides some insight into the social relationships of those times. Going from home to home, they paid their respects to all types of people, regardless of social class. At each home, they introduced themselves and lingered for a while, chatting, getting to know the family, asking about the area, and so on. And basically, within twenty-four hours, they were as popular in Vāraṇāvata as they had been in Hastināpura. The Pāṇḍavas were friendly, accessible, and unpretentious. In other words, they were natural leaders.

Of course, when they first arrived, Purochana was waiting to present the "grand new home" that he had built *"just for them."* All were polite, but as soon as he had gone, Yudhiṣṭhira started poking around, scratching walls, inspecting floor boards, and so on. It didn't take long for him to realize that Vidura's coded warning was well-founded. This wasn't a house, it was an *incendiary device!* Once lit, it would burn hot and fast!

The Pāṇḍavas were in grave danger, and they knew it. To make matters worse, they had no idea when Duryodhana's agent might strike: a day, two days, a week? This left them in an extremely vulnerable position, with escape being far more complicated than just packing their bags and walking out the door. They would need to escape secretly, without being discovered by Purochana—which, in effect, meant Duryodhana, who was now in command of the entire Kuru army. The Pāṇḍavas needed a foolproof plan, *and fast!* As it turned out, expert help was on the way from an always reliable source: ever faithful Vidura.

Although, by *dharma*, the Pāṇḍavas were Dhṛtarāṣṭra's wards, for reasons we now know well, he could never really care for them. Vidura, on the other hand, actually loved the Pāṇḍavas and was determined to protect them at all costs. He had no intention of leaving things stand with that warning back in Hastināpura. Remember that Dhṛtarāṣṭra came out blind, Pāṇḍu came out pale, but Vidura came out brilliantly intelligent. And he had a plan!

Secretly, Vidura sent a trusted agent, an expert engineer and excavator, to join the Pāṇḍavas in Vāraṇāvata. But since the entire kingdom was aware of Vidura's special affection for his nephews, he knew they would need to be sure it was *Vidura*, and no one else, that had sent them help. He knew that the Pāṇḍavas would need proof that the engineer was really on their side. Vidura thus supplied him with certain facts that only Vidura and the Pāṇḍavas could know. By providing these, the engineer was able to quell their fears and convince the Pāṇḍavas of his loyalty and good intentions.

It was now time to reveal Vidura's plan—simple in design, yet not without its challenges: the engineer would excavate a tunnel beneath the house that ran through the city and beyond its borders. To imagine this, of course, we must remember that agrarian, pre-industrial cities were not as large as those of today. So the Pāṇḍavas house was close enough to the city limits to make this kind of one-man excavation possible. Given this, and with an expert excavator on hand, the plan was solid and doable; the tunnel would allow for a secret, unseen escape. But with Purochana lurking about, watching their every move, it would be difficult to dig without being detected and jeopardizing the entire operation.

To solve the "Purochana problem," the Pāṇḍavas began to profess a passionate love for nature. They told Purochana of their need to roam the countryside each day, taking long walks, riding the plains, exploring the forests, and so on. Purochana, of course, had been ordered to not let the Pāṇḍavas out of his sight. And so, each day, as they wandered far, far away from Vāraṇāvata, wandering somewhere behind them—perhaps hiding behind every tree and bush—was Purochana *(who, it seems, had also taken his own "sudden interest" in nature!)*. Meanwhile, the excavator was free to dig and construct his tunnel. There was also a second reason for the Pāṇḍavas' daily excursions: gaining knowledge of the countryside and settling on the best route of escape. And from Vidura's cryptic message about the stars, they knew to effect a nighttime escape, making a good grasp of the terrain essential.

Eventually, a day came when the Pāṇḍavas sensed that Purochana was about to act. Of course, we can only imagine the type of life they were living up till then. It must have been a very tense period. For one thing, at least one person had to be awake guarding while the others slept; and it's certainly not much fun knowing that your next door neighbor's trying to kill you. I mean, something like that can really ruin your vacation (*Disney World would definitely lose its charm!*).

In any case, sensing that Purochana was about to make his move, the Pāṇḍavas decided to act first. It was late at night and the entire town was asleep (including their would-be assassin). Bhīma edged outside, set fire to the Pāṇḍavas' house, and also torched the next-door armory, where Purochana slept. He then joined Kuntī and his brothers in the tunnel, and together they made their escape, leaving Purochana to his fate.

Here, we don't have to feel too bad for Purochana, since he was the kind of person whose death even his mother would not lament. And Bhīma really had no choice. If the Pāṇḍavas had left Purochana alive, he would have told Duryodhana that he hadn't started the fire, leaving them dangerously exposed. So it was absolutely necessary to eliminate Purochana before they escaped.

When Kuntī and the Pāṇḍavas finally emerged from the tunnel, they were exhausted. They had lost a lot of sleep waiting for the cover of night. Then, after setting the fires, they had to really move through that tunnel. At the end, they were extremely fatigued, and still very anxious, but at least they had escaped. The nighttime air must have felt refreshing and cool. They were on their way!

And here's where the Pāṇḍavas' nature-loving ruse really paid off. It was pitch dark, but they knew exactly where they were going and how to get there—and they had "Vidura's stars" to guide them. So they moved along at a rapid pace, putting as much distance as possible between themselves and Vāraṇāvata. The text actually describes that at one point Kuntī,

Yudhiṣṭhira, Arjuna, and the twins were so exhausted that they just couldn't go on. So Bhīma, the son of Vāyu, simply swooped all five into his arms and carried them part of the way. And when they just couldn't go any further, they stopped to rest. Soon everyone fell asleep while Bhīma stood guard. Then, a very curious thing occurred.

India, back then, was filled with vast jungles; and within those remote and primitive environs lived what are called *rākṣasas*—these ferocious cannibals that come in and out of the stories in the Sanskrit texts. Well, as it happened, near to where the Pāṇḍavas were sleeping lived two particularly dangerous *rākṣasas* named Hiḍimba and Hiḍimbā *(a brother and sister act)*. And when Hiḍimba smelled (or somehow detected) that humans were in the area, suddenly, it was like, "Feast time!" Apparently, humans were a rarity in Hiḍimba's neck of the woods, so he was definitely in the mood.

(After all, he hadn't eaten humans for a long time, and you know how it is: every once in a while you want some Italian or Chinese ...!)

In any case, Hiḍimba sent his sister to scout things out, or maybe just kill a human or two and bring the carcasses to him. But when Hiḍimbā came upon the Pāṇḍavas' campsite and saw Bhīma guarding, something unexpected happened: she didn't want to eat him, she wanted to marry him! Hiḍimbā had fallen in love. And realizing that her present *rākṣasī* form was pretty ghastly *(like, every day is a "bad hair" day)*, she decided to use the *yoga* power of *kāma-rūpa* to transform herself into this stunning young lady (*à la* Pūtanā). Then, she walked right up to Bhīma and asked him to marry her. She also told him of her real identity and her brother's intentions. Bhīma, of course, wasn't at all concerned.

Meanwhile, back in the jungle, Hiḍimba was getting impatient—and hungry—thinking, "What happened to my sister? Where's my gourmet meal?"

(And, you know, it's not uncommon for people to become a little irritated when their food is late. It happens even among sadhus! *If you don't believe me, ask Durvāsa)*

Finally, Hiḍimba's patience wore thin and he went to the campsite to investigate the hold up. Of course, when he arrived, he saw his sister all decked out in this new human-type female form, talking to Bhīma. It didn't take long for Hiḍimba to figure out what was going on, and he became *enraged*: "What are you doing? Why are you flirting with my food?!"

At this point, a major fight breaks out between Hiḍimba and Bhīma, and Hiḍimba is thinking, "As soon as I finish off this character and have my meal, I'm gonna kill my sister too—because she's obviously losing it. I mean, a human? She's out of control!"

Thus far in our walk through the *Mahā-bhārata*, we haven't heard much about Bhīma or really seen him in action. We've learned that as the son of Vāyu, Bhīma possesses superhuman strength. And we know he's a born fighter—someone that just loves to fight! For Bhīma, the prospect of mixing it up with some *rākṣasa* is not a cause for anxiety. It's a preferred competitive sport, pure recreation, a pleasant way to spend a Sunday afternoon!

Thus when Hiḍimba begins making his moves, Bhīma thinks, "Finally, there'll be some fun around here to break the monotony!" Bhīma was as happy about fighting Hiḍimba as Hiḍimba was about eating Bhīma. It would be an interesting, if one-sided, match!

Bhīma and Hiḍimba circle each other, ready to attack. Suddenly Hiḍimba uproots a giant tree and tries to bring it down on Bhīma's head; but Bhīma blocks it with his arm, shattering it into pieces. Not to be outdone, Bhīma himself uproots a tree and bashes it on top of Hiḍimba. This goes on until all the trees in the area are gone! Then they start hurling giant boulders at each other until all these are gone as well. With nothing left worth throwing, Bhīma and Hiḍimba just start beating each other with their fists.

Now, with all this commotion going on, it isn't long before Arjuna wakes up, sees Bhīma fighting with this *rākṣasa*, and says something that I've always found interesting from a linguistic point of view. I'll explain.

The Sanskrit of the *Mahā-bhārata* is generally called "Classical Sanskrit." Much of it is poetic, and thus very carefully crafted. But sometimes, what breaks through in the text, and especially in the dialogue, is the impression that they're just speaking the way people really spoke back then, which is not that different from the way we speak today. In composed Sanskrit, the syntax is often very different from regular speech—as it would be, for example, when reciting a highly crafted English poem. But when you encounter this more realistic dialogical Sanskrit, you find that it's actually similar to the way we talk.

That's what struck me when I first read in Sanskrit what Arjuna tells Bhīma after waking up; and I remember it even today. He says, *tarasva mā krīḍā,* "Hurry up, don't play around!"— because Arjuna becomes irritated when he sees Bhīma having his ususal brand of fun with this *rākṣasa,* intentionally prolonging the inevitable. He tells his brother, "Stop playing around with this guy and just finish him off," because it's dangerous, it's making a lot of noise, and it could attract the wrong kind of attention.

Bhīma gets the message and does what he typically does in these fight situations: he lifts Hiḍimba up above his head and starts spinning him around faster and faster, till the blood is practically rushing out of his eyes, mouth, and nose. Then, using all the momentum of that spinning motion, Bhīma forcefully slams the man-eating giant to the ground.

(*I mean, Hiḍimba didn't even have a chance to tap out; he was just gone!*).

After all that uproar, however, the Pāṇḍavas were worried and decided to decamp; they really felt the need to move on as soon as possible. But wait a minute! There was also the matter of Hiḍimbā! Let's not forget poor, love-struck Hiḍimbā.

Hiḍimbā had been watching the whole fight from the sidelines, rooting not for her brother *(a most unlovable man-eater)*, but rather for Bhīma. Then, when everything was over and she saw the Pāṇḍavas leaving, she became utterly heartbroken. In desperation she approached Bhīma, begging him to marry her and stay. Bhīma, however, wanted nothing to do with Hiḍimbā and was even thinking of killing her or perhaps just scaring her away. But Yudhiṣṭhira, the son of Dharma (the god of justice), admonished him: "First of all, this is a woman; and, second of all, how could she be a threat when you've already taken care of her much stronger brother?"

Hidimbā thanked Yudhiṣṭhira for his kindness and then approached Kuntī with tears in her eyes: "You know how a woman suffers when she's in love like this. My desire for Bhīma is so strong that it's literally killing me. If I can't be his wife, I don't want to live. It's as simple as that!"

When Bhīma heard this, even he was somewhat moved. He

told Hidimbā, "Look, I follow Yudhiṣṭhira; whatever he says, I'll do." Yudhiṣṭhira then made the final decision: "Hidimbā can marry Bhīma, and he can give her a child; but afterwords, he must leave with us, and she must stay behind." For various practical reasons, bringing Hidimbā along just wasn't an option. This is the sort of thing that sometimes happens in the literature: a man would accept a woman, or give her a child, and the woman, in a sense, would live her life with the child.

Now, Hiḍimbā, because she had these powers, takes Bhīma on this flying honeymoon. And they beget a child named Ghaṭotkaca, who figures later in the story. Ghaṭotkaca means "pot shine" and is called this because he was bald from birth. Apparently, even though Hiḍimbā had transformed herself into a ravishing beauty, she was, genetically, still a *rākṣasī*. Thus Ghaṭotkaca bore some of the traits of his mother's actual form.

A quick aside: to take our Sanskrit analysis of Ghaṭotkaca's name a bit farther, *ghaṭa* literally means "a pot," and *utkaca* literally means "shining forth." Actually, Śaṅkara and other philosophers often used the word "*ghaṭa*" in some of their more famous analogies, like the one about the clay pot.

In any case, Hiḍimbā and Bhīma have this unique child, who becomes a great wizard with magical powers, like the ability to fly, increase and decrease his size, become invisible, and so forth. Ghaṭotkaca will also play an important role in the Battle of Kuru-kṣetra, fighting on the side of the Pāṇḍavas.

After Ghaṭotkaca's birth, as previously agreed, the Pāṇḍavas left Hiḍimbā and the boy behind and continued on until they came to a town called Ekacakra. Here, of course, they're not alone anymore; they have to intermingle with other people. And because Duryodhana's agents may be looking for them, they have to keep their identities secret. They have to hide in plain sight, because discovery means a swift and certain death. This is where the Pāṇḍavas' Himālayan upbringing as *brāhmaṇa* sages really pays off. When they have to hide, they hide as *brāhmaṇas.* And because they know what being a *brāhmaṇa* is all about, they can actually pull it off.

Siblings raised by deaf parents naturally become expert in the language of sign. When they grow up and leave the home, of course, they *speak* their language, like almost everyone else. But if they ever need to have a private conversation, they can always revert to sign language, which, in a sense, is their mother "tongue." Similarly, the Pāṇḍavas' "mother" culture, you could say, was the culture of *yogīs* and *brāhmaṇas.* Therefore, they knew exactly how to wrap their robes and exhibit all the outward signs and conduct of authentic *brāhmaṇas.* And this is exactly what they did: they disguised themselves as young *brāhmaṇas,* wearing these sort of baggy "Jedi Knight" robes (because they needed a good deal of cloth to wrap around their large, muscular frames).

(It worked for the Jedi Knights, and it worked for the Pāṇḍavas! Well, actually, it worked for the Pāṇḍavas first, didn't it? Maybe George Lucas got it from them!)

After arriving in disguise at the town of Ekacakra, the Pāṇḍavas sought shelter in the home of a very generous *brāhmaṇa,* who had a wife, a daughter, and a small boy. And, for some time, they lived very happily in this *brāhmaṇa's* home. Not long after arriving, however, the Pāṇḍavas discovered that the people of this town contended with a terrible evil—a plague upon their lives. That evil took the form of yet another *rākṣasa,* this time named Baka. And to make matters worse, the local king was weak and unable to protect them, leaving the entire town vulnerable and subject to Baka's whims. Thus, for the overall safety of the population, Ekacakra had to strike a dreadful bargain with the beast: each month, a different family would have to sacrifice a member (a father, a mother, a daughter, a son) to be eaten alive. The extent of the town's suffering is hard to imagine. It was a tragic situation.

Now, one might say, "Why did they stick around? Why didn't they just run away?" Well, it wasn't that easy. As we learn from the text, Baka wasn't the only *rākṣasa* around. The area was full of them. So anyone trying to escape ran the risk of becoming the next *rākṣasa* snack. Ekacakra, it seems, was one of those places where you could get *in,* but you could never get *out. (Wasn't the Hotel California like that?*[70]*)*

Perhaps out of politeness, the Pāṇḍavas' hosts never said a word about the town's plight; so for some period of time they just weren't aware of the situation. This changed one day when Yudhiṣṭhira, Arjuna, and the twins went out to beg alms, and Bhīma stayed home with Kuntī. (To keep up appearances, the Pāṇḍavas' daily *brahminical* routine included the begging of alms.)

In any case, on this particular day, Kuntī and Bhīma suddenly heard this terrible wailing coming from one of the rooms in the house. Wanting to find out why, they discretely made their way toward the sounds. I don't know if they had doors with doorknobs back then, or just hung cloths, but Kuntī and Bhīma got close enough to overhear this very strange conversation, punctuated by many tears: evidently, each family member was trying to convince the others, "I'm the one who should die."

---

[70] "Last thing I remember, I was running for the door; I had to find the passage back to the place I was before. Relax, said the night man, we are programmed to receive. You can check out any time you like, but you can never leave!" From "Hotel California" by The Eagles. *Hotel California.* Asylum Records 6E-103, 1976, LP album.

First they heard the father talking to his wife: "I should be the one to die, because if I die all of you will live! And it's the duty of the father to protect his family. Somehow, the Lord will help you get along. And you know the children can't live without their mother." Then they heard the mother answer: "No, I should be the one to die! If you die, then neither I nor the children will be protected, and who knows what will happen to us. I just can't face that; so it's better that I die." Then, even the daughter chimed in: "No, you're both wrong! It should be me. You both need to stay alive to take care of my little brother."

At this point, Kuntī was thinking, "What in the world is going on here?" She wasn't going to wait to find out. Entering the room without being invited, she demanded, "What's wrong here? What is all this terrible talk of dying?"

The father then told Kuntī of the town's "arrangement" with Baka, explaining that it was now their family's turn to make the sacrifice—to choose one from among themselves to be eaten alive. Imagine the horror of having to choose a member of your own family to be devoured by a giant demon. Kuntī herself wouldn't hear of it. She turned to the family and said, "None of you are going. I'm sending my son Bhīma instead!" This, however, seemed to horrify the family even more! But why? Because they were deeply committed to what can be called the culture of hospitality.

One of the wonderful things about ancient Vedic civilization is how much people valued this culture of hospitality, so much so that a common phrase of the times was, *atithi devatā*, which means that the *atithi* (the guest) in your home should be treated like *devatā* (God Himself). Let's digress for a few minutes to talk about this notion of *atithi devatā*, since hospitality was such a significant feature of Vedic society. We can start with the word *atithi*, guest.

Sanskrit, like Spanish, French, or German, is a gendered language, and *tithi*, which means "lunar day," is a feminine word. That's why the names of all the days of the month are feminine, like *Ekādaśī, Dvādaśī*, and so on—they're feminine because they're *tithis,* lunar days. And there are special *tithis* (holidays, birthdays, and so forth), where guests are ordinarily invited to one's home—like when you invite grandma over for Christmas. Here, the idea is that these important occasions are days in which guests—often family members and friends—are specifically expected. And, of course, such guests are naturally treated with great warmth and hospitality.

This, however, was not the real test of ancient Vedic hospitality. The real test was how you treated someone that was *atithi*: an uninvited guest that just showed up unexpectedly on an ordinary day. That's why such guests were called "*a-tithi*." And this is where the notion of *atithi devatā* comes in. The idea is that even such an *atithi,* to whom you have given shelter, must be treated as if he were *God*—as if God Himself had come to your home.

The more subtle point here is that God *factually has* come to your home, since God is in everyone's heart. In other words, anyone that comes to your home—be they relative, friend, or stranger—is literally a temple of God. There's a beautiful verse in the *Śrīmad-Bhāgavatam* (11.2.47) that speaks to this point:

arcāyām eva haraye
pūjāṁ yaḥ śraddhayehate
na tad-bhakteṣu cānyeṣu
sa bhaktaḥ prākṛtaḥ smṛtaḥ[71]

---

[71] See canto 11, ch. 2, vs. 47 of *Śrīmad Bhāgavatam*

Basically, this means that one who worships God in the temple, but neglects to honor that same God in the heart of every living being, is on the material, not the spiritual, platform. The idea is that the God who resides in the temple, church, mosque, or synagogue also resides in the heart of every living being. And therefore, every living body (human or otherwise) is actually a temple of God. So that's the idea. And I must say, "it's a good idea!"

Now let's return to the *brāhmaṇa* family, who had just rejected Kuntī's proposal to send Bhīma in their stead. This family was so committed to the culture of hospitality—this spiritual understanding of the Lord in the heart—that they literally said, "We would rather die than sacrifice a guest in our home." And that's when Kuntī told a roundabout truth: "Actually, I wasn't thinking of *sacrificing* my son. You see, Bhīma is actually a very powerful *yogī,* with special *mantras* that can neutralize *rākṣasas.*" Even hearing this, however, the *brāhmaṇa* family still refused Kuntī's offer.

But Kuntī, this powerful, aristocratic, and highly self-realized queen of the world, was not someone to whom you said "no." Apart from being a Yadu princess and a great devotee of Kṛṣṇa, she had spent years performing extraordinary *yoga* practices high in the Himālayas, where she had achieved great spiritual and mystical power. She also had led an absolutely sinless life. In other words, Kuntī was a force to be reckoned with. When she spoke, people were almost compelled to listen! She firmly told the family, "No more protests. This is what we're doing. And please have no fear for my son."

When the other Pāṇḍavas returned from collecting alms, they were told of all that had transpired. However, they were not very enthusiastic about Kuntī's plan. They didn't want to risk losing Bhīma, who was absolutely essential to their mission on earth: assisting Kṛṣṇa to establish just rule and rid the world of *Asuras*. But Kuntī was not pleased at her sons' reluctance and admonished them, saying, "Don't think like this! Now is the time to be *kṛta-jña*," the Sanskrit word for "grateful." *Kṛta* means, "what was done," and *jña* means, "knowing;" so, *kṛta-jña* literally means, "knowing [and not forgetting] what was done for you."

Kuntī was reminding the Pāṇḍavas that when they first came to Ekachakra after fleeing the "burning house," it was the *brāhmaṇa* and his family who took them in, gave them shelter, and allowed them to live safely and happily in disguise. Now that Baka's cruel bargain had brought death to their door, it was time for the Pāṇḍavas to step up, acknowledge this family's hospitality, and repay the debt by killing Baka. Kuntī specifically wanted Bhīma, an expert demon-killer, to do the job. And once again, it was Kuntī's irresistible will that prevailed. It was obvious who was in charge! We can imagine the Pāṇḍavas bowing their heads to mother Kuntī as Bhīma prepared himself to go.

The rules of Baka's ugly game were truly incredible! The family that won *(really, lost)* the lottery had to fill an oxcart with various foods *(it seems the man-eater fancied himself something of a gourmet and wanted plenty of side dishes to garnish his meal)*. Then, the "main course" had to drive the wagon to an appointed spot, where Baka would be waiting. This time, however, it wasn't some ordinary, shivering-in-his-boots victim that was driving the cart. It was Bhīma, the son of Vāyu.

We can now try to imagine this scene. It's nighttime, Bhīma is driving this oxcart filled with all kinds of food, and this *rākṣasa* is waiting out there to devour the whole thing: oxen, driver, food, and maybe even the cart itself *(except, perhaps, for the nails)*. Now, as he's driving along, Bhīma begins to think, "Why should I waste all this good food?" So he starts to snack, and snack, and snack ... [72]

Of course, by the time Bhīma arrives, Baka's food is almost gone. And when this huge *rākṣasa* notices the bits of remnants in the near-empty cart, he is not a happy camper. Enraged beyond belief, he screams, "You ate my food," and strikes Bhīma with a blow that would have been fatal for an ordinary human being. For Bhīma, however, it's merely like a slap from an annoying little child. Completely unfazed, he holds Baka back with one hand while eating what's left with the other. Then, after finishing his meal, and in utter contempt of this *rākṣasa*, Bhīma gets down, casually washes his hands, turns to Baka, and gives him a good smack. *(Bhīma's got style.)*

Now, of course, a big brawl breaks out that isn't too dissimilar from the one we just witnessed between Bhīma and Hidimba. And even though Bhīma can end these types of events in two seconds flat, he can never resist the opportunity for some good old-fashioned fun. The back and forth between the two rapidly rages through the tree-heaving, boulder-smashing, fist-fighting phases, with a few good chokeholds and body slams thrown in for good measure. It's a real fight. Finally, Bhīma decides, "Enough is enough; I have other things to do." And just as all great wrestlers have their one famous hold, this special thing they do, Bhīma also had his own trademark maneuver—his winning move.

He picks Baka up, spins him around at high velocity, and

---

72 Another name for Bhīma is Vrikodara, meaning "wolf-bellied" or "voracious eater."

then throws him to the ground with maximum force! But that isn't all, because Bhīma really didn't like this *rākṣasa* and all his horrible deeds. The text actually describes what happens next: Baka is lying face down, stretched out on the ground, with Bhīma at his side; then, with one arm around the *rākṣasa's* neck, one knee pressing down on his back, and the other arm stretching around his legs, Bhīma just folds Baka backwards till he breaks like a brittle twig and dies. Afterwards, he takes the body back to Ekachakra and dumps it at the city gates.

The next morning, when people woke up and came out of the city to tend their farms, they saw the *rākṣasa's* broken body and were stunned. Not only was the great and terrible Baka dead, but he had been killed in a ghastly way by someone with superhuman strength. Immediately, everyone started asking, "Whose turn was it anyway? Who could have done this?" Then they all came rushing to the *brāhmaṇa's* house to find out what happened.

Of course, all the *rākṣasas* in the area also saw Baka's body. Actually, the text says that after Bhīma killed Baka, he warned the other *rākṣasas*, "This is what's going to happen to you if you don't start behaving yourselves." And with this warning, Ekachakra became the only town in the world in which humans and *rākṣasas* actually got along. Because the *rākṣasas* had become very nice and polite, like, "Good morning Mr. Jones. And how are you today?" They never forgot what happened to Baka.

In any case, before the townfolk came looking for answers, Kuntī had already told the family what to say. So the *brāhmaṇa* informed them: "A great *yogī* was passing through our town, and I let him stay in my house. And it so happened that this *yogī* had a powerful *mantra* to control *rākṣasas*. It was with this that he went and killed Baka." After that, the town declared an annual holiday to honor the *brāhmaṇa* because of what that *yogī* had done.

And it was at this point that the ever-wise Kuntī began thinking that it was time for the Pāṇḍavas to move on. For now, the townfolk had accepted the story of the mysterious *yogī* and his demon-slaying *mantra*; but how long before they started thinking about those nice young men staying at the *brāhmaṇa's* house? True, the Pāṇḍavas played their roles with great expertise. Still, they couldn't hide the fact that they were far larger and more muscular than your average *brāhmaṇa.* Kuntī reasoned that it was only a matter of time before someone started seriously wondering whether her sons might have had something to do with Baka's death. And so, one day, she gathered the boys together and informed them that they had lingered in Ekachakra long enough, enjoying the hospitality of the village and exploring the beauty of the countryside.

By coincidence, just around the time the Pāṇḍavas were preparing their departure, a *brāhmaṇa* had arrived in town. In those days, wandering *brāhmaṇas* were a type of ancient news service. Sages were always traveling from place to place, and wherever they stopped along the way, they would share all that they had heard and seen with the locals. In exchange for charity, these *brāhmaṇas* provided medical, astrological, and other forms of ancient expertise, including, of course, the provision of spiritual knowledge. But they were also the ancient equivalent of CNN *(in this case, BNN, the "Brahminical News Network").*

It was one of these saintly "broadcasters" that happened to come to town, meet with the Pāṇḍavas, and tell them all the news of the world, including one particular bit of information that caused Kuntī and the Pāṇḍavas to adjust their plans.

Tune in next time for the full BNN report ...

Arjuna: The Impossible Shot

When we last spoke, Kuntī and the Pāṇḍavas were preparing to leave Ekachakra, fearing that Bhīma's very public killing of the *rākṣasa* Baka would attract unwanted attention. Before they left, however, a traveling *brāhmaṇa* gave news of a particular happening that greatly aroused their interest and oriented the direction of their next move—something we'll be talking about today.

Before this, however, let's go back for a few minutes to discuss how certain previous events were perceived by the rest of the world. We can begin with Vāraṇāvata and Bhīma's burning of both the armory and the Pāṇḍavas' flammable house. How did the world perceive and understand this? For one thing, when the house burned down, news spread like *wildfire* that Kuntī and the five Kuru princes had expired in the flames. This shocking turn of events, of course, was a major "headline" that *struck hard* throughout the kingdom.

But things weren't completely clear-cut; there was still some mystery surrounding these deaths, especially for Duryodhana and his crew. For one thing, Purochana had also died, leaving Duryodhana without the firsthand confirmation he expected to receive. Some also thought it odd that Purochana had died along with the Pāṇḍavas, which was definitely not part of Duryodhana's plan. And Duryodhana himself remained uncertain and perplexed due to his agent's unexpected death.

What about the ordinary citizens of Hastināpura, who loved and adored the Pāṇḍavas? How did they feel? How did they react to reports of their deaths? Already, suspicion of assassination plots had been in the air; so hearing the news, in a sense, confirmed the public's worst fears, creating a climate of unrest. We in America, who actually lived through the assassinations of the Kennedys and Martin Luther King, know firsthand how the people of Hastināpura felt—the frustration, anger, and suspicion that must have gripped them. People actually went out into the streets to blame the government for the Pāṇḍavas' deaths.

I already mentioned that there was freedom of speech in ancient Vedic civilization. People were able to openly criticize the government without fear of censure or reprisal. And here we have an example of this principle in action. People strongly suspected that the Vāraṇāvata fire was not some random accident, but rather an intentional act of arson; they also strongly suspected that Duryodhana was behind it. So they took to the streets to vent their anger, call out the government, and protest against an outrageous crime.

Now, in some versions of this story, before setting the fire, the Pāṇḍavas removed six bodies from the local morgue and laid them in the house, hoping they would be taken as proof that the Pāṇḍava family had indeed perished in the flames. As the fire blazed higher and higher, its brilliant flames, menacing sounds, and all-too-familiar smells awakened a sleeping population; the whole city came alive in the middle of the night and everyone rushed to the Pāṇḍavas' house. Back then, of course, cities weren't equipped with the sophisticated firefighting tools of today—specialized vehicles, helicopters, water dispensers, and so on. Thus the crowds could do little more than watch in horror as the inferno burned the house to the ground. And since the Pāṇḍavas were nowhere to be seen, everyone assumed the worst.

Later, after the fire had run its course and only a smoking shell was left, the remains of six badly charred bodies were discovered—burnt beyond recognition. And without modern forensics to provide a definitive answer, everyone naturally assumed that these were the bodies of Kuntī and her five sons. Word soon went out to Hastināpura that the entire Pāṇḍava family had been killed in a mysterious fire.

So far we've talked about the reactions of Duryodhana and the inhabitants of both Hastināpura and Vāraṇāvata. But what of Vidura, who had warned his nephews of the danger? How was he taking news of the fire? For one thing, even if Vidura disbelieved the death reports, with so many spies around, he had to play the part of the grief-stricken uncle.

On the other hand, there were real elements of anxiety, confusion, and strain in his so-called pretense of grief. Like Duryodhana, Vidura had received no ironclad word about the Pāṇḍavas' fate—no confirmation one way or another. He knew there was a plan in place and that his engineer had finished digging an escape tunnel. But he was completely in the dark about what had transpired after that. Had Purochana succeeded in killing the Pāṇḍavas, only to become trapped in the blaze himself? Or had the Pāṇḍavas killed Purochana and made their escape? Vidura simply didn't know.

I mean, in all the panic and adrenal intensity of their rush through that tunnel, with Purochana burning up behind them, letting Vidura know they were actually alive was not the first (or even the second) thing on their minds—nor was it as simple as just sending him a quick SMS. In the immediacy of their escape, and even after reaching Ekachakra, there was no effective way of getting a message to their uncle—no one they could trust with the secret of their identities.

So, on the one hand, we have a situation where Vidura strongly suspects but cannot confirm that the Pāṇḍava family is alive, and, on the other hand, we have a situation where Duryodhana and Dhṛtarāṣṭra strongly suspect, but cannot confirm, that they are dead. And being extremely shrewd politicians, we can imagine that Duryodhana and his men were watching Vidura like hawks, waiting for that unguarded moment, for the slightest sign of relief, triumph, or contentedness, for that one chink in his armor of grief. The bottom line is that everything was up in the air for all the important players, and the people in general were shocked, angry, and suspicious of the Kuru clan.

Here we can imagine that news must have eventually reached Duryodhana that not too far from Vāraṇāvata, on the night they were supposed to have died, a *rākṣasa* had been brutally killed—Bhīma's trademark! Of course, by that time, the Pāṇḍavas were already living with the *brāhmaṇa* family in the distant town of Ekacakra, making it more difficult for Duryodhana to connect this coincidental killing with a possible Pāṇḍava escape. The general belief was that Kuntī and the Pāṇḍavas were dead. After all, didn't they find their charred remains? Still, there were suspicions in certain quarters that the queen and her sons were *not* dead—that they had somehow survived. It remained an open mystery: they were probably dead, but ...

(You'll see why I keep emphasizing this in a few minutes.)

But let's get back to Bhīma's very public killing of Baka,

Kuntī's decision to "get out of Dodge" before it's too late,[73] and the Pāṇḍavas' chance meeting with the wandering *brāhmaṇa* just before leaving Ekachakra. Recall that in this ancient civilization, wandering sages and *brāhmaṇas* would often carry the news. They were articulate, intelligent, and able to move in high governmental circles, being of the *brahminical* class. Thus they were privy to a great deal of valuable information. They also often congregated at different "*brāhmaṇa* watering holes," where they would exchange reports—and, in this way, spread the news.

The *brāhmaṇa* who spoke with the Pāṇḍavas was among this group, and he shared some shocking yet extremely interesting news. To understand why, we need to recall Droṇa's demand that the Pāṇḍavas use all their advanced military skills and weaponry to invade the kingdom of Pāñcāla, defeat Drupada, and secure his kingdom for Droṇa. Recall also that this demand was particularly hard on the Pāṇḍavas because Drupada was one of their father's dearest friends—practically a member of the Pāṇḍu family. Unable to refuse their teacher's order, the Pāṇḍavas had no choice but to hand Drupada a stinging, humiliating defeat—all because of Droṇa's need for revenge. Then, to add insult to injury, Droṇa had offered back half the kingdom to Drupada—a cynical act of extreme condescension. With no other choice, Drupada swallowed his pride and grudgingly accepted Droṇa's "remnants," but from that day forward he had only one aim in life: to destroy Droṇa and reunite his kingdom. The question was how?

---

73 The phrase, originating in 1878, is attributed to Bat Masterson, then Sheriff of the unruly cattle town of Dodge City, Kansas. After a gunfight that killed his brother, he had had enough, and exhorted his remaining family members to "get out of Dodge" at once. As a result, the phrase has come to mean flight from a difficult or dangerous environment as quickly as possible.

Here we need to remember that Droṇa was not only a master of military science, but also in possession of a superhuman weapon given to him by Paraśurāma himself. He was thus one of the most dangerous men in the world, far too formidable to defeat with ordinary *kṣatriya* power. Realizing this, Drupada had lost his will to govern and left for the forest, determined to find some *brāhmaṇa* or yogī who could help to crush Droṇa once and for all. That was the last the Pāṇḍavas had heard of Drupada.

And now, after many starts, stops, and delayed promises, I'm finally ready to reveal the travelling *brāhmaṇa's* "headline news": the news of what happened to Drupada after leaving his kingdom and entering the forest.

For many days, Drupada searched here and there until he finally came upon two powerful *brāhmaṇas*, the brothers Yāja and Upayāja. In Sanskrit, *upa* means "small" or "little." Often, a younger brother is given his name simply by adding *upa* to the older brother's name. Indra's kid brother, for example, is named Upendra (meaning "little-Indra"); and here we have Yāja and Upayāja (meaning "little-Yāja").

In any case, imagine King Drupada, one of the most powerful *kṣatriyas* of his time, coming across these two ascetic *yogīs* in the middle of the woods. What did he do? Did he order? Did he demand? No! He humbly approached these personages in the mood of a disciple and remained as their menial servant, attending to their every need. Eventually, due to the king's sincere service, Yāja and Upayāja granted his wish for a son that would kill Droṇa! Thus, on Drupada's behalf, the brothers performed a powerful mystical sacrifice, from the fires of which came this consummate warrior named Dhṛṣṭadyumna, who literally flew out of the flames, born with the power to kill Droṇa.

But that wasn't all! From the very altar of this sacrificial fire *(and at no extra charge to Drupada)*, a type of goddess emerged (although human, she was also, in a sense, a goddess). Her temperament was fiery, and her beauty was so overwhelming that it was viewed as a creation of the gods to destroy the *Asuras*. Indeed, so great was her beauty that again and again the *Asuras* would succumb to and eventually be destroyed by it. This, of course, was Draupadī (the daughter of Drupada), also known as Pāñcālī (because her father's kingdom was Pāñcāla), Yājñasenī (because her father defended the sacred sacrifice), and Kṛṣṇā, with the long feminine *"ā"* at the end, (because she was so devoted to Kṛṣṇa).

So these were the developments that the Pāṇḍavas knew nothing about, being off in the remote town of Ekachakra, dealing with their own predicament. And to hear that Drupada, their dear most "uncle," had conjured a son who would one day kill their *guru* was too much to bear. They were shocked! Dismayed! Disturbed! It appeared that the balance of world power was about to shift, and there was more: Draupadī, whose beauty was now legendary, was about to hold a *svayaṁvara* to choose a husband.

When the *brāhmaṇa* who had conveyed all this news looked carefully at the large, muscular "*brāhmaṇas*" seated before him, he was struck with an idea: "You *brāhmaṇas* are in pretty good shape. Why don't you travel with me to Draupadī's *svayaṁvara* and compete for her hand?"

At this suggestion, the Pāṇḍavas began to think strategically. Here was this legendary beauty, the daughter of their father's closest friend. If they could somehow win Draupadī's hand, thereby forming an alliance with Drupada, they could stand up to Duryodhana with the backing of a major world power, and in this way come out of hiding. So the Pāṇḍavas had two important reasons for participating: firstly, there was Draupadī herself, this stunning, highly qualified princess, providing a romantic incentive; and secondly, there was a very practical geopolitical incentive as well.

The *brāhmaṇa's* invitation was accepted, and soon thereafter, Kuntī and her five *"brāhmaṇa"* sons started out for Draupadī's *svayaṁvara.* Along the way, they would sometimes walk alongside their new *brāhmaṇa* acquaintance and sometimes walk alone. One evening, while alone, they went to the bank of the Ganges to take bath, where they encountered Citra-ratha, the king of the *Gandharvas,* who was already bathing in its waters. Citra-ratha was somehow annoyed at their arrival and insulted them, saying, "Stay away from this river! At this time of the night the Ganges is only for *Gandharvas.*"

Recall that the *Gandharva* Citrāṅgada had killed their forefather, the son of Śāntanu, simply because he had the same name. Perhaps remembering this incident, Arjuna stepped forward and boldly replied, "Sir, the Ganges is a sacred river; anyone at any time can take shelter in her waters without restriction." With that, Citra-ratha fired a weapon at Arjuna, who, it must be admitted, was thrilled at the chance to once again display his skills.

Because he had been attacked without cause, the laws of chivalry allowed Arjuna to respond in kind and he immediately released these flaming weapons that literally knocked the *Gandharva* unconscious and burned his chariot to ashes. When he awoke, Citra-ratha—who actually turned out to be quite a good sport—told Arjuna, "My name used to be Citra-ratha (one who rides in a colorful chariot), but now you can call me Dagdha-ratha (one whose chariot burned up)!"

After this, the journey continued until the Pāṇḍavas finally reached the kingdom of the Pāñcālas, where they took up residence in the house of a potter and began living the sort of *brahminical* life they had led in Ekacakra. And because they expertly adopted the dress, mannerisms, and lifestyle of genuine *brāhmaṇas*, they went about their affairs without being recognized by the general population. Finally, the day of Draupadī's *svayaṁvara* arrived, and the Pāṇḍavas made their way to the event.

Svayaṁvaras were elaborate affairs, and Drupada had spared no expense to accommodate his royal guests and display the richness and opulence of his kingdom. The king's palace, the *svayaṁvara* arena, and the specially built guest quarters were all architectural wonders, adorned with varieties of golden and jeweled ornaments, flower garlands, flags, festoons, and so on. Then there were the many arriving royal entourages: *kṣatriya* kings and princes, attired in their most glorious outfits, riding here and there on golden chariots, giant elephants, and graceful steeds, each accompanied by his own military guard. And let's not forget the accompanying queens and princesses, along with their ladies in waiting, who had also come to see the great event.

Apart from the *kṣatriyas*, there were many, many *brāhmaṇas,* who had come from far and wide to witness the competition and receive charity from the king. For the *brāhmaṇa* class, which lived on charity, great events like Draupadī's *svayaṁvara* were economically important activities—opportunities for the king to display his largesse by showering these priests, advisors, and teachers of society with varieties of gifts and donations.

Of course, when it came to giving away his beautiful

daughter, Drupada's secret, long-held dream was that she marry one of Pāṇḍu's sons, whom he loved as if they were his own. That dream, however, had been dashed with news of the Vāraṇāvata fire and the apparent deaths of the Pāṇḍavas and Queen Kuntī. Still, somewhere in the back of his mind, Drupada held onto a small sliver of hope that the rumors were false—that somehow or other they had all survived.

Although the text doesn't explicitly mention it, we can assume that since Drupada was close to Pāṇḍu, he also was close to Vidura, and knew that he was especially looking out for the family's safety. Whatever the case, Drupada's suspicion that the Pāṇḍavas were still alive must have been somewhat strong since he and Draupadī had arranged a *svayaṁvara* that especially favored the Pāṇḍavas. That challenge was in two parts: the bow and the impossible shot!

As with Rāma at Sītā's *svayaṁvara* and Kṛṣṇa at the sacrificial arena in Mathurā, the first segment of the competition involved bending and stringing an oversized, extremely inflexible bow that no ordinary human being could even lift, let alone string! Anyone able to accomplish this tremendous feat of strength, next had to execute a feat of archery that was even more impossible.

High above the competitor's head was a revolving wheel, and beyond that, a small target. While concentrating on the target's reflection in a turbulent pool of water, the archer had to lift this giant bow over and behind his head, pull back its stiffly held string, and shoot an arrow between the spinning spokes to the middle of the target. No amateurs here, please! Even for a skilled archer, this was a daunting task!

In the stands sat Drupada, Draupadī, Dhṛṣṭadyumna and many royal guests, along with exalted members of the *brahminical* community. Crowds of ordinary people also gathered to observe these dazzling affairs, sitting in trees, peeking through lattices, and pressing against barriers, while others looked down at the proceedings from the tops of surrounding roofs.

Because of Draupadī's legendary beauty, all the important princes of the world had come to compete for her hand. And, of course, among these were the Pāṇḍavas' great enemies, Duryodhana, Karṇa, and other members of the Kuru clan. In the guise of *brāhmaṇas*, the Pāṇḍavas were there as well, seated among those of the *brahminical* class.

Draupadī's brother, Dhṛṣṭadyumna, stood and announced the details of the challenge and the contest began. The results, however, couldn't have been more disappointing as prince after prince stepped forward and then almost immediately returned to the stands, having failed to string the bow. More often than not, in the middle of the attempt, the whole bow would somehow snap free, sending a hapless prince or king flying backwards onto the ground. There, he'd lay unconscious, his jewels, bangles, and headdress scattered in the dust. After a few minutes he'd wake, as if from a dream, collect his belongings, and make his way back to his seat.

We can imagine how these proud young *kṣatriyas* felt as they picked themselves up, dusted themselves off, and returned in shame to the stands, pretending that the laughter had nothing to do with them. Sitting back down, trying to exude as much dignity as possible, they might have said something like, "Hey, I only half-tried; I didn't really want to string that bow anyway. I mean, the girl's not *that* pretty, is she?"

In this way, all the more ordinary princes were humiliated

one after another; then, even the greatest kings and princes of the world failed to string that bow—including Duryodhana himself. This scandalous result meant that not even one among them had qualified to move on to the next phase: the impossible shot.

Let's pause and take a breath, because I'm now going to mention a truly monumental moment in the *Mahā-bhārata*: the very first time that Kṛṣṇa and His elder brother Balarāma appear in its pages, seated among the *kṣatriyas*, observing all the goings-on at Draupadī's *svayaṁvara*. What's interesting here is that even though the Pāṇḍavas are completely disguised, wearing baggy *brahminical ("Jedi")* robes, with their hair tied in some sort of special *brahminical* way, and so on, as soon as Kṛṣṇa glimpses them, He turns to Balarāma and says, "Look, there are the Pāṇḍavas. That one over there's Yudhiṣṭhira, there's Bhīma, that's Arjuna, and those are the twin heroes, Nakula and Sahadeva."

This is something that I have always found striking since there is no indication that Kṛṣṇa ever laid eyes on the Pāṇḍavas prior to this event. From the very first time that Kṛṣṇa appears, the *Mahā-bhārata* makes it clear that He is not an ordinary human being: Kṛṣṇa is perfectly aware of everyone's identity—and far, far more than that.

In any case, after all the most famous kings in the world have been either brought to their knees or thrown to the ground by trying to bend this incredibly stiff bow, the *brāhmaṇas* begin coaxing Arjuna, "Why don't *you* give it a go? What have you got to lose?" And Arjuna, who has been carefully observing Draupadī's beauty and outstanding qualities, is eager to give it a try. He steps forward and walks toward the bow. The crowd's reaction is mixed.

The *brāhmaṇas,* of course, are really getting a kick out of this turn of events: "Hey look, it's one of our guys!" Back in ancient times, when *brāhmaṇas* got really excited and wanted to cheer, they would do this funny thing: they would take off their *chādars* (top cloths) and wave them around.

(Back then, you know, there weren't any stadium horns and they hadn't yet invented "the wave;"[74] *so* brāhmaṇas *just wildly waved their top cloths).*

The *kṣatriyas,* on the other hand, were jokingly dismissive, but also irritated at the audacity of this *brāhmaṇa* "upstart!" They sniggered, mocked, and sneered: "You guys just keep waving your little cloths. We're the most powerful humans in the world and we couldn't string that bow! What do you think one little *brāhmaṇa* can do? Besides, this event isn't for *brāhmaṇas* in the first place. If you know what's good for you, you'll just stick to ringing your bells, chanting your *mantras,* and making your fires!" There was definite tension in the air, but these *kṣatriyas* weren't overly concerned; they were thinking, "This is ridiculous; this is just some *'schlemiel.'*"[75]

So the crowd reacts in various ways as this unknown *brāhmaṇa* in strange baggy robes approaches the bow, with the *kṣatriyas* half-expecting him to trip over his own clothes. But when Arjuna deftly bends, strings, and arms the giant bow without even breaking a sweat, the boisterous crowd is stunned to silence, as every eye is riveted on the scene below!

---

[74] "The Wave" (also known as the "Mexican wave") is a type of synchronized group cheer popular at American football and baseball stadiums, where, one after another, contiguous sections of fans briefly rise, raise their hands, and then sit down, creating the appearance of a huge wave undulating from one end of the stadium to the other.

[75] A Yiddish term for an inept, clumsy person, a bungler, or a dolt. Yiddish is a Germanic language, originally spoken by the Jews of Central and then Eastern Europe.

Then, with penetrating focus, Arjuna meditates on the target's quivering reflection in the water, carefully positioning his bow and drawing its string. He appears almost frozen in time as every person in that arena holds their breath and looks on. Finally, Arjuna releases the arrow, which shoots past the spinning wheel, striking the target dead center!

Amazement! Astonishment! Pandemonium! The crowd erupts as the ordinary onlookers and *brāhmaṇas* break into spontaneous cheers! They're loving it! The *kṣatriyas,* on the other hand, are furious: "We give you *brāhmaṇas* all this charity, all these alms and gifts. And now, on top of that, you want to steal our women?!" They are positively livid with rage and want to kill this mysterious *brāhmaṇa*.

As I mentioned before, even when a regular *kṣatriya* king or prince wins the day and takes his bride, he usually has to fight his way out of the arena. But here we have an even more explosive situation: someone who really shouldn't have won at all! We can only imagine how slighted, angry, and humiliated these proud warriors felt, having been outdone in a contest of martial skill and strength by a *brāhmaṇa*. They rushed out of the stands to attack Arjuna, who had been garlanded by Draupadī and was about to leave the arena with his prize. And what happened next makes for a kind of farcical scene.

In a sincere attempt to defend one of their own, all these scrawny, little *brāhmaṇas* poured out of the stands with their tiny water pots (*kamaṇḍalūs*) and bamboo rods (*daṇḍas*) to fight off these powerful, heavily armed *kṣatriyas*.

(You know, bop the king on the head with a water pot, poke him in the belly with a bamboo stick! There's actually a lot of humor in the Sanskrit text, if you relax a bit when you read.)

In any case, because these are *brāhmaṇas (and most* brāhmaṇas *are actually kind of uncoordinated, especially when it comes to fighting!)*, Duryodhana goes over and basically toys with them, keeping them at bay just to make sure they don't hurt themselves. Arjuna, however, is a different matter: the *"brāhmaṇa"* who bent the bow, hit the target, and was about to walk off with Draupadī, the most beautiful princess in the world.

Shortly before the melee broke out, Yudhiṣṭhira and the twins had left the event to check on their mother at the potter's shop. So only Arjuna and Bhīma are present when things go ballistic and Karṇa rushes toward Arjuna, brandishing some sort of weapon. Bhīma, of course, is also posing as a sort of oversized *brāhmaṇa*. But when he sees his brother being attacked, he immediately steps forward. And just by his stance, people begin to suspect that he's actually a *kṣatriya*—that this guy really knows how to fight!

In any case, Karṇa decides to teach this big *brāhmaṇa* a lesson and attacks Bhīma with a burst of arrows. Undaunted, Bhīma calmly holds his ground and counterattacks with his own barrage. Suddenly, it's Bhīma and Arjuna on one side and all these somewhat reluctant warriors on the other—reluctant because they're fighting *brāhmaṇas*, and *kṣatriyas* just don't do that! Then again, these two don't battle like ordinary *brāhmaṇas*; their skills are deadly, and it's requiring maximum effort just to keep them at bay. So this wild skirmish is going back and forth on the arena grounds while a number of other kings are angrily chasing Drupada through the stands for giving his daughter to a *brāhmaṇa*. So now the king of Pāñcāla is basically running for his life in his own ceremonial arena! Like I said, it's a pretty farcical scene.

Anyway, to make a long story short, Bhīma and Arjuna gradually fight their way out of the arena and make it back to the potter's house with the beautiful Draupadī in tow. Recall that Draupadī had placed the ceremonial garland on Arjuna, technically accepting him. It was basically a "done deal," so she naturally went with him.

By this time, Drupada had secured his own safety by taking shelter of the *brāhmaṇas*. He then asked his son, Dhṛṣṭadyumna, to follow those two *brāhmaṇas* and discover their actual identities. Because it suddenly dawned on Drupada that in all the excitement at the arena—the hitting of the target, the boisterous crowds, the garlanding, the melee, and so on—he had handed over his daughter to some random stranger: "I have absolutely no idea who just took my daughter! Dhṛṣṭadyumna, find out all you can about that *brāhmaṇa*. I mean, who *is* that guy?"

So Dhṛṣṭadyumna somehow finds the potter's house and begins to spy on the inhabitants. First, he notices that there are a total of five, not two, *brāhmaṇas*, and that none of them have typical *brāhmaṇa* bodies. To the contrary, when seen disrobed, these are large, muscular men, built like warriors, and with typical warrior scars (marks on the arm from regularly shooting arrows). He also manages to overhear their conversations, all of which seem to be about war, weapons, battle strategies, fighting techniques, and so on. No talk here of *mantras*, *mudras*, fire sacrifices, the Vedas, or anything like that!

For Dhṛṣṭadyumna, the answer is obvious, so he goes back to Drupada and reports, "Father, I don't think these *brāhmaṇas* are *brāhmaṇas*; I think they're *kṣatriyas*! Also, the two that fought their way out of the arena, and maybe even all five, seem to be brothers." Because he had never met the Pāṇḍavas,

Dhṛṣṭadyumna was unable to recognize them. Recall that like Vyāsa, Dhṛṣṭadyumna and Draupadī had taken celestial births, meaning that they started out not as infants, but rather as mature young adults. That's why, although appearing older, Dhṛṣṭadyumna had never met the Pāṇḍavas: he was only recently born. However, when Drupada heard this description, his longstanding hope returned, and he dared to consider, "Five, not two? Brothers? What if these are the Pāṇḍavas?"

After a *svayaṁvara*, the father of the bride generally prepares an elaborate reception for the happy couple. But in ancient Vedic civilization, there were different ways of receiving people from different sectors of society. Typically, there was a *brahminical* reception, a *kṣatriya* reception, a *vaiśya* reception, and a *śūdra* reception. And since Drupada had given his daughter away to a total stranger—who held himself out as a *brāhmaṇa* but appeared to be something else—he was unsure of what type of reception to prepare. Maybe the guy was just a real tough *śūdra*! Drupada's interesting solution was to prepare receptions for all four *varṇas*, just in case.

(And then, it's like diplomacy: "When they get here, we'll figure out who they are. And when we know, we'll just press the right varṇa button, and all will be well.")

All this leads to another of my favorite *Mahā-bhārata* scenes. Drupada sends word, inviting Arjuna and his family to be received at the palace. By this time, all the other *kṣatriyas* have calmed down and returned home, so there's no more need of costumes, pretense, and hiding—not from their greatest friend and well-wisher, "uncle" Drupada. On the appointed day, the Pāṇḍavas remove their baggy robes, groom their hair, don their princely garbs, and stride into Drupada's palace like newly minted kings—glorious phoenixes, apparently arisen from the ashes! Queen Kuntī accompanies them, looking glorious as ever!

For so long they had to walk and talk like *brāhmaṇas*, adopting the dress, speech, mannerisms, and activities of this class. Now that's over, and they can once again be who they are: the descendants of Pāṇḍu, the descendants of the Yadus, the descendants of the gods! The princes and the heir apparent of the Kuru dynasty!

When they enter the reception hall, everyone that glimpses them immediately understands that these are important personages. Yudhiṣṭhira, without even waiting to be asked, sits in a seat meant exclusively for royalty, and no one utters a word in protest. They all instinctively acknowledge the appropriateness of this gesture.

Then Drupada, seeking confirmation of the obvious, asks these royals who they are, revealing his secret wish that his daughter marry a son of Pāṇḍu. With great dignity and a slight bow of the head, Yudhiṣṭhira answers: "My lord, you will not be disappointed. We are indeed the Pāṇḍavas." And although it is not explicitly mentioned in the text, we can imagine that numerous tears of joy were shed that day. At long last, the Pāṇḍavas had returned!

After the reception, when the festivities had all but died down, the Pāṇḍavas had one more revelation for Drupada, and it was a real shocker! We can assume that Drupada was asked to sit down!

And on that dramatic note, we'll end for today.

Yudhiṣṭira: Reversal of Fortunes

When we last met, Kuntī and the Pāṇḍavas had revealed their true identities to Drupada and were just about to disclose another shocking bit of news. Before revealing what Drupada was told, however, I'll need to provide some context. To do so, I'll need to turn back the clock and explain what happened after Arjuna's brilliant *tour de force*.

Recall that Arjuna had been garlanded by Draupadī, that he and Bhīma had fought their way out of the arena, and that all three had returned to the potter's shop, where Kuntī and the Pāṇḍavas had been staying. While her sons attended the *svayaṁvara,* Kuntī had chosen to stay behind. Perhaps not wanting to bother with a disguise, she would wait to hear what happened when the Pāṇḍavas returned.

This brings us to one of the most remarkable aspects of the *Mahā-bhārata*, at least for me. When Arjuna, Bhīma, and Draupadī arrived at the potter's shop, all five brothers were in high spirits. After all, Arjuna had just won the hand of Draupadī with an extraordinary feat of skill. And here she was, standing before them, this ravishing celestial beauty! The mood that day was celebratory, joyful, and care free! In the midst of it all, one of the Pāṇḍavas playfully called out, "Mother, wait till you see today's alms [meaning Draupadī]. The collection really went well!" And Kuntī, who had heard but never turned to look at her sons, responded as she always did when they collected alms as *brāhmaṇas*: "That's nice. Now divide the collection equally among yourselves." In an instant, laughter turned to gasps, and then to silence. But why? What had just happened?

To understand the Pāṇḍavas' sudden silence, it is necessary to grasp how seriously these ancients took their own and others' words—to grasp, in other words, the difference between an oral society, in which there are no written documents, and a literate society, in which things are commonly written down. This is a whole field of study and scholarship, but the relevant point here is that in a literate society, in matters of serious consequence, one draws up a document and signs it. One puts it in writing! My guru, Śrīla Prabhupāda, would sometimes jokingly quote the old English adage: "You can say any damned thing you like, but don't put it in writing."

In other words, in a modern literate society such as ours, if one person claims that another person has made a commitment to a certain transaction or course of action, the first thing that will be asked is, "Do you have documentation? Do you have it *in writing*?" And as a result of this reliance, oral communications (especially the giving of one's word or promise) have lost much of their power and importance—although they still retain some legal force in certain contexts.

Now let's get in our time machines for a minute and transport ourselves back to a time where nothing is written. Everything is oral. A time in which your word is morally, ethically, and legally your bond *(as binding as a signed document)*. In a society such as this, your personal honor, your inner sense of integrity, your public respectability, and your social standing are all wrapped up in *your "word"*—in meaning what you say when you say it!

If we can put ourselves in the shoes of these ancient people, if we can feel about the spoken word as they did, then we can better grasp the Pāṇḍavas' reaction after Kuntī said, "That's nice. Now divide the collection equally among yourselves." Nowadays, if your mother had said this in similar circumstances, you'd just think she hadn't gotten the joke. Or maybe you'd just tell her to turn around and see that you weren't talking about alms, you were talking about your brother's beautiful bride. But back then, even though Kuntī's utterance was clearly based on a wrong impression, once spoken, it could not be easily retracted—not for someone who prized her word above all else. Hence, the Pāṇḍavas' silence.

There's another thing I've noticed in the *Mahā-bhārata* that relates to this incident and reminds me of my own youthful experiences when growing up. It revolves around the "generation gap" that always seems to exist between parents and children regardless of time or place. It's practically universal that each new generation develops values, meanings, and standards that to some degree differ from those of the previous generation. I think everyone knows what I mean here. In various ways and to various degrees, we are just not like our parents.

In looking back at ancient societies, modern persons generally picture them as going on for centuries, if not millennia, without too much change. But the *Mahā-bhārata* happens to take place as the world is rushing into a change of *yuga*—a watershed event!

Today's age is one in which many things are undergoing rapid change: our values, beliefs, and preferences; the way we live, communicate, and interact; the way we view each other and the world, and so on. Well, it wasn't that much different thousands of years ago (approximately 5,100 years ago, according to Aryabhatta).[76] One great age, the *Dvāpara-yuga,* was ending, and another great age, the *Kali-yuga,* was beginning; and because of this transition, everything else was in transition as well. Thus, in the *Mahā-bhārata*—the history of those living through this change—one can actually detect a difference in values between older and younger generations.

Grandfather Bhīṣma, for example, can be considered to hold an older generational view. Once he gave his word—as with his vow of celibacy—nothing (no consequence) could make him budge: come hell or high water, come the destruction of the entire universe, he would not break his word. And we can see this in Kuntī as well. Recall that one of Kuntī's most endearing qualities was her devotion to elders. Indeed, it was her faithful service to Durvāsā that melted this elder *yogī's* heart and prompted him to grant her that famous boon. And when it came to her word, Kuntī, like Bhīṣma, had very strong convictions: whatever you say, that's it; the consequences don't matter.

Interestingly, in contrast to both Bhīṣma and Kuntī, the younger generation, including Kṛṣṇa and the Pāṇḍavas, are far more pragmatic in the sense that they want to see justice in the world. What really matters is what happens to people; that's their overriding moral concern. And they don't want to get hung up on technicalities. First and foremost, things really must be just—consequences matter!

In any case, when Kuntī had told her sons to divide whatever they had brought, she happened to be doing something, and her

---

[76] Aryabhatta (476 AD-550 AD), as you may recall, is considered one of the greatest mathematicians/astronomers of all time and a founder of modern trigonometry.

back was turned; she hadn't yet seen Draupadī. But when her words were followed by deafing silence, she realized something was wrong and turned to see what kind of "collection" they had brought. And, of course, there stood Draupadī. But again, why the silence? Because, knowing their mother, the Pāṇḍavas understood the implications of her utterance.

Yudhiṣṭira, as the leading brother and heir to the throne, tried to explain that it was only a lighthearted joke, and that Arjuna alone had succeeded in winning the hand of Draupadī. Although Yudhiṣṭira had much to gain in a shared marriage to this beautiful, highly qualified princess, he really tried to explain why his mother's words didn't apply in this case. But Kuntī wasn't having it. Like Bhīṣma before her, she insisted that even though her words may have been based on some kind of misunderstanding, she had uttered them as a mother, as the head of the family. Her words must be honored no matter what, and to make a long story short, the five Pāṇḍavas ultimately accepted Kuntī's decision.

The *Mahā-bhārata*, of course, contains numerous cases of polygamy—especially of kings marrying many wives. But *polyandry*, where a woman marries several husbands, was quite controversial, even five thousand years ago. I mean, if *we* find this surprising, and a sort of "Oh, my God" moment, imagine what it was like five thousand years ago, and not the least for Draupadī's father.

Drupada, of course, naturally assumed that Arjuna was "the lucky guy," since it was he who had strung the bow and hit the target. But then Yudhiṣṭira explained, "Actually we have a unique *dharma* within our family." And here Drupada might have thought he was referring to a system that was common even in Europe at a certain point: the eldest son or daughter is to marry first, then the next, and so on. So Drupada says, "Well, whatever. You're all Pāṇḍavas, you know. Any Pāṇḍava is fine by me." Yudhiṣṭira finally tried to very gently break the news: "You see, sir, it won't be *one* of us, it will be *all five*! We're all going to marry Draupadī. At this, Drupada was genuinely shocked. But somehow or other he eventually came to accept this unusual arrangement. They were, after all, *"the Pāṇḍavas!"*

Before continuing with our narrative, let's take a few minutes to look at this from a slightly different angle. Ultimately, the ancient Vedic texts (or *śāstras*) explain that God (Kṛṣṇa) actually orchestrated all these events as part of His *līlā* (pastimes). So why did things happen in this extraordinary way?

One point is that Draupadī's beauty was so remarkable that it literally became a lethal weapon in the struggle against the *Asuras*. In fact, one gentleman—who we already know quite well—was so infatuated, so bewitched by Draupadī's beauty, that it led him to perform all kinds of abominable deeds. That gentleman *(and I use the term loosely)* was none other than Duryodhana, who never got over losing Draupadī to Arjuna, and whose passion for this princess burned hotter and hotter with the passage of time. The text specifically mentions that when Duryodhana first saw Draupadī at her *svayaṁvara*, he really fell hard, and being an *Asura*, he was extremely angry, jealous, and bitter that his arch-rivals, the Pāṇḍavas, had obtained her hand.

In a more esoteric sense, the spell cast by Draupadī's beauty can be viewed as Draupadī's role in Kṛṣṇa's mission to save the Earth. Duryodhana was a formidable *Asura*, whose clear intention was to participate in the conspiracy to take over the world. And although his obsession with Draupadī never diverted him from his *asuric* mission, it certainly made him more reckless, thus exposing him and rendering him more vulnerable.

In other words, the original plan of the *Asuras* was to follow and manipulate *dharma*—which is something like using the power of the Force to promote its Dark Side. So, in a sense, Duryodhana was going to do this no matter what. But his obsessive attachment to Draupadī, and the bitter anger he felt at losing her, unmasked his intentions and caused him to act more transparently—revealing his true colors for all to see.

At a later point in the *Mahā-bhārata,* during a gambling match, Duryodhana and his cohorts (who were also entranced by Draupadī's beauty) will condemn themselves for behaving in an extremely reprehensible way toward the princess. Because of their inappropriate conduct, all these *Asuras* will be cursed to die!

Returning now to the marriage between the Pāṇḍavas and Draupadī, there was another, more pragmatic, reason for Kuntī's radical decision. The success of the *Suras'* mission to defeat the *Asuras* depended on the Pāṇḍavas remaining united. If only one of the Pāṇḍavas married such an astonishing and powerful beauty, this could lead to dissension. And so, to assure that the Pāṇḍavas stayed absolutely united, somehow this arrangement was made.

It is also important to remember that the Pāṇḍavas were self-realized souls. They were aware of their mission on Earth, but they were also aware that this planet was not their ultimate home. They would stay, but not for long. They were not actually earthlings. Indeed, this is true not only of the Pāṇḍavas, but of each and every one of us as well. It is also one of the *Gītā's* main points:

dehino 'smin yathā dehe
kaumāraṁ yauvanaṁ jarā
tathā dehāntara-prāptir
dhīras tatra na muhyati

"As in the body, the embodied soul experiences childhood, youth, and old age, so too, one attains another body. This does not confuse the wise".[77]

Every soul should realize that we have to leave this world. We are all just visiting here, and when our tourist visa runs out, the body we have borrowed must be returned to nature. Being great devotees of Kṛṣṇa (God), the Pāṇḍavas, Kuntī, and Draupadī were keenly aware of these facts; thus, they were simply working as a united community to accomplish their mission on Earth.

Another interesting feature of this remarkable arrangement is that it tends to balance things out in terms of gender roles. The Sanskrit texts cite many instances of men marrying more than one woman, and here we have an instance of a woman marrying more than one man. Ancient Vedic civilization was not always just a man's world.

Now, apart from its private household advantages, this union had far-reaching geopolitical implications as well. By marrying Draupadī, the Pāṇḍavas had married into one of the most powerful ancient dynasties in the world: the Pāñcāla kingdom. With Drupada's powerful *kṣatriya* army at their disposal, the Pāṇḍavas, already a force to be reckoned with, would now be unbeatable. The Pāṇḍavas were no longer alone. A dramatic shift in world power had occurred. Let's look into

---

[77] From ch. 2, v. 13 of *A Comprehensive Guide to Bhagavad-Gītā*

this alliance a bit more.

Recall that when Droṇa was attempting to conquer Pāñcāla, it was only through the prowess of the Pāṇḍavas that he ultimately achieved success. Now, things had dramatically changed. The Pāṇḍavas were no longer fighting for Droṇa, who was part of the Kuru camp; they had joined forces with Drupada, Droṇa's bitter enemy, and together they posed an immediate existential threat to the Kurus.

Think about it: if you try to kill a group of people, but fail, and those people know that it was you who tried to kill them, you have a problem. Well, this was the exact problem that Duryodhana had with respect to the Pāṇḍavas. They knew that he was behind the failed Vāraṇāvata plot, and *he* knew that *they* knew! This only heightened Kuru fears that an unstoppable Pāñchāla army, headed by Drupada and the five Pāṇḍavas, might invade their kingdom at any time. It was an unprecedented crisis, requiring immediate attention. An emergency meeting was convened, attended by the usual major figures: Dhṛtarāṣṭra, Duryodhana, Droṇa, Bhīṣma, Vidura, perhaps Kṛpa, and so on.

Before the meeting, or perhaps during a recess, an interesting private conversation took place that gives some insight into Duryodhana's despicable character. He was talking to Karṇa, expressing his fear of having a direct, warrior-to-warrior face-off with the Pāṇḍavas. To avoid this, he was proposing every dirty trick in the book, from an ambush, to a cowardly attack from the rear, to stirring up brotherly jealousy over Draupadī, and so forth. But Karṇa wasn't interested in such spineless tactics: "Forget all these sneaky plots and maneuvers. Just get out there and confront them head on. Fight like a proper warrior!" The actual Sanskrit word that Karṇa uses is *vikramaḥ*, which literally means "step out"— also a way of saying, "Have courage. Go, be a man!"

The conference ended with a decision by the Kuru leaders to send Vidura to Pāñchāla as their ambassador—the logical choice and best hope for bringing about a peaceful solution. After all, Vidura had been the Pāṇḍavas' well-wisher, protector, and confidant ever since they came down from the mountains to Hastināpura as little boys; he was thus a trusted, revered, and much loved figure in their lives. The Kurus knew that anything he proposed would be taken into serious consideration. His mission was to avoid war by proposing that the Kuru kingdom be divided between the Pāṇḍavas and the Kurus, and ruled accordingly.

One ironical aside: When the Pāṇḍavas completed their military training, Droṇa used them to conquer and then divide Drupada's kingdom. After this, however, there is not a word in the text indicating that Droṇa ever governed, or even visited, his half of the Pāñchāla kingdom. From this we can assume that after Drupada emerged from the forest with his two children, one of which was endowed with the ability to kill Droṇa, the lost half of his kingdom quietly reverted back to him. Now, ironically, the shoe was on the other foot! Drupada not only had all of Pāñchāla, he also had the Pāṇḍavas—the very warriors that had once helped to divide his kingdom. And now, under threat of severe consequences, it was the Kuru empire (of which Droṇa was a part) that stood to be divided! That, at any rate, was the proposal that Vidura carried to Pāñchāla.

It was, like, "Hey, that whole thing in Vāraṇāvata, you know, with the burning house? That was just a terrible misunderstanding, an unfortunate mistake. After all, let's not forget that we're all Kurus here; we're all part of the same family. So we'll take half the kingdom and you take the other. And from now on, we'll all just work together! One big happy dynasty." In Yiddish, that's called *chutzpah*![78]

We can imagine how this proposal went down with *kṣatriyas* like Bhīma, who ·knew that the Pāṇḍavas and Drupada had the advantage: "Do you believe this blankety-blank nonsense?! Let's teach these blankety-blanks a good lesson! Let's attack right now and take it all!" Ultimately, however, cooler heads prevailed. Yudhiṣṭira consulted with Drupada, and then they both spoke to uncle Vidura, to whom Yudhiṣṭira was deeply devoted. The proposed arrangement was accepted but, as usual with Duryodhana, the Pāṇḍavas got the short end of the stick.

In what turned out to be an extremely cynical agreement, Duryodhana and Dhṛtarāṣṭra retained rule of Hastināpura, the traditional Kuru capital, with all its riches, opulences, buildings, gardens, and so on. And what did the Pāṇḍavas receive? The "extraordinary opportunity" to build a kingdom from scratch on an undeveloped piece of real estate in the middle of nowhere! This wilderness, known as Khāṇḍava-Prastha, was the half-kingdom Yudhiṣṭira spiritedly agreed to accept.

So the Pāṇḍavas traveled to Khāṇḍava-Prastha with Draupadī and began clearing land, constructing buildings, and generally establishing their kingdom (factually, they were excellent managers). And because their rule was so sublime

---

[78] *Chutzpah* is a Talmudic word that made its way into Yiddish, and eventually became a part of American slang. It comes from the verbal root "to peel," and thus suggests barefacedness, arrogance, impudence, and sheer cheek.

and just, people of all classes began flocking there. Within a short period of time, the city, which they named Indraprastha, had developed into a beautiful, thriving metropolis, filled with all types of *brāhmaṇas, kṣatriyas*, merchants, craftsmen, and workers. The Pāṇḍavas were greatly loved by the people, the arts were flourishing, and the city had become a major center of trade. Having sprung up almost overnight, Indraprastha soon established itself as one of the great cities of the world.

So the Pāṇḍavas ended up building this fabulous city, which, as it turns out, is the current location of New Delhi, the capital of India. Khāṇḍava-Prastha (now Indraprastha) was on the Yamunā river and Hastināpura was on the Ganges. So the great city that arose back then remains a great city even today.

In any case, when the literature recounts these epic battles between the *Suras* and the *Asuras*, a common theme emerges: the attempt by the *Asuras* to eliminate the *brāhmaṇas*, sages, and *yogīs* whose spiritual practices and commitment to *dharma* strengthen Vedic civilization. This is an important point. It was not only the warriors that protected and maintained this ancient society; the great sages and *brāhmaṇas* played a major role as well. Thus, if one wanted to undermine or destabilize the social fabric, killing the *brahminical* class was sometimes more important than killing the king. The kings depended on their *gurus* (teachers) for wisdom, sometimes for diplomatic and strategic advice, and especially to keep their kingdoms aligned with *dharma*. In this way they would assure that the forces of the universe continued to act on their behalf.

Thus, for the *Asuras*, wiping out this highest social class was a vital part of their plan to take over the Earth. But there was a problem: how to do this without themselves violating *dharma,* and thereby dooming their efforts. The *Asuras* came up with a very clever workaround (mentioned before): certain of them would take birth as forest-dwelling animals so they could "legally" attack and kill the *brāhmaṇas*, sages, and *yogīs* that resided in their vicinity.

According to *paśu-dharma* (the law governing animal conduct), because it is in the nature of forest beasts to attack and kill humans, they can do so without incurring bad reactions. Thus, by taking birth as animals, the *Asuras* could get away with what would have been a heinous crime for a human being.

This brings us to an incident that occurred in the vicinity of Khāṇḍava-Prastha after the Pāṇḍavas had arrived: a great fire that burned the Khāṇḍava forest to the ground, killing many of the animals that resided there. When first reading of this event in the *Mahā-bhārata*, it struck me that at least some of the "animals" consumed in that fire might have been the *Asuras* mentioned above—the ones that had taken birth as animals to "legally" annihilate the *brahminical* class. I was thinking that these *Asuras* might have been headquartered in that forest. Later, while reading the text in Sanskrit, I actually came upon an obscure, largely unknown, verse that confirmed this suspicion.

Now, about that fire. There's a popular Hindu version of this event that has somehow made its way into the *Mahā-bhārata* over the years. As the story goes, certain kings had offered such a large amount of ghee (clarified butter) into the sacrificial fire that Agni, the god of fire, got a *cosmic case of indigestion*. Needing a digestive aid, he "consumed" the Khāṇḍava forest, which was rich in herbs, thus burning it to the ground.

To me, however, there's something about this story that doesn't quite square with the values of those times. Having a fit of belching doesn't seem like much of a justification for burning down a whole forest and killing numerous animals. The real story, I think, can be found in the text itself, if one carefully looks: the point about the *Asuras* in the form of animals.

In this connection, the *Mahā-bhārata* describes how Kṛṣṇa, Arjuna and some of the *kṣatriya* ladies travel to the banks of the Yamunā for a few days of vacation.[79] It seems that even back then they had special resort areas where people would go for relaxation, recreation, and sport. In Dvārakā, for example, Kṛṣṇa would go to Raivataka Mountain.

Anyway, in the midst of their vacationing, a red-headed, red-bearded *brāhmaṇa* (or someone appearing to be *brāhmaṇa*) suddenly approaches Kṛṣṇa and Arjuna, begging for alms.[80] And since everything about this *brāhmaṇa* indicates that he is a learned, respectable sage, they are instantly inclined to assist him in any way they can. With that, the "*brāhmaṇa*" immediately transforms into his true identity. He is Agni, the god of fire, who informs Kṛṣṇa and Arjuna that the nearby Khāṇḍava forest must be burned to the ground. And for his "alms" he requests that they assist by preventing

---

[79] These *kṣatriyās* (warrior ladies) were not ordinary. Some engaged in wrestling matches and other types of warrior sports. So the typical Hindu stereotype of the "good woman" did not always apply when it came to these ancient *kṣatriyā* ladies. Kṛṣṇa's sister Subhadrā, for example, was an expert charioteer. This is not to say that these women were man-like. Not at all! They were very beautiful, refined ladies, with all kinds of abilities. But it's good to remember that ancient Vedic culture is not necessarily equivalent to later Indian culture.

[80] It is interesting to note that in the texts of this ancient Indo-European civilization, figures such as Indra and Nārada Muni are described as being blond-headed.

"certain animals" from escaping the forest's flames.

Here we can recall that the *Suras* (the gods) have descended in various forms to save planet Earth from the *Asuras*—some of whom have taken birth as animals, according to the *Mahā-bhārata* (here's that connection again). Their center was in the Khāṇḍava forest, and Agni is now going to create this fire to destroy them.

With Kṛṣṇa and Arjuna stationed at different ends of the forest to seal off the main escape routes, Agni whirls himself into this gigantic, burning (Old Testament-styled) pillar of fire, and proceeds to consume the Khāṇḍava forest along with all the *Asuras* that were residing there—dealing a significant blow to their plans.

In any case, with Indraprastha firmly established as one of the world's great capitals and Yudhiṣṭira firmly established as its king, Kṛṣṇa strongly urged him to perform the Rājasūya sacrifice, the great offering of kings. This, Kṛṣṇa knew, would confirm that Yudhiṣṭira was the rightful heir to the Kuru throne. The Rājasūya was essential to Yudhiṣṭira's success—and to Kṛṣṇa's design for ultimate victory—because any king that could perform that great sacrifice would thereby establish himself as the *king* of kings, the emperor of the world!

But in order to perform this sacrifice (without being ignored, and thus making a complete fool of himself), a king first had to send a "challenge horse" throughout the land, to all the great kings of the world, indicating, "accept me as your emperor or prepare to fight!" To make this challenge, Yudhiṣṭira dispatched his brothers in the four directions: Arjuna to the North, Bhīma to the East, Nakula to the West, and

Sahadeva to the South.[81]

The idea was not so much to conquer as it was to inform these kings of Yudhiṣṭira's intention to execute the Rājasūya sacrifice, and to collect taxes to fund the great event. Payment of the tax indicated acknowledgement of Yudhiṣṭira as king of kings. Of course, refusal certainly meant a fight. But, as it turned out, almost all the kings accepted Yudhiṣṭira's rule: first, because nobody wanted to challenge the Pāṇḍavas' great power; and second, because they realized that Yudhiṣṭira was capable of restoring *dharmic* order to the world.

Among all these kings, however, there was one holdout, one extremely powerful *Asura* who would never accept Yudhiṣṭira's rule without a fight. His name was Jarāsandha, the king of Magadha, and for the next few minutes we'll talk of his ultimate demise.

We all remember Kaṁsa, who imprisoned his own sister, killed her infant children, and went after Kṛṣṇa with a vengeance—that is, until Kṛṣṇa ended him with an effortless toss from the top of a stadium. Well, Jarāsandha, the king of Magadha, was Kaṁsa's best friend, to the point of giving two of his daughters to be Kaṁsa's wives. Thus, when told by his daughters that Kaṁsa had been killed by Kṛṣṇa, Jarāsandha became filled with rage and a desire for revenge. From that moment on, he made the killing of Kṛṣṇa and the entire Yadu dynasty his top priority.

---

81 Recall that Sahadeva, the youngest of the Pāṇḍavas and the son of the Aśvinīs, was incredibly good looking. Because of this, when he arrived at one Southern kingdom, everyone was so entranced by his good looks that he was greeted the way we greet our rock stars and celebrities today. The crowds were evidently so enthralled by his appearance that they wouldn't leave him alone. Finally, he had to ask them to please calm down and allow him to make his challenge to the king—a very serious matter indeed.

At the time, Kṛṣṇa was a youth living in Mathurā, the Yadu capital. So Jarāsandha gathered his massive army—thousands of chariots, elephants, and soldiers—and launched an attack! Taking a small force with Them, Kṛṣṇa and Balarāma rode out to meet the challenge. And although Kṛṣṇa could have easily killed Jarāsandha, putting a swift end to the problem, He had something else in mind: destroy Jarāsandha's entire army—every elephant, horse, and man—leaving Jarāsandha as the sole survivor, the last man standing; then, allow him to return to Magadha, gather more troops, and attack again.

By playing with Jarāsandha in this way, Kṛṣṇa was able to destroy army after army, thus ridding the world of huge numbers of *Asuras*. Seventeen times Jarāsandha returned to Magadha, recruited a giant military force, attacked Mathurā, and was left standing alone on the battlefield, surrounded by the blood, guts, and body parts of another decimated army. Seventeen times, he was captured and dismissively released in an insulting, humiliating manner.

Finally, seeing that Jarāsandha and his armies were almost entirely depleted in all respects, and wanting to spare the Yadus further distress from yet another futile attack, Kṛṣṇa constructed Dvārakā: a fabulous city in the middle of the ocean, off the Western coast of India (the part closest to the Greek world).[82] He then transported the entire population of Mathurā to this new oceanic abode.

---

82 Although one can never be sure, there is at least a reasonable possibility that Kṛṣṇa's Dvārakā is the city of Plato's tale of Atlantis—an island city that was eventually reclaimed by the sea. I mention the Dvārakā-Atlantis connection because all the Sanskrit scriptures teach that at one point the ocean rose and covered Dvārakā—something that archaeology has recently confirmed. And since there was certainly contact between the Greeks and the Persian Empire, which was on the border of India, some have speculated that Dvārakā and the fabled city of Atlantis are one and the same.

Sometime later, after requesting Yudhiṣṭira to perform the Rājasūya sacrifice, Kṛṣṇa was sitting in Dvārakā with His royal counsel and several Yadu elders when the great sage Nārada informed Him of a terrible tragedy. In the course of his drive to conquer kingdoms in different parts of the world, Jarāsandha had forcibly captured thousands of kings who would not submit to his rule, imprisoning them in mountain caves. The literature describes Jarāsandha as a gigantic, extremely formidable, and imposing figure—more powerful than "ten-thousand elephants" (a common way of describing a warrior of superior strength). His plan was to make a human sacrifice of these kings to Goddess Dūrgā by offering their severed pieces to her image. (This, of course, was not Dūrgā's desire, but rather Jarāsandha's grizzly concoction!)

It was these captured kings that had sent Nārada to Dvārakā with a message for Kṛṣṇa: "Please, you're our last hope. If you don't save us, we will soon meet a horrible, ghastly death." The message even contained a heartbreaking plea from the kings' wives and children. This took place right around the time that Yudhiṣṭira had invited Kṛṣṇa to Indraprastha to attend the Rājasūya sacrifice. So it seems that the Yadus were confronted with two pressing matters at the same time. What to do?

To resolve the matter, Kṛṣṇa sought the counsel of Uddhava, one of His most intelligent advisors; and Uddhava came up with a solution that fed two birds with one scone *(to put it nonviolently)*. Here is what he proposed: "According to *dharma,* the Rājasūya sacrifice can be performed only by one who has gained victory over all kings; but in the case of Yudhiṣṭira, we have a holdout who also happens to have imprisoned thousands of Yadu kings. Therefore, killing

Jarāsandha must be our first priority, as this will both free the kings and enable the Rājasūya to go forward." Uddhava then provided Kṛṣṇa with a perfect plan for killing such a formidable enemy. Here's what happened next, beginning with an obscure sect known as Vratyas.

Vratyas were wandering ascetics, at times taken to be *brāhmaṇas*, who traveled and begged alms in the region of Jarāsandha's Magadha kingdom (today's Bihar). They lived in the hills, outside the pale of the dominant Vedic religion, where they practiced their own brand of austerities and religious rites; they were also known to be a somewhat unruly lot. Disguised in the garb of these local Vratya *brāhmaṇas,* Kṛṣṇa, Bhīma, and Arjuna traveled to Girivraja, the capital of the Magadha kingdom, to beg a favor from Jarāsandha, who was renowned for having never refused a *brāhmaṇa's* request. Of course, these so-called Vratyas would soon be making a very *non-brahminical* request: the *"favor"* of a fight!

The *Mahā-bhārata* describes that when Kṛṣṇa, Bhīma, and Arjuna arrived, they didn't go through the city's entrance gates. Girivraja means "surrounded by hills," and located on one such hill were all the ritualistic items, ingredients, and paraphernalia to be used in Jarāsandha's horrendous human offering to the Goddess Dūrgā. Because even for these sorts of ghastly sacrifices, all types of *brahminical* rites were still required. So Kṛṣṇa, Bhīma, and Arjuna went to the top of this hill and basically laid waste to everything up there.

They then climbed down and stealthily entered Girivraja. Of course, news soon reached Jarāsandha that some unruly Vratya *brāhmaṇas* had come down from the hills and were tearing up the town, destroying public property, taking whatever they wanted from the marketplace, and creating a general disturbance. It was similar to the time that Kṛṣṇa, Balarāma, and the cowherd boys entered Mathurā to kill Kaṁsa. In other words, Kṛṣṇa, Bhīma, and Arjuna displayed complete contempt and disregard for the so-called law and order of Jarāsandha's kingdom.

After this, they entered Jarāsandha's palace at the exact time he was scheduled to receive *brāhmaṇas*. Despite his being a major *Asura*, Jarāsandha was a strict follower of *dharma*, who prided himself on his perfect record of charity to the *brahminical* class. But he quickly noticed that these three *"brāhmaṇa"* troublemakers weren't *brāhmaṇas* at all. There was something about their voices, their demeanor, their physique that didn't quite fit with their dress; these and other signs led Jarāsandha to conclude that these individuals were actually *kṣatriyas*—and familiar ones at that! Still, since they had come as *brāhmaṇas* begging alms, he decided to act according to *dharma* and grant them whatever they desired.

Then, after going to all this trouble of disguising themselves, what happens next always amazed me: Kṛṣṇa immediately says, "Guess what! We're not actually *brāhmaṇas* and we're not here to beg some fruits, grains, or cows. My companions are the Pāṇḍavas, Bhīma and Arjuna, and I am your old enemy Kṛṣṇa. We've travelled a long, long way to be with you today, begging for only one thing: a fight to the death!"

In good sporting spirit, Jarāsandha simply laughed and immediately granted their request. But he refused to fight Kṛṣṇa, who he called a coward, hiding in the middle of the sea; nor would he fight Arjuna, the younger, smaller, and supposedly weaker of the two brothers. In Bhīma, however, he saw a worthy opponent. Bringing two large clubs, he led the party outside the city gates for the fight.

To understand what happens next, we need to know a bit about Jarāsandha's unusual birth—something hinted at by the very meaning of his name. Jarā refers to the witch (or *rākṣasī*) who bore that name, and the Sanskrit word *sandhi* means "placing things together." The *Mahā-bhārata* explains that, being childless, Jarāsandha's father, King Bṛhadratha, somehow won the favor of a *brāhmaṇa* who blessed the parents with success in begetting a son. Shockingly, however, the child came out not only stillborn, but as two separated, perfectly symmetrical halves of an infant body—from top to bottom! The sight was so grotesque and appalling that the horrified mother ordered her nurse to take the pieces and just toss them somewhere in the forest.

There they were found by Jarā, a powerful sorceress, who began playing around with the pieces, noticing that they were perfectly formed halves. Using "the dark side of the Force" (my favorite analogy), she placed the pieces together, and *voilà:* the child came to life! Hence, the name Jarāsandha—"put together by Jarā."

In any case, once they got outside the city gates, this terrible, violent fight broke out between Bhīma and Jarāsandha, who kept bashing each other again and again with these heavy clubs—not just for days, but for weeks on end, until club after club was left shattered on the ground. During the day, the two would fight; but at night, out of mutual respect, they would sit together, break bread, and commiserate, following *kṣatriya dharma*. In this way, the contest went on and on with neither party gaining the upper hand.

Finally, Kṛṣṇa thought, "This is getting tiresome. We have to end this so we can move forward! We have to kill Jarāsandha and release all those kings so that Yudhiṣṭira's Rājasūya can take place." Knowing the details of Jarāsandha's strange birth, Kṛṣṇa held up a fork-shaped twig, got Bhīma's attention, and slowly pulled the twig apart until it peeled in two. Bhīma quickly grasped Kṛṣṇa's hint and immediately threw Jarāsandha down, pressed one leg to the ground, took hold of the other leg, and tore his body along the seam that had been long ago sealed by Jarā's magic—literally ripping Jarāsandha apart. Jarāsandha was dead and all the kings were set free to return to their respective kingdoms. Then Kṛṣṇa, Bhīma, and Arjuna left for Indraprastha to give Yudhiṣṭira the good news.

The Rājasūya sacrifice was attended by many gods of the universe, such as Brahmā, Śiva, and Indra. Many of the greatest sages and *brāhmaṇas* were there as well, along with numerous kings, queens, princes, and princesses from lands both near and far. Included among these, of course, were all the leading figures of the Kuru dynasty: elders such as Bhīṣma, Dhṛtarāṣṭra, and Vidura, teachers and generals such as Droṇācārya and Kṛpācārya, and even Duryodhana, the Pāṇḍavas' arch-enemy, who really had no choice but to attend.

In a sense, the performance of the Rājasūya sacrifice was a win-win situation for both the Pāṇḍavas and their rivals, since it served to re-establish the Kurus as the world's most powerful dynasty. As they say, a rising tide lifts all boats! And it was nice to see many of these powerful warriors taking on various humble duties to help make the sacrifice a success. Bhīma, of course, took charge of the kitchen *(since he definitely knew about "good meals")*; Duryodhana agreed to manage the treasury; Nakula and Sahadeva took care of the elders, and so on and so forth. Interestingly, Kṛṣṇa took the humble service of washing the feet of all the arriving guests.

Traditionally, the Rājasūya sacrifice began with a special

inaugural ceremony in which the assembly of gods, kings, and learned *brāhmaṇas* would elect an honorary president to receive first honors: the *greatest* personality among all those great personalities! The question of "who" was put before the assembly, and all the attendees were given the chance to nominate their favorite candidate.

At one point during this process, Bhīṣma (according to the *Mahā-bhārata)* or Sahadeva (according to the *Śrīmad-Bhāgavatam)*—there might have been a number of speeches—stood up and urged the assembly to elect Kṛṣṇa, arguing that it would be absurd to consider anyone other than Him to receive such an honor: "Honored guests, are we really even going to discuss this? Kṛṣṇa is here, and who can be equal to or greater than Kṛṣṇa! Kṛṣṇa is Puruṣottama, the Supreme Person! He is the Soul of the entire cosmos, now only playing the part of a Yadu prince. That is why He, and only He, should be the first to be honored." Hearing these words, the whole assembly burst into applause, and everyone began shouting, "Well spoken! Well spoken!" Everyone concurred, and then King Yudhiṣṭira personally worshipped his dear most Kṛṣṇa as prescribed by *dharma*.

Now, amid all the hand-clapping and uproarious praise, one sulking figure remained seated with a bitter, twisted scowl on his face: Kṛṣṇa's hateful cousin Śiśupāla, a major *Asura*, who is said to have despised Kṛṣṇa from his very birth.[83] Indeed, his propensity for offending Kṛṣṇa was so great that Kṛṣṇa once remarked that He would allow Śiśupāla one-hundred insults, but after that, no more!

---

83 In studying the *Mahā-bhārata,* one finds many incidents taking place between cousins, mostly related through the different sisters of Vasudeva, Kṛṣṇa's father. One of Vasudeva's sisters, of course, is Kuntī, making Kṛṣṇa and the Pāṇḍavas cousins, who are also cousins of Duryodhana, their sworn enemy.

In any case, when Śiśupāla saw Kṛṣṇa being honored and worshipped by the greatest personalities in the world—and even in the universe—he became so outraged that he literally lost control *(he definitely had some serious anger-management issues).* In the middle of the ceremony, he suddenly stood up and began ranting and raving—insulting Kṛṣṇa in every possible way. Actually, some of the things Śiśupāla said were sort of comical because they had a double-meaning that Kṛṣṇa's devotees often appreciate.

Śiśupāla, for example, tried to cast aspersions on Kṛṣṇa's social status, saying, "We don't even know His actual *varṇa.* He was born a *kṣatriya*, grew up as a *vaiśya*, and now He's again acting as a *kṣatriya* prince. So nobody knows where He comes from; nobody knows His true *varṇa.*" Now in ancient Vedic culture, this was a major insult. But to a devotee of Kṛṣṇa, it can be seen as a type of unintended glorification. One point about Kṛṣṇa (or God) is that He truly has no status in the *varṇa* system, or any other system, because He is entirely beyond them all: the Original Person, the Cause of all causes, and so on.

In any case, during Śiśupāla's long, rambling tirade, Kṛṣṇa sat untroubled, patiently listening without the least bit of concern. Kṛṣṇa's *kṣatriya* friends, on the other hand, were not about to stand for Śiśupāla's impudence. Some left in protest, while Bhīṣma, the Pāṇḍavas, and others readied their weapons, as Śiśupāla wildly drew his, preparing to do battle with them all.

Now, the last thing anyone wants at the start of the greatest sacrifice in the world is a battle between *kṣatriyas*. These were passionate warriors, many of whom were at odds; but they had set aside their differences to peacefully attend this important religious event. However, when Śiśupāla began hurling insults at Kṛṣṇa, their blood began to boil, and their *kṣatriya* natures emerged. That's when Kṛṣṇa stepped in and asked His friends not to bother with Śiśupāla, assuring them that He would handle the situation Himself.

Kṛṣṇa then called forth His most famous weapon, the *Sudarśana Cakra*—this beautiful, brilliantly shining disc that spins with inconceivable speed *(one often sees it depicted in Indian art).* Being invoked, this irresistible *Cakra* appeared, whirling rapidly around Kṛṣṇa's finger. Then, right before everyone's eyes, Kṛṣṇa released His weapon, which traveled like lightning, *giving Śiśupāla a haircut just below the chin!* The entire assembly was amazed, but what happened next was even more astonishing. Indeed, it has become one of the more famous episodes of ancient Vedic history, often referred to in the Sanskrit texts.

Within sight of all the assembled guests, the soul of Śiśupāla emerged from his body and merged into the body of Kṛṣṇa. Thus, everyone there witnessed this unique passing, which is talked about even today in communities that know about these stories.

This incident also exemplifies one of the principles in these texts: if Kṛṣṇa kills someone, He gives them liberation. They don't go to hell for eternal punishment; they are actually liberated! In Śiśupāla's case, he was granted what is known as *sāyujya-mukti* (merging into the body of God)—the first of five types of liberation mentioned in the texts.[84] And that was the

---

[84] In the purport to ch. 2, v. 266 of the *Caitanya-Caritāmṛta,* Śrīla Prabhupada defines each type of liberation. "*Sālokya* means that after material liberation, one is promoted to the planet where the Supreme Personality of Godhead resides, *sāmīpya* means remaining an associate of the Supreme Personality of Godhead, *sārūpya* means attaining a four-handed form exactly like that of the Lord, *sārṣṭi* means attaining opulences like those of the Supreme Lord,

end of Śiśupāla's earthly existence.

Afterwards, as Kṛṣṇa desired, the Rājasūya sacrifice went on to triumphant conclusion, thus establishing Yudhiṣṭira as the emperor of the world. Everyone was satisfied! Everyone was overjoyed! Everyone, that is, with the exception of that one person who could never swallow his pride, subdue his ambition, or curb his envy of the Pāṇḍavas: Duryodhana!

---

and *sāyujya* means merging into the Brahman effulgence of the Lord. These are the five types of liberation" A.C. Bhaktivedanta Swami Prabhupada, *Caitanya-Caritāmṛta*, *Madhya-Līlā*, *Vol.*1 (Mumbai: Bhaktivedanta Book Trust, 1996), 69

Duryodhana: The Ill-Fated Coup

When we last met, we saw that much had been done to diminish both the power and the presence of *Asuras* on Earth: the alliance of the Pāṇḍavas and King Drupada, which led to the division of the Kuru kingdom; Agni's burning of the Khāṇḍava forest, which destroyed many *Asuras* in the form of animals; the utter destruction of seventeen large, well-equipped *Asura* armies; the killing of both Jarāsandha and Śiśupāla; and, the performance of the Rājasūya sacrifice, which established Yudhiṣṭira—and not Duryodhana—as the emperor of the world.

And with the name Duryodhana, we identify the person who was most unhappy about Yudhiṣṭira's post-Rājasūya ascent. After all, his entire life's mission was to thwart the rise of Yudhiṣṭira and secure the Kuru throne for himself—an aim that had just suffered a severe setback. At the moment, however, there was nothing to do but grin and bear it. Being far more rational than Śiśupāla, Duryodhana knew that his only hope for ultimate victory was to go with the flow and wait for the energy to change, allowing for another whack at evil. As it turns out, he wouldn't have to wait too long.

When the festivities were over and all the great personalities had returned to their respective homes, members of the inner family stayed behind for a few days. During this period, something happened to Duryodhana that sparked his rage and rekindled his obsessive need to destroy the Pāṇḍavas. It all took place in the Pāṇḍavas' remarkable palace, which had been built by Maya Dānava, this famous celestial craftsman. Not only were the opulences, riches, and furnishings of this palace far beyond anything seen in this world, but it also contained various built-in illusions that especially acted upon pretentious fools.

It all started when Yudhiṣṭira was showing Duryodhana around the palace and they entered the section containing all these mystical constructions. One of these was an area of solid flooring made to look like an area of water. Not noticing the deception, Duryodhana walked across while lifting his cloth so it wouldn't get wet—something that elicited not a few indiscrete chuckles from those around. Imagine this big, proud, powerful warrior, in all the regalia of a Kuru prince, daintily lifting his dress while tip-toeing across a perfectly solid floor. Then the party came to an area that looked like a solid floor but was actually water. You can guess what happened next: trying not to make the same embarrassing mistake twice, Duryodhana boldly stepped forward, head held high, and summarily toppled headlong into the drink. Two acts of utter buffoonery!

Here the text describes how the ladies of the palace burst into uncontrollable laughter, because it really was quite comical! Yudhiṣṭira, of course, felt embarrassed for Duryodhana and tried to shush the laughter, but Kṛṣṇa kept encouraging it, telling Yudhiṣṭira, "No, no! It's all right; let them laugh." This was, after all, the same Duryodhana that had several times tried to murder the Pāṇḍavas. So Kṛṣṇa wasn't all that sympathetic to his plight.

In any case, Duryodhana, now drenched to the bone, was completely mortified, and his demonic nature immediately came out. To him, this was no laughing matter. In a huff, he immediately quit the palace, then the whole of Indraprastha, and hurried back to his own city, Hastināpura, which, of course, he had usurped! To be so shamed, so demeaned, so humiliated in front of so many lords and ladies, was more than he could bear. And so he sank into a deep depression, losing his appetite for food, sports, socializing, *and even assassination plots*. Indeed, his condition was so severe that his friends and relatives became seriously concerned about his mental and physical well-being. Even more than before, Duryodhana had become a truly miserable, wretched creature. That's when good old uncle Śakuni stepped in. A word about him.

Śakuni is the brother of Gāndhārī, Duryodhana's exalted mother; both are from Afghanistan, which at the time was part of the immediate Vedic civilization. Now Śakuni had a reputation for being an expert gambler, especially when it came to throwing dice. And when he sees that both Dhṛtarāṣṭra and Gāndhārī are extremely concerned about their eldest son, whose health is verging on collapse, Śakuni goes to Duryodhana with a plan for turning things around. Basically, he advises, "Don't get *mad*, get *even*. We can fix this! And here's how: have your father order Yudhiṣṭira and the Pāṇḍavas to Hastināpura for a gambling match. And at that match, we'll strip them of everything they've gained! *We'll take it all!*"

Now, Śakuni was not only an expert gambler, he was also an expert cheat—not the first time that the two went hand-in-hand. Hence his confidence in the outcome! And, of course, both Dhṛtarāṣṭra and Duryodhana were totally on-board with Śakuni's underhanded scheme.

It was shortly after the Rājasūya sacrifice that the Pāṇḍavas received Dhṛtarāṣṭra's request and traveled to Hastināpura for the big Yudhiṣṭira-Śakuni matchup. But why, after gaining so much, would Yudhiṣṭira take the gamble, especially against a wily old dicer like Śakuni, who was known for his cheating ways? For one thing, it was a principle among *kṣatriyas* that one cannot simply turn away from a challenge; once called out, a warrior had to stand up, no matter what! Secondly, the challenge to the match came directly from Dhṛtarāṣṭra, the Pāṇḍavas' so-called surrogate father, whose request they would hardly refuse, being of such noble hearts.

In any case, to make a long story short, Śakuni uses every dicing trick in the book to basically rob Yudhiṣṭira of all that he possesses: his riches, his lands, his kingdom, his weapons—and ultimately, the services of his own brothers.

Now, I can almost hear everyone say, "Wait a minute, his own brothers? What do you mean, his own brothers?" I'll try to explain.

Nowadays, if someone formally owes you money, that debt (or financial instrument) becomes a completely negotiable thing: it can be sold, auctioned, traded, pawned, or whatever, because that instrument is as good as money. Well, ancient times were not that different: all ancient civilizations, whether Roman, Greek, Indian, or Chinese, had negotiable political and military debts. And if you study the nature of feudal law, or just the way the world worked prior to the Industrial Revolution, the Pāṇḍavas' fealty to Yudhiṣṭira, their sworn obligation to serve his interests at all costs, was considered a type of possession. In other words, that "obligation," that "debt," was a negotiable commodity; it could be put up as stakes in a gambling match like lands, riches, weapons, or anything else.

Here, I think, there's a common misunderstanding that ancient Vedic civilization permitted the gambling away of human beings. This, however, was not the case. The thing that was transferred to the winner of the match was not the *person*, but rather the person's *obligation* or *oath*.

So Yudhiṣṭira gambled his brothers' *oaths* to serve him and lost. Imagine! He lost his own brothers. And, you know, gambling is an addiction—it's like a fever. And Yudhiṣṭira, even though he was Dharmarāja, the king of virtue, was sort of trapped in this feverish situation. And just to twist the knife, every time Śakuni beat Yudhiṣṭira, he would cry out, "*Jitam* (it's won)!" "Your kingdom? *Jitam*! Your weapons? *Jitam*! Your brothers' oath of service? *Jitam*!" In this way, Śakuni took every single thing away from Yudhiṣṭira, save one. And now we come to Draupadī!

(By the way, the Sanskrit *ji,* the root of *jitam*, is also the root of *jaya,* an expression we all commonly use, meaning "victory to," "glory to," and so on.)

Several Hindu versions of what happened to Draupadī in the gambling hall tell that Yudhiṣṭira gambled her away like he did his brothers. However, after my own studies and readings of various *Mahā-bhārata* texts, I personally don't think that's exactly correct. In any case, we certainly know that once the Pāṇḍavas lost their kingdom, their weapons, and even their own autonomy, they were effectively powerless. It was then that Duryodhana and his brothers took advantage of the situation by forcibly dragging Draupadī into the gambling hall: not a place for a woman, let alone this most qualified and noble Kuru princess!

Even if things had stopped with this, it still would have been considered an unprecedented offense; men's gambling halls back then were not much better than they are today. But things didn't stop there. Duryodhana and his crew wanted to see Draupadī publicly humiliated and shamed! Indeed, many versions of this story relay their attempt to disrobe her before the entire assembly of men.

One small point here: When reading the actual Sanskrit, it becomes clear that this is not an erotic story. At the time of the incident, Draupadi happened to be sequestered due to her menstrual period, and was sitting alone in a private room, wrapped in a simple, modest cloth (*eka vastra*).

Let's also remember that Draupadī was no ordinary woman. She was practically a goddess, born from the altar of a fire sacrifice—this fiery, beautiful woman! And, as I mentioned, Draupadī was born with such beauty that she would ultimately cause the destruction of the *Asuras* and the undoing of their mission on Earth. The *Asuras* simply could not resist her beauty. This, of course, included Duryodhana, who never overcame his bitter anger at losing Draupadī to Arjuna, and who remained obsessed with the thought of having her for himself.

Here we can point out an interesting contrast. The Pāṇḍavas, who actually *did* have Draupadī as their wife, were not at all desirous of enjoying her. These are great souls, highly enlightened beings, and personal associates of Kṛṣṇa, the Supreme Being. This may sound a bit clichéd, but the Pāṇḍavas and Draupadī had a genuine spiritual relationship—a relationship not of temporary bodies, but of eternal souls. Duryodhana, on the other hand, only desired to enjoy Draupadī and exploit her for his own personal and political ends.

In any case, to convey Draupadī to the hall, Duryodhana initially sends a member of the royal staff. And this poor guy, not very high up on the totem pole, wants no part of it, realizing that Duryodhana is about make an incredibly foolish mistake. He just stands there, not wanting to go, until Duryodhana commands: "Go and get her ... *Now!*" So he reluctantly makes his way too Draupadī's sequestered quarters and humbly tries to explain why he's been sent. Draupadī, of course, is not about to budge—not even an inch! So the poor, luckless staffer has to return to his superiors with the bad news: Draupadī will not come! It seems he preferred the wrath of Duryodhana to messing with a goddess.

Of course, with Duryodhana and his crew, it's never that easy. This time, it's his brother, Prince Duḥśāsana, who volunteers to get the job done. He's a chip off the old block: something like Duryodhana, but much, much worse. Duḥśāsana literally means "bad instructions"—so he's Mr. Bad Instructions. He's also a brutal beast, who has the audacity to march straight into Draupadī's private chambers, grab her by the hair, and literally drag her across the palace grounds and into the gambling hall.

Step by reckless step, these arrogant, foolhardy *kṣatriyas* were forging their own inevitable doom, and they didn't even see it! Indeed, the *Śrīmad-Bhāgavatam* contains a powerful statement concerning their fate: *rājñaḥ kaca-sparśa-kṣatāyuṣaḥ,* "By roughly touching the hair of the queen, they cut down their duration of life."[85] Think of it! Just by touching Draupadī's hair, they hastened their own deaths.

(By the way, the Sanskrit word *ayur* means "duration of life," as in the word *Ayurveda*, which literally means "knowledge of *prolonging* the duration of life.")

In any case, Duḥśāsana dragged Draupadī before this assembly of gamblers. Then, according to many accounts, he forcibly tried to strip the cloth from her body while the weaponless Pāṇḍavas gritted their teeth and helplessly watched. Duryodhana had won their oaths of allegiance in the gambling match, and thus the Pāṇḍavas no longer had the right to act independently on Draupadī's behalf. They were also

---

[85] See canto 1, ch. 8, v. 5 of *Śrīmad Bhāgavatam.*

surrounded by thousands of highly armed enemies, including *Asuras* with supernatural powers, making any such attempt a sheer act of suicide. The Pāṇḍavas were disciplined enough to show restraint, even in this most difficult of circumstances, knowing that their day would come.

Meanwhile, elders like Bhīṣma, Dhṛtarāṣṭra, and Droṇa, who had the power and authority to bring this horror to an end, stood by silently and did nothing—a significant moral flaw for which their stature suffered. And remember, this is a goddess! As we will see, nature itself is going to react against the savagery and brutality of all these men.

As if this was not enough, Duryodhana managed to inflame the Pāṇḍavas' rage even more. He was very proud because he evidently had this really fantastic warrior *"bod,"* and was especially proud of his thighs, which he considered to be very powerful and attractive.

(I mean, nowadays, some people even get calf implants; so vanity can make one truly stupid.)

In any case, while his cohorts were trying to strip away Draupadī's clothing, Duryodhana pulled back his *kṣatriya* dress and, with a disgusting gesture, revealed his thigh. We can just imagine the expression on his face as he did this while glaring at Draupadī! In response, Bhīma called out, "Exactly on that lovely thigh of yours, that's where I'm going to smash you when the time comes! I'm going to break that thigh and kill you!" Bhīma then turned his attention to Duḥśāsana, swearing that he would one day rip his beating heart from his chest, drink his blood, and then wash Draupadī's hair with it!

(Of course, one can wonder whether Bhīma really uttered this very Gothic vow, or whether it was added later, during some sort of "Clint Eastwood/Dirty Harry" phase of Indian history. Did

they really do that sort of thing back then?)

In any case, among all the Kurus assembled in that infamous hall that day, only Vidura stood up and condemned the outrage, basically speaking the plain truth, "Today you Kurus have destroyed yourselves by touching and dishonoring this noble queen; today you have sown the seeds of your own inevitable doom."

Vidura's stark warning, of course, remained unheeded, and Draupadī was left without a champion to protect her—or at least put a halt to these grotesque proceedings. The Pāṇḍavas had lost their weapons and were vastly outnumbered, and Bhīṣma and Droṇa had elected to remain silent—to their everlasting shame.

Here one can ask why Bhīṣma and Droṇa refused to intervene at seeing the humiliation of Draupadi? Bhīṣma, as I mentioned earlier, was a deontological ethicist—meaning that, for him, the act itself is everything, regardless of the consequences. In other words, if you know that by telling the truth innocent people will be slaughtered, you must still tell the truth regardless!

(Amazingly enough, Immanuel Kant actually held this view, which is surprising since he seemed to be quite bright otherwise.)

In any case, according to the *Mahā-bhārata*, it was this line of thinking that caused Bhīṣma to place legal technicalities above moral action. His reasoning went something like this: Since Yudhiṣṭira had gambled both himself and the Pāṇḍavas away in terms of their feudal obligations, they were now, in a sense, the Kurus' "possessions"—a status that automatically called into question the status of Draupadī. Who now "possessed" her? If the Pāṇḍavas had already lost themselves, how could they still possess Draupadī? Legally, Draupadī must "belong" to whoever "owns" the Pāṇḍavas. So on one side we have this goddess, this enlightened being, this great devotee of Kṛṣṇa, who is being horribly abused, and on the other side we have grandfather Bhīṣma, with his legalistic perspective, doing nothing to save the day.

Kṛṣṇa's position when it comes to such matters is very different. For Him, if something is wrong or unjust, it should not be done—period! No technicalities! Telling the truth, for example, may be an important principle. But if telling the truth will get innocent people killed, lying or withholding knowledge is a justifiable response.

As for Droṇa, he literally owed everything—title, possessions, lands, and so on—to the largesse of the Kurus. In the *Bhagavad-gītā*, Arjuna himself identifies people like Bhīṣma and Droṇa as *artha kāma*, "people who covet profit." He says: *hatvārtha-kāmāṃs tu gurūn ihaiva, bhuñjīya bhogān rudhira-pradigdhān*: "Even though they are *artha kāma*, "pursuing their own interest," "they are still *gurus*." Then he literally says, "If we kill them, we will enjoy spoils tainted by blood."[86]

Getting back to Draupadī's plight, she was literally left without shelter. Neither Bhīṣma, nor Droṇa, nor even her own husbands, the Pāṇḍavas, were able to help. She thus turned to Kṛṣṇa Himself, the shelter of all living beings. Draupadī, in fact, is so much identified with Kṛṣṇa, that she is commonly referred to as Kṛṣṇā (the feminine form). And, in the end, Kṛṣṇa obviously saved her.

There's a very popular version of this story, which is also found in several editions of the *Mahā-bhārata*. As these big, powerful warriors try to pull Draupadī's covering from her

---

[86] From ch. 2, v. 5 of *A Comprehensive Guide to Bhagavad-Gītā.*

body, Draupadī obviously tugs back, trying to protect her honor as best she can. Finally, when she sees that her effort is futile, that there's no way to fight against these *kṣatriyas*, she simply throws her arms in the air and appeals to Kṛṣṇa for protection. And Kṛṣṇa responds in a singular way—by supplying an unlimited number of cloths, continuously replacing one after another, so that Draupadī's body always remains covered. The faster they pull, the faster the new cloths come—hundreds and hundreds, in diverse colors—until all these great Kuru warriors are so worn and weakened that they simply give up, almost collapsing to the ground.

This, of course, is one of the great scenes of the *bhakti* tradition: Draupadī crying out to Kṛṣṇa and Kṛṣṇa responding. Indeed, there are numerous depictions of this scene in Indian art, usually showing a large pile of cloths on the floor, with all these big, big warriors looking exhausted and confused.

Here the text mentions that the despicable treatment of Draupadī had been such an offense against *dharma* (something the *Asuras* had been trying to avoid) that nature itself began to cry out against it, displaying all types of inauspicious omens and signs—and these were no laughing matter. Even the mighty Romans and Greeks, with their impressive advances in philosophy, military science, architecture, and engineering, still took omens very seriously, as did every other civilization in the ancient world. Omens were viewed as genuine indicators of future events, of the favorable and the unfavorable, the timely and the untimely, and so forth. The Romans, for instance, would never go to battle without first checking the signs to see if things boded well for a successful outcome.

And here, in the case of Draupadī, who had been so severly violated by the Kuru clan, all the worst possible omens began to appear: jackals crying loudly, answered by the braying of asses and the shrieking of terrible birds. It was as if nature itself had been violated by the violation of this goddess!

On top of this, Draupadī herself specifically cursed the Kurus. And when someone with the power of Draupadī utters a curse, you can be sure that whatever she utters will come to pass. But before the specifics of this now famous curse, we'll talk a bit more about the offense itself.

In Vedic culture as well as in Buddhism, the body is a very powerful symbol—a type of sacred symbolic physiology or anatomy. And among the various parts of the anatomy, the feet are especially important as a symbol of humility. That is why one finds innumerable prayers and songs about the "lotus feet" of the *guru*, the "lotus feet" of Kṛṣṇa, and so forth. Because the feet are the lowest part of the body, adoring or touching them, praying or bowing to them, and so on, is considered the greatest act of humility, indicating that one completely surrenders oneself, as a soul, to God—or to God's representative.

And just as the feet—the body's lowest part—are a powerful symbol of submission, so the head (or hair)—the body's highest part, is also an extremely powerful symbol. This brings us back to the specific offense against Draupadī. To touch someone's head in an aggressive or insulting manner is considered the greatest possible offense, just as touching someone's feet in a submissive or adoring manner is considered the greatest act of humility. And there are many, many stories about this in the Sanskrit literature.

Now, hopefully, we can better comprehend why the Kurus' misdeeds were so grave. They had dared to touch Draupadī's head, to untie her hair, to drag her by the hair, and so on, which was the greatest possible offense. And because of this,

Draupadī uttered the following curse: "What you have done to me today, all your wives will one day do." But what does this mean?

In Vedic civilization, when a woman's husband dies, to symbolize her mourning, she unties and loosens her hair. Thus, by issuing this curse, Draupadī was basically condemning to death anyone that in any way participated in this great offense! The text further says that when Kṛṣṇa heard this curse, He immediately declared that it would be enforced. And Kṛṣṇa's declarations can never be thwarted—they always come to pass!

In other words, at the very hour of their apparent triumph in stealing everything from the Pāṇḍavas and insulting their wife, the Kurus had actually laid the groundwork for their own eventual destruction. Theirs was a pyrrhic victory, if ever there was one! And this was beginning to dawn on Dhṛtarāṣṭra, who was sitting there listening as all these events unfolded. Finally, when he realized that the Kurus were actually self-destructing, he decided to intervene and put a halt to all the nonsense. Though blind (in more ways than one), he was, after all, the king.

In studying the relationship between Dhṛtarāṣṭra and Duryodhana, one sees Duryodhana always making independent decisions and encroaching upon his father's power. And the relationship went through various phases as Duryodhana grew up, with his father first ordering, then arguing, and finally pleading with his ever more reckless son to cease and desist. In one sense, a son's desire to "be his own man" is a very natural thing as he reaches maturity and his father's getting older—especially in families that wield a lot of power. This time, however, there would be no pleadings, no appeals. Dhṛtarāṣṭra simply declared, "This is over; it's finished!" He was terrified that this whole Draupadī affair would end up destroying the entire dynasty (something the astrologers predicted about Duryodhana at the time of his birth). So Dhṛtarāṣṭra gently called Draupadī to come before him and began treating her with gushing kindness, as if she was his own dear daughter.

Of course, as long as Dhṛtarāṣṭra believed that the Kurus would get away with their abusive conduct, there was none of this "daughter stuff;" but now that he feared for his sons and his dynasty, he began treating Draupadī with kid gloves, saying, "Please, I'll give you anything you like; ask anything, and it's yours!" And Draupadī was not shy about her demands: "I want my husbands to be free of their obligation to the Kurus, and I want everything they lost in this gambling match to be returned." Dhṛtarāṣṭra replied, "Granted! Is there anything else?" And Draupadī said, "No! That'll do."

By this, she basically put Dhṛtarāṣṭra on notice that she wanted everything back that had been stolen, but would not accept anything beyond that. In other words, she did not want Dhṛtarāṣṭra's charity. *Kṣatriyas,* in general, were very strong on this point. They would not take charity, considering it to be a humiliating act.

And so, having received back all that they had lost, including their pledges of obedience, the Pāṇḍavas leave the Kuru capital of Hastināpura and begin the journey back to Indraprastha. Shortly after they've gone, however, Duryodhana goes almost crazy with panic: "Father, don't you understand? After what we've done here today, there'll be no stopping these Pāṇḍavas. From now on, they will be our sworn enemies. We can only imagine what they will do to us if left with the power to do it."

(Perhaps Duryodhana was thinking of Bhīma here, and feeling a definite twinge in that thigh of his!)

In any case, he somehow or other convinces Dhṛtarāṣṭra to call back the Pāṇḍavas, who were still on the road to Indraprastha. And, amazingly, after all they had been through, the Pāṇḍavas actually agreed to return to Hastināpura for one more throw of the dice. As *kṣatriyas*, they just didn't have it in them to resist either a challenge or their uncle's order.

This time around, there was no insulting of Draupadī, no shouts of *jitam*—nothing of the sort. Just one throw of the dice, with the loser being sentenced to twelve years of exile in the forest and one year of living incognito in any of the world's great kingdoms. The key here is that the losers had to spend that last year living among large numbers of people without being detected. Otherwise, they'd have to spend another twelve years of exile in the forest.

I don't think anyone will be surprised to learn the name of Yudhiṣṭira's opponent in this new high-stakes match. None other than Śakuni, who had earlier cheated him out of all that he possessed. With everything riding on one throw of the dice, the match was over before it began, and the Pāṇḍavas soon found themselves heading toward the forest for thirteen years of exile. And with that begins the great book of the *Mahābhārata* called the *Vana-pārva*, the *Forest Book*.

The terrible events of the day, however, represent a complete game changer—a real turning point—for the Pāṇḍavas. The lessons learned that day will never again be forgotten. It's interesting that during all those times that Duryodhana insulted them, offended them, threatened them, and even tried to kill them, somehow or other their early *brahminical* training kept kicking in, and the Pāṇḍavas always showed tolerance and restraint, depending on Kṛṣṇa. But when Duryodhana, Duḥśāsana, and the others offended Draupadī, that was the last straw. For themselves, the Pāṇḍavas could tolerate so many things, but when Draupadī was offended, that they would not tolerate.

Here the text clearly describes that as the Pāṇḍavas were leaving Hastināpura, having lost their kingdom for many years, they were in a completely different mood: it was no more "Mr. Nice Guy!" To a person, they all vowed that if the Kurus refused to return their kingdom after the passage of thirteen years, they would answer with war. And this is really the first time in the text that the Pāṇḍavas aggressively proclaim, "There will be war and you will be destroyed." So the grave mistreatment of Draupadī changed them—it completely changed their consciousness. From that point on, the Pāṇḍavas were not going to tolerate anything else from the Kurus.

The citizens, of course, were very depressed to see the Pāṇḍavas leaving Hastināpura, knowing they would be gone for many, many years. Indeed, as they made their way from Hastināpura to the Kamyaka forest, where they would reside for the next twelve years, numerous *brāhmaṇas* travelled along, intent on staying with them in the woods. But the Pāṇḍavas tried to discourage them, saying, "We're just not in a position to take care of you. Please go back to the city and wait for us there." You know, if you're out alone in the forest, where money and credit cards are of little value, you basically have to live on whatever nature provides, which is probably not enough to feed hundreds of *brāhmaṇas*.

Before moving away from these topics, recall that during the Kurus' attempt to disrobe Draupadī, she first tried to protect her honor by clinging to her cloth covering. Finally, when she saw that her own efforts would never be enough, she stopped struggling, threw her arms in the air, and prayed to Kṛṣṇa for protection. In response, Kṛṣṇa miraculously supplied an unlimited quantity of cloth, which exhausted the Kurus and kept Draupadī's honor intact.

Sometime after this incident, Draupadī asked Kṛṣṇa why He only indirectly intervened rather than personally coming to save her. And Kṛṣṇa explained, "I was unable to come because My own city, Dvārakā, was under attack." Here we can ask, why couldn't Kṛṣṇa, the omnipotent, omnipresent Supreme Being, be in two places at the same time?

In answer, what the ancient texts tell us over and over again is that Kṛṣṇa was playing the part of an ordinary human being. In Canto One, Chapter Eight of the *Śrīmad-Bhāgavatam,* there's a famous set of Sanskrit prayers, offered by Queen Kuntī to Kṛṣṇa just after the battle of Kurukṣetra. And in the second of these truly exquisite prayers, she likens Kṛṣṇa to an actor dressed in a costume (*naṭo nāṭyadharo yathā*).[87] Her point is that Kṛṣṇa came to this world and played the part of a human being, just as an actor takes on a particular role in a theatrical production. But why does Kṛṣṇa (or God) do this?

For one thing, Kṛṣṇa respects our free will, and so does not want to bring us back to His eternal abode unless we really want to be there out of spontaneous, voluntary, pure, and unmotivated love. Those that are drawn to God only for the sake of benefits and opulences are generally motivated not by love, but rather by their own selfish, material interests.

Therefore, Kṛṣṇa comes and acts in an ordinary way so that people who are not inclined to accept Him will not be

---

87 See canto 1, ch. 8, v. 19 of *Śrīmad-Bhāgavatam.*

disturbed in their "faith." Here it is important to clarify that atheism is also a type of faith, as Kṛṣṇa points out in the *Gītā*. In fact, a negative belief—believing that something is *not* the case—is equally a belief, according to any system of logic. So Kṛṣṇa came and acted like an ordinary human being. Although, when there was need, He would do incredible things that only Kṛṣṇa could do. Still, for the most part, He simply played His part. He simply played His role.

Another point about Kṛṣṇa is that He is equal to everyone, something that is frequently mentioned in literatures like the *Śrīmad-Bhāgavatam* and *Bhagavad-gītā*. In the *Gītā*, for instance, Kṛṣṇa famously says, *ye yathā māṁ prapadyante tāṁs tathaiva bhajāmy aham,* "However anyone approaches Me, I accept them in just that way."[88]

Thus, despite the fact that Kṛṣṇa took the side of the Pāṇḍavas or fought against this or that *Asura*, He factually reciprocates with all beings equally. Because the Pāṇḍavas loved Kṛṣṇa, and wanted His help and support, He responded to them in just that way. And because the *Asuras* were committing unjust acts against others, against the will of the Supreme, Kṛṣṇa responded by stepping in to stop them.

It's not that Kṛṣṇa has self-esteem issues, and thus punishes someone for being against Him. It's not that if you don't believe in Kṛṣṇa, you're sent to hell for eternity or something like that. No! Kṛṣṇa is actually impartial! As he again explains further on in the *Gītā, samo 'haṁ sarva-bhūteṣu na me dveṣyo 'sti na priyaḥ,* "I am equal to all beings; I neither hate nor favor."[89] Kṛṣṇa reciprocates with all souls according to their own behavior.

---

[88] From ch. 4, v. 11 of *A Comprehensive Guide to Bhagavad-Gītā*, 165.
[89] *Ibid.* ch. 9, v. 29, 183.

In any case, Kṛṣṇa answered Draupadī's question by explaining that while the events in Hastināpura were taking place, His own city of Dvārakā had come under attack from an *Asura* named Śālva. Remember that Dvārakā was built in the middle of the sea just to avoid attacks. But Śālva had this amazing flying ship, which enabled him to attack the island city from the sky.

Śālva's airship also had a variety of mystical capacities. It was large, almost like a flying village in which people could actually live. And it was stealthy in the sense that it could appear in one place, disappear, and then appear somewhere else—it had the power of invisibility. It also contained deadly supernatural weapons to unleash upon a foe.

Now, Kṛṣṇa happened to be away when Śālva attacked. But, to make a long story short, He quickly returned, killed Śālva, and destroyed his airship. And that's what Kṛṣṇa was doing when Draupadī was being disrobed.

That's it for today. Tomorrow, we join the Pāṇḍavas and Draupadī in the Kamyaka forest.

The Pāṇḍavas: In and Out of Exile

Yesterday, we left the Pāṇḍavas as they were entering the forest to begin their years of exile. And, in a sense, things have come full circle. They grew up high in the Himālaya Mountains, living an extremely simple life as young ascetic *yogīs.* Now, after enjoying all the opulences of a kingdom, and even an empire, they're back where they started—back to a simple, spartan life in the wilderness. And it is precisely because of their background that the Pāṇḍavas are able to pull this off without losing their "*dharma*-cool"—something that not many would be able to do.

Think of Karṇa, for example. When he felt frustrated because he couldn't work at his level, doing something that matched his abilities and true status, what did he do? He lied to the *avatāra* Paraśurāma. Then, for no clearly discernable reason, he became the self-declared enemy of the noble, spotless Pāṇḍavas. And what of Duryodhana and Dhṛtarāṣṭra? When they faced the prospect of losing a kingdom that wasn't theirs to begin with, what did they do? They embarked upon a tiring series of usurpations, manipulations, and failed assassinations, all to gain the throne by hook or by crook.

The example of the Pāṇḍavas couldn't be more different. They marry this wonderful, beautiful princess, make an alliance with one of the strongest dynasties on earth, develop their own flourishing kingdom, and successfully perform the greatest sacrifice in the world, establishing Yudhiṣṭira as the king of kings! Then they are cheated out of it all by a rigged game of dice and forced to live in the wilderness for twelve long years—literally going from riches to rags. And, I mean, back then, the forest literally meant *the forest*! This was no comfortable family outing to the Great Smoky Mountains, with its lodges, bed-and-breakfasts, grocery stores, and so on. So how did the Pāṇḍavas cope? By gracefully accepting their fate and living peacefully in the forest—making the best of a bad bargain and placing their trust in Kṛṣṇa. And, on the positive side, Draupadī's presence could brighten even the darkest day.

This brings us to the *Mahā-bhārata*'s *Vana-pārva*, or *Forest Book*, which basically recounts the Pāṇḍavas' years of exile. What happened out there in the forest for all those years—and with all that time on their hands?

For one thing, the Pāṇḍavas weren't always alone, since many great sages and other prominent personalities would occasionally stop by for a visit—including Vyāsa, who visited them on a number of occasions, and even Kṛṣṇa Himself. And whenever this or that sage dropped by, they would always try to lift the Pāṇḍavas' spirits and encourage their hopes—often through the telling of tales. Thus a portion of the *Vana-pārva* consists of stories about other places, other times, and other kings that are somehow relevant to the Pāṇḍavas' situation. And among these tales, perhaps the most famous is that of Nala and Damayantī, told to Yudhiṣṭira by the renowned sage Vṛhadaśva.

One interesting aside: More than a hundred years ago, the *Harvard Oriental Series* published a Sanskrit reader named *Lanman's Reader* (after the professor of the same name). Since that time, many generations of students have studied Sanskrit using this reader, the first story of which is that of *Nala and*

Damayantī. It begins, *āsīd rājā, nalo nāma*, "There was a king named Nala," and numerous Sanskrit students graduated from Harvard knowing this passage by heart!

And so, in a highly abridged form, here's the story and how it came to be told:

Despite the fact that the Pāṇḍavas had a real knack for adjusting to the rigors of forest life, there was one among them who was not a happy camper: King Yudhiṣṭira, who was wracked with guilt and deeply disheartened, seeing himself as the sole cause of their current misfortunes. Thus, when the great sage Vṛhadaśva stopped by for a visit, Yudhiṣṭira laid his troubles at the sage's feet, seeking guidance, understanding, and relief. It was in response to this humble plea that Vṛhadaśva recounted the history of *Nala* and *Damayantī*--famed for being one of the great romantic tales of the *Mahābhārata*.

Nala, king of Niśāda, was one of the great *kṣatriyas* of his time, known not only for being an extraordinary horseman, but also for being a master of the culinary arts. And Damayantī, an astonishing beauty, was his highly qualified wife and queen. Together, they were a real "power couple," bringing justice, peace, and prosperity to their kingdom. Having fallen in love simply by hearing of each other's wonderful qualities, they had married, bore two children, and lived a charmed life—until fate stepped in and blew everything apart!

Here I'll have to skip the details, but suffice it to say that, like Yudhiṣṭira, Nala was lured by his own brother into a crooked gambling match, where he lost every single thing he owned. He was then summarily kicked out of his own kingdom with *less* than the shirt on his back. That's right! Nala and Damayantī were exiled with only one piece of cloth between them—one shared cloth to cover their naked bodies. And so, wrapped together in this way, disgraced, and with no other shelter, they began wandering toward the forest.

Nala, of course, was filled with self-loathing and regret, and didn't want his wife to share an undeserved fate. Thus, along the way, he kept pleading with Damayantī to return to Vidarbha, her father's kingdom. But Damayantī wouldn't hear of it! She refused to abandon Nala. When they finally reached the wilds of the forest—hungry, dirty, and exhausted—they took refuge in a crude traveler's shed, where Damayantī quickly fell into a deep sleep, covered by their single cloth.

And here we come to this truly heartbreaking scene in the jungle. Nala can't sleep. He just keeps thinking of his own foolishness, and all the terrible reversals that he and Damayantī have suffered: the loss of a kingdom, the desertion of friends, the grueling trip to the jungle. Death looks better than this. And he especially can't stand the thought of Damayantī suffering the deprivations and dangers that lay ahead. But he also knows that she will never willingly leave him. What to do?

After hours of difficult, tortured reflection, Nala finally decides upon a drastic measure that he hopes will force his wife to return to her family in Vidarbha. In the middle of the night, he quietly approaches a sleeping Damayantī, cuts off half the cloth for himself, and leaves—or tries to, anyway. The text describes how he leaves and then returns again and again. He can't quite bring himself to do it. He's obviously a really conflicted guy. What if she doesn't make it back to her family? What if she's eaten by a tiger instead? Finally, he's, like, totally emotionally drained. Seeing no other course and knowing that Damayantī will be protected by the power of her own virtue, Nala once and for all departs.

When she wakes up the next morning, Damayantī finds herself alone in the middle of a very dangerous nowhere. Petrified with fright, she calls for Nala, but nothing. Now she's really in a panic, and just starts running helter-skelter in all directions—looking behind every tree, jumping at every sound, screaming out Nala's name. But Nala is nowhere to be seen. She'll have to survive on her own.

At this point in the narrative, Nala and Damayantī have their own individual adventures, as destiny gradually leads them back to each other and the full restoration of their kingdom. The story's so long that there's really only time to touch upon a few highlights.

For one thing, the text offers some amazing descriptions of the jungle itself. Here's just a little taste. It contained lions, leopards, tigers, bears, and wild boars, as well as varieties of deer, birds, flowers, bamboos, and trees—including trees of mango, palm, and date. There were also numberless mountains, filled with various ores, as well as groves, glens, rivers, and lakes. But it was also a place of grave danger, infested with all kinds of snakes, goblins, thieves, and *rākṣasas*. It was both an enchanting and a frightening place.

In any case, let's follow Damayantī for a while as I list some of the things that happened to her. At the start, she was almost crushed to death by a giant python, and then almost raped by the huntsman who "rescued" her. She then joined a caravan of merchants, where she was almost trampled to death by a herd of maddened elephants. Finally, she traveled with a few surviving *brāhmaṇas* to the Cedi kingdom of Subāhu, where her elegance and beauty caught the eye of the queen mother. Hiding her true identity, Damayantī presented herself as a maidservant and became the companion of princess Sunanda, the queen mother's daughter. Eventually, through a series of very interesting and dramatic events, everyone discovers Damayantī's true identity, and she returns to her father's kingdom of Vidarbha, where she is reunited with her two children.

Before we move on to Nala, I should mention a curious thing that occurred when Damayantī was still in the jungle. At one point, while deep in the forest, she came upon an idyllic ashram, peopled by sages like Vāsiṣṭha, Bhṛgu, and Atri. After hearing her story, these sages, who could actually see the future, envisioned Damayantī and Nala reigning in Niśāda, surrounded by friends, relatives, children, and prosperous citizens. Damayantī's heart filled with hope. Then, within the blinking of an eye, the entire scene vanished from her sight: quaint hermitage, sages, sacred river, all types of birds and flowers—everything *gone*! And Damayantī was left wondering, "Was it all a dream?"

Turning now to Nala, we find that his jungle "holiday" was not nearly as varied and eventful as Damayantī's, although it was every bit as dramatic! Basically, it consisted of one event.

After deserting Damayantī, Nala wandered for some time, till he came upon a huge forest fire, from which he heard repeated cries for help. And, oddly enough, those cries seemed to come from some creature that actually knew his name: "Nala, help me! Good King Nala, *help*!" Following the call, Nala rushed into the flames where he found a great Nāga sitting like a coiled statue on the ground, all due to the curse of Narada.[90]

---

[90] *Nāga* is the Sanskrit word for a class of beings who take the form of very great snakes. *Nāgas* are generally revered and worshiped in Hinduism, Buddhism, and Jainism as nature spirits and the protectors of springs, wells, and rivers as well as for fertility and prosperity. Narada Muni, the one who uttered the curse against the *nāga,* is the son of Lord Brahma. He is exalted

The Nāga's name was Karkoṭaka, and he promised that if Nala helped him escape the flames, he would help Nala escape his exile. Nala agreed, but as soon as Karkoṭaka was out of danger, he returned the favor by biting Nala on the neck, transforming the handsome king into an exceedingly unattractive dwarf. Nala was obviously upset, but the Nāga told him he had done this to help Nala travel incognito. He also gave Nala two celestial garments, which would return him to his old handsome self as soon as he put them on and meditated on Karkoṭaka, the king of snakes.

Karkoṭaka then told Nala to immediately go to Ayodhya and present himself to King Ṛtuparṇa, a champion dicer, saying, "I am Bāhuka, an expert charioteer and horseman" *(remember, this was one of Nala's defining features).* Karkoṭaka continued, "That king will become your friend and make you a master of dice in exchange for your knowledge of horses. Not long after that, you'll be reunited with Damayantī and regain your prosperity and kingdom." All that the king of snakes predicted did indeed come true. Here, very briefly, is how it happened.

With the help of a *brāhmaṇa* named Parṇāda, Damayantī discovers Nala's whereabouts, although reports of his unsightly appearance *do* leave some doubt in her mind. Knowing that Nala will never come to her as a dethroned king, Damayantī devises a trick to both lure King Ṛtuparṇa and send a big wake-up call to her reluctant husband (now posing as Bāhuka): she delivers word *only* to Ayodhya that since Nala is

---

in Vedic texts as one of the twelve *mahājanas,* or great authorities on eternal truth. He is also often considered the original spiritual master and intercedes prolifically throughout Vedic history to assist in advancing the Lord's pastimes as well as in helping orchestrate the spiritual progress of countless great saints and sages. His so-called "curses" are always blessings in disguise in order to spark higher purpose and consciousness.

nowhere to be found, she will hold a *svayaṁvara* to select a new husband—an event that will be held in Vidarbha on the very next day.

Now, when King Ṛtuparṇa hears that one of the most beautiful women in the world is again available, he becomes determined to have her; and when Nala hears that his beloved wife had basically given up on him, he becomes determined to drive the king! At this point, a bargain is struck: if Nala promises to get the king to Vidarbha on time, the king will immediately teach Nala the science of dice. When the two arrive in Vidarbha on time, however, they are surprised to see not a single sign that a *svayaṁvara* is being held: no festivities, no decorations, no kings and princes, no learned *brāhmaṇas* chanting *mantras*—nothing. It was just an ordinary, quiet morning at the palace. Of course, Ṛtuparṇa's no dummy and immediately understands that something's up. He pretends he's just there for a friendly visit, and he and Nala are shown to their quarters.

Now, as soon as Damayantī knows that Ṛtuparṇa and Bāhuka have arrived, she sets in motion a series of tests and inquries designed to penetrate the mystery of the charioteer. And when she is convinced that this homely little character is none other than her dear most Nala, she calls him to her chamber. When Nala arrives, he at once wraps himself in Karkotaka's celestial clothes and meditates on the king of snakes. Then, right before Damayantī's eyes, Nala reverts to his former handsome self.

Finally reunited, the two lovers are overwhelmed by all kinds of competing emotions, as tears of sorrow, regret, forgiveness, and joy mix together and spill to the chamber floor. It's been four years since Nala's disappearance, and as news of his return spreads, there's great joy and celebration among all the inhabitants of Vidarbha.

One month later, Nala sets out for Niśāda with a small accompanying force. As soon as he arrives, Nala tempts his brother with a false tale of his "fabulous new fortune" and challenges him to another game of dice. Needless to say, he easily defeats his disloyal brother, wins back his kingdom, and then sends for Damayantī and their children—who had remained behind in Vidarbha. Of course, many days of joyous celebration follow the return of the rightful king and queen, who rule Niśāda with kindness and justice for many years to come. And that, in a nutshell, is the story of Nala and Damayantī.

Now, remember, the sage Vṛhadaśva was telling this story to Yudhiṣṭira to help him gain some perspective. To put a cap on the story and encourage the king, Vṛhadaśva pointed to the life of Nala, saying, "Like him, you lost a kingdom; but also like him, everything will work out in the end. You, your brothers, and your wife will certainly regain your kingdom, opulence, and status. And consider: when Nala lost everything, he had to suffer his fate alone, going through all kinds of trials and tribulations. You, on the other hand, are sporting each day in this enchanting forest with your bothers and the beautiful Draupadī; and you are regularly visited by wonderful sages and personalities, including Vyāsa, and even Kṛṣṇa Himself. Kick out this lamentation, and instead count your many blessings."

The sage reminded Yudhiṣṭira that sober persons, who are advanced in spiritual knowledge, never hanker and never lament, but are steady in both loss and gain, victory and defeat. Then, as an extra added bonus, Vṛhadaśva taught Yudhiṣṭira the science of dicing, making him a master of the game *(also like Nala)*. In the future, if challenged, the outcome would be quite different indeed. After this, the sage proceeded to a sacred river for a well-deserved bath.

This is a fairly good example of the types of tales and adventures described in the *Vana-pārva*. The bottom line is that during their years of exile, the Pāṇḍavas had one amazing adventure after another, many of which involved Bhīma, whose activities are always highly chivalrous and entertaining! Unfortunately, I can only touch upon a couple more today.

At one point, for instance, the Pāṇḍavas and Draupadī climb the Himālaya Mountains to locate a special gateway to heaven (or *Svarga-dvāram*). *Svarga* is the world of Indra, the administrative head of the gods. Indra, if you recall, also happens to be Arjuna's father. On another occasion, Arjuna visited *Svarga* alone, to obtain celestial weapons in preparation for war. The Pāṇḍavas didn't believe for a minute that Duryodhana would hand back their kingdom at the end of thirteen years. They knew there would be more tricks, deceptions, and lopsided deals. So Arjuna was planning for the worst.

Kuntī, by the way, who was now quite a bit older, didn't accompany her sons to the forest, but rather stayed behind in Hastināpura under the care of Vidura, thus avoiding the rigors and austerities of forest life. So it was just the Pāṇḍavas and Draupadī.

In any case, let's get back to the main thread of our narrative with one more *Vana-pārva* tale—this time involving our favorite usurper himself: Duryodhana, who had received word through his network of spies about the precise location of the Pāṇḍavas and had decided to go there to further taunt and humiliate them. Unfortunately, while traveling through the forest he came upon a Gandharva king, who battled, defeated, and arrested the unlucky *Asura*.

Meanwhile, the Pāṇḍavas had heard that Duryodhana was looking for them, and they had gone out to find *him* instead—which they did, embarrassingly under the control of this Gandharva. As fate would have it, this was the same Gandharva that Arjuna had almost destroyed on the way to Draupadī's *svayaṁvara* (we discussed this the other day, if you remember).[91] Thus, out of gratitude to Arjuna, who had once spared *his* life, the Gandharva agreed to release Duryodhana into the Pāṇḍavas' hands—a bitter, stinging humiliation for this hateful, envious *Asura*! Much, much worse than death!

(I mean, he is *an Asura. And Asuras really* do *have some serious character problems.)*

And so Duryodhana, who was previously apoplectic at seeing the Pāṇḍavas' opulence and success, is now absolutely devastated that Arjuna—of all people—has saved his life. Without the slightest hint of gratitude, without the slightest bit of remorse over past misdeeds, Duryodhana basically decides to kill himself. He simply cannot live with the shame of being saved by Arjuna. It was just too much!

Instead, he will sit down and fast until death—a technique known as *prāyopaviṣṭe*, often employed by *yogīs* who are desirous of leaving this world. They just sit down in *yoga* posture, fix their minds on the Absolute, and continue fasting until the soul leaves the body. Droṇa, for instance, eventually departs in this way. And this is what Duryodhana now decides to do. However, before things get too out of hand, something happens that I've always found very interesting *(something similar to a modern-day "intervention")*.

---

91 See Chapter 9.

Certain *Asuras* that did not take birth on Earth have been monitoring the whole invasion from some sort of *Asura* Command Central. And when they see Duryodhana performing *prāyopaviṣṭe*, they become alarmed and mystically transfer him—or at least his mind—to their particular location.

The idea is that Duryodhana needs a bit of a pep talk to get him back on his feet. So they remind him of his importance to the *Asura* mission, give him a few pats on the back, and send him on his way with renewed enthusiasm for the mission.

Again, this story is just a small taste of all that is recorded about those forest years, which flew by one after another till the time came to live incognito. The Pāṇḍavas, of course, had been thinking about this for quite some time, trying to figure out the best place to go. Finally, they settled on the kingdom of Virāṭa,[92] a former ally. Having thus resolved the matter of "where," the next question was "who" each would be during their year of concealment.

Yudhiṣṭira began, telling the others that he would present himself as the *brāhmaṇa* Kaṅka, a king's counselor and gambling coach (since he himself was now a master of dice). Next came Bhīma, who said that he would present himself as Vallabha, a king's cook, skilled in all things culinary—and especially in the making of curries. Nakula would become Granthika, a king's keeper of horses; his twin brother Sahadeva would become Tantripāla, a king's keeper of cows; and Draupadī would disguise herself as a *sairindhrī*—a servant girl, skilled as a queen's beautician and hair dresser.

But of all the diguises and false identities assumed by the Pāṇḍavas, Arjuna's was certainly the most flamboyant! With

---

[92] According to modern scholars, the kingdom of Virāṭa was located in the area of Rajasthan, just northeast of modern-day Jaipur.

bangles on both arms to conceal the telltale scars of a bowman, and wearing brilliant earrings, a female dress, and long braided hair, Arjuna would pose as Bṛhannala the eunuch, this very effeminate dance instructor for royal princesses and the like. He obviously had to behave in an extremely effeminate way, otherwise no king would ever entrust unmarried virgin girls to his care. Here we can imagine seeing Arjuna in this outlandish costume, prancing about with a mincing gait, speaking in high, girlish tones, and so on. As I mentioned, the *Mahā-bhārata* is not without its humor.

There's a Hindu story that Arjuna had been cursed to spend one year as an *actual* eunuch—meaning a year in which he had factually lost his male anatomy. But I'm not entirely convinced that this is accurate. It's just as likely that he was only *pretending* to be "someone of the third sex" (as the text puts it).

In any case, having decided on the "where" and the "who" of their incognito year, the Pāṇḍavas and Draupadī set out for the kingdom of Virāṭa and eventually arrive outside its gates. However, they are still carrying their weapons, including the renowned Gāṇḍīva—a bow given to Arjuna by the god Agni, which is mentioned in the *Bhagavad-gītā* itself.[93] And obviously, they can't just waltz into Virāṭa with these powerful *kṣatriya* weapons, pretending to be cooks, *brāhmaṇas,* and so on. They will have to find a secure place to hide them for one whole year. And to part with their spectacular weapons—a warrior's most precious possession—is a very hard thing for the Pāṇḍavas to do!

---

[93] In one of the most dramatic moments of the *Gītā,* occurring in the first chapter, Arjuna is so overcome by grief that, *gāṇḍīvaṃ sraṁsate hastāt,* "Gāṇḍīva is slipping from [his] hand." From ch. 1 v. 29 of *A Comprehensive Guide to Bhagavad-Gītā.*

They begin searching the vicinity, and it's Arjuna who finds the perfect spot: a giant Śamī tree, located next to a desolate cremation site, surrounded by a forest filled with snakes and wild beasts. In other words, a very inauspicious place according to the superstitions of those times—a place (and a tree) that all would fear to approach.

So the Pāṇḍavas gather their weapons, and Nakula climbs high into the Śamī tree to tie their bows, swords, quivers, and arrows onto its strongest, most obscure branches. Then, to make double-sure that their weapons will be safe, the Pāṇḍavas hang a corpse in the tree, knowing that its stench will make the place even more uninviting. After this, donning their various costumes and disguises, the Pāṇḍavas and Draupadī enter the city one by one.[94]

So, what happened during that year? Did the Pāṇḍavas escape detection? To make a long story short, everyone perfectly assumed their various identities and roles, and they were able to successfully maintain their cover for the entire year. Towards the end, however, there was one incident that could have exposed them all.

The problem, as usual, revolved around Draupadī's devastating beauty, which always provoked an uncontrolled reaction from the *Asuras*—one of which just happened to be the queen's own brother, Kīcaka, the commander of Virāṭa's armies. To be honest, it was actually due to Kīcaka's expert

---

[94] Although the *Mahā-bhārata* doesn't explicitly mention that they entered one at a time, to me, this is a logical assumption. By the time they had to live incognito, everyone in the world knew that the Pāṇḍavas and Draupadī would need to live somewhere in disguise for another year. If five big guys and a lady suddenly showed up in some kingdom, people wouldn't need to be rocket scientists to figure things out. I'm assuming the Pāṇḍavas were intelligent enough to understand this and to act accordingly.

command that Virāṭa enjoyed a certain level of independence from Kuru rule.

All that glory, however, didn't prevent this *Asura* from being a real jerk when it came to the abuse of power. Apparently, he took one look at Draupadī and literally flipped into carnal overdrive, to say the least. And to make matters worse, because Draupadī was in the role of a *sairindhrī,* Kīcaka felt an immense sense of entitlement, like, "I'm brother-in-law to the king, the commander of his armies, and she's just some lowly serving girl. I can do what I want with her."

Kīcaka then began making one disgusting overture after another, using the most lewd and lascivious language. But Draupadī paid him no mind. Finally, in frustration, he decided to take her by force, and Draupadī, noticing his escalating aggression, became seriously alarmed. Secretly, she consulted her husbands, who put their heads together and soon came up with a plan. Draupadī was to tell Kīcaka that she could no longer resist his "charms," and now desired him as much as he desired her. She was ready to submit! The only thing left was to meet on the dancehall couch in the dead of night, and she would finally be his.

After waiting impatiently all day, finally the midnight hour strikes, and Kīcaka rushes to the dancehall to find Draupadī waiting in the dark on the couch. He approaches and there's this really hilarious scene—which, I think, was intended—where Kīcaka starts spewing all this pseudo-love poetry and even starts caressing Draupadī's body. At this, however, the blanket that's covering "Draupadī" starts to move, and a silhouette suddenly springs up, but it looks a lot bigger than Draupadī—and for good reason. It's not Draupadī at all. It's Bhīma! And Kīcaka is in big trouble!

As usual with Bhīma, a fight quickly ensues, but after what Kīcaka has done, Bhīma doesn't want to hand him an easy death. He really doesn't like this guy and wants to kill him with a bit of flair—something memorable, like when he broke Baka in two by bending him backwards.[95] So Bhīma starts relentlessly pounding Kīcaka's body over and over until he literally beats Kīcaka's head, arms, and legs into his torso, ending up with a big, round "medicine ball" of flesh. From this killing, however, another complication arose.

Kīcaka had been admired by all for his great strength and fighting prowess. So when people awake in the morning and discover his ball of a body, you can imagine their reaction. You can also imagine how quickly word of Kīcaka's death spread to Duryodhana's neck of the woods. Although Duryodhana had no idea the Pāṇḍavas had been staying in Virāṭa, Kīcaka's death affords him a different type of opportunity: the chance to smash and subjugate the free state of Virāṭa once and for all, now that its chief protector is gone.

Duryodhana immediately calls for Bhīṣma, Droṇa, and the other Kuru generals, and tells them to gather their troops for "a walk in the park"—the effortless conquest of Virāṭa's headless army. But, like so many things in Duryodhana's life, this was not to be! As it turns out, his arrival at the outskirts of the city coincided with the expiration of the thirteenth year of the Pāṇḍavas' exile, which had passed without detection of their true identities. The Pāṇḍavas were finally free! Free from the terms of the bet! Free to once again be themselves!

So the Kurus are there at the outskirts of the city, and almost immediately they begin their attack. Seeing them, the

---

[95] See Chapter 8.

king's son Uttara—this swaggering young prince with absolutely no battle experience—begins spouting all this over-the-top warrior hyperbole: "I can defeat all of them by myself! They're nothing compared to me!" But when Arjuna responds with a surprising, "Okay! Let's do it," prince Uttara has more than a little regret about his bragging big mouth!

Then Arjuna (in the ridiculous guise of a eunuch) literally drags the reluctant prince onto his chariot and swiftly drives to the Śamī tree, where (if you remember) all the Pāṇḍavas' weapons are stashed. And what follows is this really great scene. But to properly appreciate it, we need to understand a few things.

According to the *Mahā-bhārata* and other Sanskrit texts, many thousands of years ago a very advanced form of technology was available to certain individuals, largely due to the frequent intercourse between Earth and the higher worlds. It wasn't like the hard, scientific, industrial technology of today, with its heavy dependence on various ores, minerals, and oil. You know, like those big "Star Wars" ships that take 35 minutes to pass overhead. It wasn't that sort of metallic, machine-driven technology. Rather, it was a technology based on *yoga* and the manipulation of the great elements of the universe: earth, water, fire, air, and space. And it employed vibrations of sound—the chanting of *mantras*.

Now, when Arjuna takes down all these pulsating, glowing weapons, invested with all these sophisticated, supernatural powers, Uttara is astonished just to look at them. He's never seen such weapons in his life—emblems of this advanced technology. And, of course, he has no idea that they belong to the Pāṇḍavas, of whom the eunuch Bṛhannala is one.

In the meantime, the Kurus have begun their attack. Using

a fairly typical military strategy (even adopted by Alexander the Great), Duryodhana dispatches a modest group of soldiers to attack from one side, thus drawing most of Virāṭa's defenders away from the center. Then, with hardly any opposition left, he directs the main body of his army to attack that center—charging straight toward the city gates.

Seeing this, Arjuna knows that he has to act at once, regardless of the odds. He takes up Gāṇḍīva and twangs its string, setting off a vibration so powerful that it travels all the way to the Kurus—warriors who have heard that sound before and know exactly what it means! But here? Now? Arjuna? They were stunned, and there was even some confusion in the ranks.

Arjuna, by the way, is still disguised as a eunuch, with dress, earrings, bangles, and long braided hair. And there's no time to change! Grabbing Uttara and gathering up his weapons, he jumps onto the chariot and takes off, driving furiously into the heart of the Kuru army. But when Uttara actually sees these legendary generals, all his feigned bravado melts away, to be replaced by sheer terror! Almost hysterical with fright, he starts screaming at Arjuna, "Get me out of here! This is suicide! Please! Just get me *out*!" But Arjuna just keeps charging ahead, at one point switching places with Uttara and telling him to just drive on.

Meanwhile, all the Kuru generals are watching this lone chariot coming straight at them, captained by a lady in a dress with long braided hair. At a certain point, however, Arjuna discards his costume and everyone realizes that the sound they had heard wasn't an anomaly. Arjuna is here, and he's coming toward them, wielding Gāṇḍīva! Duryodhana and the others immediately start calculating: "Let's see, one year incognito ... And what's the date? Oh my God! The year's up!"

Now, we can just imagine how Arjuna must have been feeling. It's been twelve long years in the forest, and one year playing dress-up as a eunuch. So there's all this pent-up anger, all these bottled up emotions—all directed at Duryodhana and his cohorts! I mean, even under ordinary circumstances, Arjuna is extremely formidable! But now, after thirteen years of simmering rage, he's not only formidable, he's overwhelming! Single-handedly, he devastates the entire Kuru army. Nobody can touch him! Nobody can challenge him! He just drives them all away.

More importantly, however, the year of hiding is up for *all* the Pāṇḍavas! After thirteen years in exile, they've completed their vow, they're back, and they want everything that was theirs returned. These are no longer the innocent, wide-eyed Pāṇḍavas of earlier times. They are matured, hardened *kṣatriyas*. And they are angry, especially over the treatment of Draupadī. This will never be forgotten; they have no more qualms! They want their rightful share or they want war! It is no less a Kuru crisis than when the Pāṇḍavas came out of hiding after Draupadī's *svayaṁvara*—perhaps even more so.

At this point in the *Mahā-bhārata* there's an entire book that outlines all various diplomatic efforts that were made in order to avoid war. Interestingly, people that are only familiar with the *Bhagavad-gītā* often want to know why, in a so-called spiritual book, Kṛṣṇa is encouraging Arjuna to fight. And, of course, in response to this challenge, I generally explain that the apparent system of government in ancient times was what we would call constitutional monarchy—for example, Britain's *Magna Carta*.

Absolute monarchy is a form of government that didn't

become popular in Europe until the 1600s. Perhaps the most prominent example is Louis XIV, who declared, *"l'état c'est moi"* ("I am the State")—a declaration that ultimately led to the French Revolution. Indeed, absolute monarchy led to the end of monarchy in general, because it constituted a type of oppressive overreach on the part of the king. Prior to this outrageous breach of power, however, the monarchy was more constitutional in nature.

In fact, if you study the history of the Mogul Empire in India, you'll come across the name Akbar (1556-1605), considered by many scholars to have been the greatest of the Mogul emperors. Akbar was very enthusiastic about Vedic culture, and had reached various agreements and accords with India's indigenous populations, assuring that both cultures could live side-by-side in relative peace. Aurangzeb (1658-1707), on the other hand, was one of the great villains of history, and the last effective Mogul emperor. A religious fanatic who basically suspended all the conciliatory measures that Akbar and others had established, Aurangzeb became an absolutist monarch. He spent the entirety of his reign attacking other kingdoms, and was perpetually at war—trying to stamp out every other religion. The result was that soon after Aurangzeb, the Mogul Empire collapsed.

So we can draw lessons from both Europe and the Moguls that when the monarchy becomes too heavy, too oppressive, the reaction among the oppressed is very strong, and the monarchy becomes weakened. We can see this dynamic at work in individual relationships as well. When one partner becomes too controlling, the relationship is often destroyed.

In contrast, ancient Vedic civilization was governed by a *constitutional* monarchy, and it was this that Duryodhana had violated. In most countries of the world, if someone usurps the government and suspends the constitution, that is viewed as reasonable grounds for armed resistance. Well, this is precisely what Duryodhana had done! He had violated established law (*dharma*) by taking the throne from the rightful heir, who had already been declared king of kings. Almost any reasonable person would considered this solid grounds for war!

But it went beyond this. After all that Duryodhana had put them through, the only thing the Pāṇḍavas wanted was the return of their half-kingdom. They didn't want to attack; they didn't want Hastināpura. They simply asked, "Return what's rightfully ours." And even this, Duryodhana refused to do! He didn't care about the rules; he didn't care about *dharma*. All he cared about was holding on to power!

Indeed, when advised by Bhīṣma and Droṇa to make peace with the Pāṇḍavas and return their lands, Duryodhana steadfastly refused. The Pāṇḍavas themselves even said, "Look! We're *kṣatriyas*; it is our *dharma* to rule. If we don't act as *kṣatriyas,* we can't follow our *dharma*. Just give us five villages, and we'll leave it at that." It is at this point that Duryodhana famously replied, "I won't give them land enough for the placement of a pin." In other words, nothing!

Now, as I mentioned, prior to the great battle and Kṛṣṇa's *Bhagavad-gītā*, there were many attempts at diplomacy, primarily by Vidura, and ultimately by Kṛṣṇa Himself—who became a leading figure in trying to avoid war. This is important! Prior to speaking the *Bhagavad-gītā*, where He encouraged Arjuna to fight as a matter of duty, Kṛṣṇa had traveled to Hastināpura as a special ambassador, seeking to bring about peace, seeking to resolve matters without bloodshed. And, of course, all *sane* persons welcomed Him and recognized who He was—all, that is, with the exception of Duryodhana and Karṇa, who dared to seek Kṛṣṇa's arrest! I mean, even if you take Kṛṣṇa to be an ordinary envoy, trying to arrest such a person is highly unethical—and perhaps even criminal—according to all standards of international law.

To avoid war, Kṛṣṇa even revealed a portion of His *virāṭ-rūpa* (cosmic form) to Duryodhana, just to prove that the Kurus would lose this war. By that time, however, Duryodhana had become so maddened by ambition, envy, and anger, that he thought, "This isn't really the *virāṭ-rūpa.* This is just Kṛṣṇa making some magic!" He wasn't able to recognize Kṛṣṇa's supreme position.

It's similar to that famous scene in the *Old Testament* where Moses comes before the Pharaoh and pleads, "Let my people go!" He then throws down his staff, which turns into a serpent right before the Pharaoh's eyes. Like Duryodhana, the Pharaoh accuses Moses of trickery, and calls upon his magicians to duplicate the feat. The Pharaoh was unable to recognize the hand of God, just as Duryodhana was unable to recognize Kṛṣṇa.

The bottom line is that all attempts at diplomacy fail, and, with no alternative in sight, there's going to be war. The Pāṇḍavas don't want it, and have compromised time and again to avoid it. Now, there's nothing left but to fight: first, to save the world from the *Asuras*; and second, to restore government by *dharma*—the rule of law.

I've several times mentioned that *dharma* means the divine law governing the universe, but it can also mean "the law" in a more ordinary sense. Thus we find throughout this ancient culture—throughout this story—that people cite "*dharma*" just as we moderns cite "the law." Ancient Vedic civilization, in other words, was very much consciousness of living according to an objective set of laws, which is just the opposite of an absolute monarchy, where the king simply says, "Off with their heads," and goes about doing whatever he wants.

Duryodhana has crossed the line and refuses to budge. So there's going to be war! That's the reality! And the next portion of the *Mahā-bhārata* describes the intense efforts by the Pāṇḍavas and the Kurus to secure allies. There are only a certain number of great kingdoms in that part of the world, so both sides are doing all they can to persuade those kingdoms to fight for them.

Ultimately, eighteen great armies will assemble—the Sanskrit word is *akṣauhiṇī,* which signifies a full army, consisting of so many thousands of infantrymen, so many thousands of chariots, cavalrymen, elephants, and so on. And the text says that eighteen such armies fought against each other in the battle of Kuru-kṣetra: eleven on the side of Duryodhana; and seven on the side of the Pāṇḍavas. So there were eighteen *akṣauhiṇīs,* the battle lasted eighteen days, and the *Mahā-bhārata* consists of eighteen books. *(So this is the tale of the eighteen!)*

One note about these alliances: In some cases, they could feel a bit tenuous. Both Droṇa and Bhīṣma, for example, were very affectionate toward the Pāṇḍavas. In the case of Droṇa, Arjuna had been his favorite student; and Bhīṣma, like Vidura, had been involved in the Pāṇḍavas' lives since there were children. So there were extremely strong emotional ties between the Pāṇḍavas and two of the primary leaders of Duryodhana's army.

That's why, in the first chapter of the *Bhagavad-gītā,*

Duryodhana goes to Droṇa to allay lingering doubts about Droṇa's loyalty and commitment. He wants to make sure that Droṇa's still with him. The verse reads:

dṛṣṭvā tu pāṇḍavānīkaṁ
vyūḍhaṁ duryodhanas tadā
ācāryam upasaṅgamya
rājā vacanam abravīt

"Seeing the Pāṇḍava army deployed, King Duryodhana approached his teacher and spoke these words."[96]

Then, a little later, in verse ten, we see a more confident Duryodhana bragging about the power of his own army:

aparyāptaṁ tad asmākaṁ
balaṁ bhīṣmābhirakṣitam
paryāptaṁ tv idam eteṣāṁ
balaṁ bhīmābhirakṣitam

"Shielded by Bhīṣma, our force is complete; but their force, guarded by Bhīma, is wanting."[97]

Kṛṣṇa has agreed not to personally fight in the battle, but will drive Arjuna's chariot. With the two armies assembled, Arjuna asks Kṛṣṇa to drive between them both so that he can observe the entire field. It's at this point that the *Bhagavad-gītā* begins.

---

[96] From ch. 1, v. 2 of *A Comprehensive Guide to Bhagavad-Gītā*
[97] *Ibid,* ch. 1, v. 10

Arjuna surveys the Kuru armies and sees great personalities that he has known his entire life, and who are very dear to him: his *guru* Droṇa (and back then the *guru*-disciple relationship was extremely strong and intimate); his legendary grandfather, Bhīṣma, who practically raised him as a child when he had lost his father; his cousins; and various other friends and relations. The situation is reminiscent of the American Civil War, where family members, sometimes even brothers, had to face each other from opposite sides of the fight—especially near the border areas.

Here, the *Gīta* recounts that when Arjuna beheld all his friends and relations standing in both armies, he despaired and spoke to Kṛṣṇa with great pity, saying, "Oh Kṛṣṇa, seeing our own people standing near, eager to fight, my limbs weaken and my mouth dries up. My body trembles, my hairs stand up, Gāṇḍīva slips from my hands and, truly, my skin burns."[98]

So here we see Arjuna having an unprecedented lapse. It's not a loss of nerve; he wasn't afraid. It was something else, relating to the way the Pāṇḍavas had been raised during their formative years. Remember, they were born in the Himālaya Mountains, and lived there throughout their youth, brought up as little *brāhmaṇas*, little *yogīs*. And if you think about it, the tendency of the *brāhmaṇa* class, the tendency of great sages and *yogīs*, is to simply tolerate. Indeed, that's one of the main *yoga* teachings: don't be attached to this world; be tolerant; be equipoised; surmount the dualities of attachment and hate, victory and defeat, loss and gain. So there was always this little undertone inside the Pāṇḍavas, murmuring, "Why are we doing all this? Why are we fighting like this?"

---

[98] *Ibid*, ch. 1, vv. 28-29

Of course, on a deeper level, they understood that they were assisting Kṛṣṇa's mission to deliver the righteous, destroy the *Asuras*, and restore *dharma*; they knew the world was at stake. But inside, in terms of their own desires and emotions, the Pāṇḍavas were thinking, "Personally, I don't care. Personally, I don't even want a kingdom." These were genuinely great souls, enlightened *yogīs,* and intimate friends of Kṛṣṇa.

But as Arjuna looks over the battlefield, suddenly these emotions—which have always been subordinated to his *dharma,* his need to protect the world—rise to the surface and overwhelm him. That's when Arjuna gives up his bow and arrows, sits down on his chariot, and frankly tells Kṛṣṇa, "I just can't do it; I just can't fight."

That's it for today. Tomorrow, with both sides poised for action, we'll see how the Mahā-bhārata *ends.*

The Battle of Kuru-kṣetra

There's a famous work among scholars of Indian literature called the *Dhvanyaloka*, written over a millennium ago by Anandavardhana. Among other things, Anandavardhana is credited with the development of a formal literary theory that was extremely influential in Indian history among poets, writers, and so on. I mention this because in the *Dhvanyaloka*, Anandavardhana cites the *Mahā-bhārata* as the best example of a perfect literature.

In keeping with his theory, Anandavardhana's analysis of the *Mahā-bhārata* focuses on the work's *rasa*, a Sanskrit word that literally means, "flavor or taste." *Rasa* is used in Dhvani theory to indicate the predominant emotion of a literary work, such as conjugal love, parental love, friendship, or the love of a servant or child for the master or parent. And when it specifically comes to the *Mahā-bhārata,* Anandavardhana says that the work's central emotion is *śānti,* or peace—an interesting choice, especially since we are about to describe an extremely violent series of events. My attempt in this last lecture will be to explain how the *Mahā-bhārata* can be viewed as a literature that ultimately teaches peace, even while containing so much personal turmoil, political conflict, and violence.

At the start of these talks, I mentioned that the *Mahā-bhārata* takes place (and teaches us) at three different levels. First of all, as part of the history of the Earth, it is the story of a great dynastic struggle, involving human kings and princes, familial intrigues, dramatic turns of events, and so on. And second, it is a cosmic story, because most of the great personalities of the *Mahā-bhārata* actually came from higher worlds. Ultimately, however, the *Mahā-bhārata* is a spiritual narrative, because it contains the *Bhagavad-gītā*, the great spiritual text of the Vedic culture.

Thus far we've spent a lot of time talking about the Earthly level—the history of the dynasty's main figures as well as the plots, betrayals, reversals, and everything else that led the Pāṇḍavas and the Kurus to the field of war. We've also talked quite a bit about the cosmic level—the battle between the *Suras* and the *Asuras* in the higher worlds, the *Asura* insurgency, the earthly births of *Asuras* like Duryodhana, Kaṁsa and Jarāsandha, and so forth. But, thus far, we've only touched upon the spiritual aspect of the *Mahā-bhārata*. I'd like to talk a little more about that now.

To ultimately understand the *Mahā-bhārata*—and why, in eighteen days of battle, millions of warriors lost their lives—we have to understand what this work tells us about the ultimate purpose of life, especially as expressed in the *Bhagavad-gītā*, the very heart of the great epic. There we learn that the ultimate purpose of life is not to enjoy this world, but rather to attain (or, more accurately, *rediscover*) our eternal nature, although the Vedas also do teach a way to be happy and live properly in this world.

The word "dis-cover" literally means "to uncover;" and, in the *Bhagavad-gītā*, Kṛṣṇa refers to the soul (or consciousness) as being covered. My teacher, Śrīla Prabhupāda, used to say that when a diamond falls into mud and you try to scoop it up, you appear to be holding only mud. But when you wash away that muddy coating (or *cleanse* the diamond), you *discover* that the diamond is still there. Compare this, for example, to pulverizing a diamond and flinging the powder into the sea; in that case, there's nothing to wash off and uncover—it's simply gone.

In the *Bhagavad-gītā*, when Kṛṣṇa compares matter and spirit, He describes matter as something that is endlessly mutable, endlessly transforming: one thing changes into another. In contrast, the soul (or consciousness) is said to be unchanging and immutable. It is present and remains unchanged throughout all processes of transformation. In other words, we never really lose ourselves; we are always eternally intact. But consciousness (or awareness) of our eternal nature becomes covered. And to discover oneself is to remove that covering and to see who we really are.

Interestingly, the *Mahā-bhārata,* which offers many elaborate descriptions of apparently worldly affairs, does not want to encourage us to remain in this world. The text can be viewed as having two paradoxical (but not contradictory) purposes. A paradox is an *apparent* contradiction that can be resolved—yet, there is still this tension. The pre-Socratic philosopher Herodotus famously noted that although a strung bow may appear to be at rest, the actual power of the bow comes from the tension between its two ends—a tension that is created by the string. In the same way, paradoxes create powerful tensions that propel us forward.

So the *Mahā-bhārata* and all the great Vedic literatures have two apparently contradictory purposes, the first of which is to attract our interest. Because if we're not drawn into the text, we won't be able to take advantage of the "spiritual medicine" contained therein. Indeed, no one is going to derive benefit from a book they've never read and never heard of. So, first of all, there's a conscious attempt to engage us, to draw us in.

In fact, it's even more profound than that. There's not only a conscious attempt to *tell* an intriguing, adventurous tale. On a higher level, there's actually a conscious attempt by Kṛṣṇa (God) to bring certain activities to the Earth—to factually enact various pastimes in this world. Both the *Śrīmad-Bhāgavatam* and the *Mahā-bhārata* mention again and again that Kṛṣṇa is theatrical. He's the greatest dramatist, the greatest actor; and when He descends, He puts on a fantastic show in order to draw us into these activities and ultimately engage us spiritually. Thus, in the act of watching, reading, or hearing these astonishing stories, we are actually practicing *yoga* and self-realization—simply by hearing these stories! This is the conscious purpose of these texts, as declared over and over by the texts themselves.

In summary, the conscious purpose of Sanskrit works like the *Mahā-bhārata* is twofold: 1) to satisfy our natural desire to hear great stories, so that instead of busying ourselves with mundane topics, devoid of spiritual benefit, we can progress in self-realization; and, 2) to lift us out of material consciousness and ultimately restore us to our eternal home, beyond this world. The *Śrīmad-Bhāgavatam* actually uses the Sanskrit word *okas* ("home") in this connection.[99] So the *Mahā-bhārata* and similar Sanskrit literatures are books that want to interest us in the happenings of this world while simultaneously lifting us out of it.

In fact, the great epic teaches that even if one has the supreme good fortune of traveling from universe to universe

---

99 From the Sanskrit word *okas*, of course, we have the Greek word *ecos*, from which the English word "ecology" is derived.

as an associate of Kṛṣṇa, a participant in the story, a part of Kṛṣṇa's "traveling road show," ultimately this temporary world of *saṁsāra* is a place of suffering, struggle, and death (as the Buddhists always point out). It is not our permanent home. In other words, the *Mahā-bhārata* wants to attract us, to show us amazing things, but not in a way that reinforces our desire to stay here.

As for the great personalities that took part in the *Mahā-bhārata*, the greatest of them were actually conscious of why they were here. Let's say, for example, that somewhere in the world a major armed invasion is taking place, and in response the government sends in a sizeable military force to deal with the situation. And they end up battling it out in some sleepy little town—(*you know, one of those one-horse towns with a post office and, I don't know: a* yoga *center?)*. Suddenly that quiet little town is filled with thousands of troops, special forces, helicopters, tanks, and so on, and it becomes the scene of a terrible confrontation between the two sides. Indeed, many of the greatest battles in history took place in insignificant little towns that no one had heard of before.

Similarly, as I've mentioned before, the sleepy little backwater planet we call Earth became the focus of this great cosmic conflict between the *Suras* (godly beings) and the *Asuras* (their opposites). Both sides had come from higher celestial realms, and as the *Asuras* began taking birth on this planet, so too did the *Suras*—as a kind of cosmic SWAT team or counteracting force. Eventually, the *Suras* triumphed, but once the conflict was over and the danger had been overcome, the troops that remained became another type of burden, and thus Kṛṣṇa arranged for their departure as well.

To better understand the situation, let's return to that

sleepy little town. Before there was a military conflict, people had been living there, raising families, and peacefully going about their lives. Suddenly, thousands of forces invaded their peaceful space, which was transformed into a militarized zone, with weapons, machinery, armed troops, and the like. What if, when the conflict was over and the danger had entirely passed, the generals decided to permanently maintain thousands troops on Main Street? How would the townspeople react? Would they be pleased with the fact that their town had been turned into a permanent armed encampment or would they want the force to return to its base so they could resume their normal lives? The answer, I think, is obvious.

This theme actually arises again and again in these great Vedic stories. And you find Kṛṣṇa Himself saying, "I came to this world to relieve the burden of the Earth. But now, if My own devotees, My own associates, remain here, they themselves will become the burden of the Earth because they are so powerful."[100] Remember, these were superhuman beings.

Therefore, in the battle of Kuru-kṣetra, great souls on both sides—and especially on the Pāṇḍavas' side—understood that once their mission was over, they had to leave, meaning they had to die. Of course, death is not death for someone whose eyes are open. It is simply a *relocation* from one place to another. Now, for example, we're here, in this pavilion, and soon we'll leave to go down to the sidewalk or some other room. When we leave we don't die, we simply change locations.

In the same way, for those whose eyes are open spiritually, leaving the body when our *natural* demise occurs *(I don't want*

---

[100] The Disciples of A.C. Bhaktivedanta Swami Prabhupada, canto 11, ch. 1, v. 3 of *Śrīmad-Bhāgavatam* (Los Angeles: Bhaktivedanta Book Trust, 1987), 6-7.

to encourage suicide!) is just like changing rooms. Or, as Kṛṣṇa explains in the *Gītā, vāsāṁsi jīrṇāni yathā vihāya*. It is just like changing dress—like donning new clothes after discarding those that are worn.[101] Well, many of the great souls that came to Earth to assist Kṛṣṇa had this understanding. They understood that they had received special bodies for a special mission, and once that mission was over they had to give back those bodies and return to the place from which they came.

And again, this is the *Mahā-bhārata* fulfilling those twin paradoxical purposes. It is drawing us in, attracting us, getting us into the story, and yet it is reminding us that we shouldn't stay rotating in this world forever, but rather should go back to our real home, which is spiritual and eternal. And with that bit of background we can move on to the battle itself.

According to the *Mahā-bhārata*, the battle of Kuru-kṣetra lasted eighteen days. And the book describing this event, the *Bhīṣma-parva*, contains detailed descriptions of each day's goings-on, including details of all the major attacks, confrontations, intrigues, battlefield deaths, and so on. Obviously, with only around 25 minutes left on the clock, I'll only be able to touch upon a few of these incidents, while skipping over most of the particulars.

The Pāṇḍavas' general was Dhṛṣṭadyumna. And on the Kuru's side, the first general was Bhīṣma, their greatest warrior, the son of Gaṅgā. Bhīṣma, of course, fought valiantly, and often the Pāṇḍavas would all fight against him; he was simply unstoppable. Indeed, by the end of the first day, Bhīṣma had actually done incredible damage to the Pāṇḍava army.

Recall that when Bhīṣma was younger, his moral

---

[101] H.D. Goswami, ch. 2, v. 22 of *A Comprehensive Guide to Bhagavad-Gītā with Literal Translation* (Gainesville: Krishna West, Inc., 2015), 156.

philosophy was, "I don't care about the consequences, I don't lie, I tell the truth. I keep my promises no matter what! And whatever comes from that is not my problem." Well, there's a point during the battle where Kṛṣṇa personally teaches Bhīṣma that consequences matter.

At the outset, Kṛṣṇa had promised that He would restrict Himself to driving Arjuna's chariot and would not personally take part in the fighting. Bhīṣma, however, was determined to force Kṛṣṇa to break that promise by so threatening Arjuna's life that Kṛṣṇa would have to intervene to save him. Clearly this was a major departure—a new version of Bhīṣma. His aim was to reveal Kṛṣṇa's love for His devotee by showing not how He keeps a vow, but rather how He breaks it. Bhīṣma knew that when it finally came down to it, Kṛṣṇa would give up anything to save those who love Him.

So Bhīṣma mounts this ferocious attack against Arjuna, and Arjuna is really in danger. And then a very famous scene occurs, which has been depicted over and over in numerous Indian works of art. The battlefield is littered with all kinds of smashed chariot parts, weapons, and so on—all this debris of fighting. And when Kṛṣṇa sees that Bhīṣma is really going after Arjuna and pressing his life, He jumps from His chariot, grabs a chariot wheel that's lying on the ground, transforms it into a spinning *cakra,* and rushes toward Bhīṣma, breaking His vow in order to protect Arjuna.

In the *Śrīmad-Bhāgavatam*, there's a whole chapter dedicated to the passing of Bhīṣma, and in that chapter there are a series of truly exquisite prayers offered by Bhīṣma to Kṛṣṇa just before leaving this world—prayers in which Bhīṣma reveals himself to be a highly elevated devotee of Kṛṣṇa. And in those prayers, Bhīṣma explains that this vision of Kṛṣṇa charging him in battle is the sight he always longed to see. Here's a sample of the prayers related to this incident:

> "On the battlefield [where Śrī Kṛṣṇa attended Arjuna out of friendship], the flowing hair of Lord Kṛṣṇa turned ashen due to the dust raised by the hoofs of the horses. And because of His labor, beads of sweat wetted His face. All these decorations, intensified by the wounds dealt by my sharp arrows, were enjoyed by Him ... Fulfilling my vow and sacrificing His own promise, He got down from the chariot, took up its wheel, and ran towards me hurriedly, just as a lion goes to kill an elephant. He even dropped His outer garment on the way ... On the battlefield He charged me, as if angry because of the wounds dealt by my sharp arrows. His shield was scattered, and His body was smeared with blood due to the wounds. At the moment of death, let my ultimate attraction be to Śrī Kṛṣṇa, the Personality of Godhead. I concentrate my mind upon the chariot driver of Arjuna who stood with a whip in His right hand and a bridle rope in His left, who was very careful to give protection to Arjuna's chariot by all means. Those who saw Him on the Battlefield of Kurukṣetra attained their original forms after death."[102]

Everyone has their own unique relationship with God; indeed, the notion that there are different ways to love God is a very strong point in the teachings. For example, some

---

[102] Online Bhaktivedanta VedaBase, *Śrīmad-Bhāgavatam,* canto 1, ch. 9, vv. 34, 37-39; http://www.vedabase.com/en/sb.

devotees of Kṛṣṇa want God as their conjugal lover, an idea mirrored to some degree in mystic Christianity's bridal mysticism. In this form of mystic devotion, one sees the Lord as one's lover, and one sees oneself as the bride of God. Something of this sort also existed in Spain around a thousand years ago, in mystic forms of Judaism.

Then there's parental love for Kṛṣṇa, or *vātsalya-rasa*, where one becomes the parent of God, in the sense that parents can't ever forget their children, although children do sometimes forget their parents. So if you develop this type of parental love for God you can never forget Him, even for a moment. Then there's the relationship of friendship, like Arjuna's relationship with Kṛṣṇa.

Now Bhīṣma, because he was a thorough warrior, longed to have this vision of Kṛṣṇa charging toward him on the battlefield with deadly force. He admired Kṛṣṇa's chivalry, and thus he longed to see Kṛṣṇa in that form. Kṛṣṇa, however, would never act with such aggression, being deeply respectful of Bhīṣma's position as the grandsire of the Kuru dynasty. Therefore, Bhīṣma provoked Kṛṣṇa, forcing Him to break His vow, because he wanted to see Kṛṣṇa in that chivalrous mood—and also wanted to show that Kṛṣṇa will do anything to protect those that love Him.

Kṛṣṇa was able to save Arjuna without actually harming Bhīṣma, but eventually Śikhaṇḍī, who had been Ambā in his previous life, finally kills Bhīṣma—as he was born to do. Recall that in Chapter Three we discussed the tragic tale of Princess Ambā, whose chastity was unjustly questioned by Bhīṣma, even when she was telling the truth. Bhīṣma had destroyed Ambā's life as a queen, and thus she performed severe austerities to earn the ability to kill him in a future life.

When Bhīṣma met Śikhaṇḍī on the battlefield, he understood that he had been responsible for destroying this persons previous life and recognized Śikhaṇḍī as the one who would be the cause of his death. At the beginning of the battle, Bhīṣma had told Yudhiṣṭhira that he himself would tell the Pāṇḍavas how to kill him when the time came. And we all know that, above all else, Bhīṣma was a warrior of his word.

Thus, on the eve of the ninth day of fighting, after seeing Bhīṣma once again decimate the Pāṇḍava army, Yudhiṣṭhira went with his brothers to obtain this vital information. We can just imagine how difficult it must have been to ask this of their dear grandfather, knowing that it would lead to his demise. But, as Bhīṣma himself pointed out, as long as he remained alive, victory would continue to elude the Pāṇḍavas. There was literally no choice, and both Bhīṣma and Yudhiṣṭhira knew it. So Bhīṣma told Yudhiṣṭhira what he needed to know.

Bhīṣma had vowed that he would never under any circumstance fight against a woman, even if under attack. This, he told Yudhiṣṭhira, included Śikhaṇḍī, who was once a woman, as everyone knew. Bhīṣma instructed Yudhiṣṭhira to have Śikhaṇḍī lead the charge against him with Arjuna close behind. "Once I see Śikhaṇḍī, I'll lay down my arms and Arjuna can have his way with me." On the next day of fighting, that's exactly what happened.

Taking the lead, with Arjuna, Bhīma, and other great warriors following behind, Śikhaṇḍī charges Bhīṣma, piercing him with a flurry of arrows. But Bhīṣma continues battling on, killing thousands of Pāṇḍava troops, although he absolutely refuses to fight with or counteract Śikhaṇḍī. Finally, only Śikhaṇḍī and Arjuna are left to battle against Bhīṣma, with both releasing volleys of arrows that find their mark. Things go back and forth for some time till Bhīṣma decides, "now's the time." Seeing Śikhaṇḍī in the lead, he lowers his arms, basically allowing Śikhaṇḍī and Arjuna to pierce through his vital organs with their arrows. Bhīṣma falls from his chariot and ends up lying face upwards, suspended on a bed of arrows—a very famous scene, often depicted in Indian art. The text actually says that Bhīṣma's body was shot through with so many arrows that nowhere was there a space more than two fingers wide.

Seeing Bhīṣma in that condition, all the great Pāṇḍava and Kuru warriors came forward, because he was their grandfather and he was lying there, thirsty. So Arjuna, who understood Bhīṣma's need, shot an arrow into the ground and water gushed up, giving the fallen general a drink of natural spring water. The significant thing here is that at this point Bhīṣma doesn't actually pass away; he just lays there alive on that bed of arrows, although permanently neutralized in terms of his participation in the battle. We'll return to this scene in a few minutes to discuss the whys and wherefores of this extraordinary development.

In any case, once Bhīṣma is out of the picture, Droṇa takes charge of the Kuru army—this *brāhmaṇa* with a real taste for violence and politics. And, as we know, he was also an extremely difficult person to kill—except, of course, for Dhṛṣṭadyumna, who has taken birth just for that purpose, and who eventually does kill Droṇa. With both Bhīṣma and Droṇa gone, Śalya next takes command, with Karṇa as his charioteer. Śalya was the uncle of the Pāṇḍavas; but, for various reasons, he was obliged to fight for the other side. In any case, he didn't last very long, and then Karṇa took over as first general—an opportunity he had long awaited.

At this point, Karṇa knew that the Pāṇḍavas were his brothers. It was actually Kṛṣṇa who told Karṇa of his true parentage back before the war, when He was using all means of diplomacy and persuasion to prevent armed conflict. As I mentioned before, people who read the *Bhagavad-gītā* often think that Kṛṣṇa is a hawk—that He just wants war. But actually Kṛṣṇa made many efforts, trying everything possible to prevent the war, short of interfering with the free will of other souls. It was during these efforts that He one day brought Karṇa onto His chariot and revealed that Karṇa was actually the son of Kuntī.

So Kṛṣṇa, Kuntī, the Pāṇḍavas—all of them—were doing everything possible to avoid war. And Karṇa was factually moved, although he would not (or could not) go back on his pledge to fight for Duryodhana. He did, however, pledge not to kill any Pāṇḍava other than Arjuna, promising Kuntī that she would still have five sons after the battle. As I've mentioned several times before, no reason is ever given in the *Mahā-bhārata* to explain why Karṇa had such hostility toward Arjuna.

In any case, finally, the supreme pay-per-view fight takes place between Karṇa and Arjuna. Now remember, according to great teachers like Madhvācārya, the *Mahā-bhārata* is a text that has been influenced over time by various reciters, scribes, and so forth. Thus, in one version of this fight, we find Karṇa being booby-trapped by so many curses that there's really no fight at all. All these curses sort of kick in and Karṇa basically self-destructs.

Personally, I don't think that's what really happened; I think there was actually a fight and Arjuna won. As evidence, it can be pointed out that this was not the first time that Karṇa and Arjuna had encountered each other in a contest of skills. For example, at Draupadī's *svayaṁvara,* Karṇa was bested by a disguised Arjuna. Here, of course, he had no idea that it was Arjuna who had outdone him in every way. Then there was the battle just as the Pāṇḍavas' "incognito year" had come to an end, where Arjuna singlehandedly repelled the attempt by Duryodhana, Karṇa, and a large Kuru force to conquer the kingdom of Virāṭa. Here, again, Karṇa was defeated by Arjuna. In any case, whichever version one chooses to accept, on that day at Kuru-kṣetra, Karṇa lost his life.

Ultimately, when the eighteen days of fighting had come to an end, and the battle had been won by the Pāṇḍavas, there were very few warriors left on either side. The five Pāṇḍavas had survived. Then, a final blow! Aśvatthāmā, the son of Droṇa, committed a particularly heinous act. Breaking the rules of chivalry, he killed the five sleeping sons of Draupadī.

But again, in order to understand all this violence, it is important to understand that the purpose of the *Mahā-bhārata* is to draw us into the action while simultaneously convincing us that our eternal home is not inside a tenuous material body in the material world. As Kṛṣṇa repeatedly explains to Arjuna in the *Bhagavad-gītā,* we have far better options waiting for us beyond this temporary world. We have our eternal life in a spiritual realm that surpasses our wildest dreams.

After the war, of course, Yudhiṣṭhira is so guilt-ridden and traumatized by the destruction and loss of life that neither the instructions of Vyāsa nor even the pacifying words of Kṛṣṇa can console him. Thinking that so many millions had died just so that he could become king, he returns to the scene of the battle, where Bhīṣma is still lying alive on that bed of arrows, long after the attack that had put him there—something that I promised to explain.

In the *Bhagavad-gītā* it is said that *yogīs* come back who leave this world during the *dakṣiṇāyana*, when the sun is traveling toward the south (obviously in the Northern Hemisphere); and that *yogīs* do not come back who leave this world when the sun is traveling to the north. So the battle basically took place in November, perhaps early December. And Bhīṣma, who was blessed by his father with the *yogīc* ability to die at will, actually laid there waiting for this auspicious time to arrive—the time when the sun came out of the winter solstice and was heading back toward the north.

Thus when Yudhiṣṭhira arrived at Kuru-kṣetra, accompanied by his brothers, Kṛṣṇa, and other great personalities, he saw Bhīṣma lying there, preparing to pass away. Actually, Yudhiṣṭhira had gone to the scene of the battle to honor Grandfather Bhīṣma and receive wisdom from him before Bhīṣma left this world. And ultimately, it was only Bhīṣma who could console Yudhiṣṭhira and convince him to give up his grief and rule for the sake the Earth.

As with the description of Kṛṣṇa's charge, Bhīṣma's pacifying words are eloquently captured in several verses from that same *Bhāgavatam* chapter:

> Oh, what terrible sufferings and what terrible injustices you good souls suffer for being the sons of religion personified. You did not deserve to remain alive under those tribulations, yet you were protected by the *brāhmaṇas*, God and religion ... In my opinion, this is all due to inevitable time, under whose control everyone in every planet is carried,

> just as the clouds are carried by the wind. Oh, how wonderful is the influence of inevitable time! It is irreversible — otherwise, how can there be reverses in the presence of King Yudhiṣṭhira, the son of the demigod controlling religion; Bhīma, the great fighter with a club; the great bowman Arjuna with his mighty weapon Gāṇḍīva; and above all, the Lord, the direct well-wisher of the Pāṇḍavas? O King, no one can know the plan of the Lord [Śrī Kṛṣṇa]. Even though great philosophers inquire exhaustively, they are bewildered. O best among the descendants of Bharata [Yudhiṣṭhira], I maintain, therefore, that all this is within the plan of the Lord. Accepting the inconceivable plan of the Lord, you must follow it. You are now the appointed administrative head, and, my lord, you should now take care of those subjects who are now rendered helpless.[103]

So, what *was* the post-war situation on Earth? First of all, India was the center of a great landmass, so political chaos reigned over a very wide area. The Pāṇḍavas were now the official rulers, but many kings had been killed, the treasury had been exhausted, and the government was basically bankrupt. This is directly discussed in the *Mahā-bhārata*.

Then it was revealed to the Pāṇḍavas that long, long ago in a previous *yuga*, a king had performed a great sacrifice high in the Himālaya Mountains. This was an age even greater than that of the Pāṇḍavas—a time of extraordinary opulence, in which everything was made of gold, including all the

---

103 Online Bhaktivedanta VedaBase, *Śrīmad-Bhāgavatam,* canto 1, ch. 9, vv. 12, 14-17; http://www.vedabase.com/en/sb.

paraphernalia used in the performance of the king's sacrifice. And, according to knowledgeable sources, this huge store of gold was still up there in the mountains, forgotten and waiting to be recovered. Needless to say, the Pāṇḍavas were able to secure that gold and use it to replenish the central treasury and reconstitute the government. Then, to further establish political order and solidify his role as the legitimate ruler, Yudhiṣṭhira decided to perform the great *Aśvamedha* Sacrifice (which is something like the *Rājasūya* Sacrifice discussed earlier).

The process was very simple. As with the *Rājasūya* sacrifice, Yudhiṣṭhira sent his brothers to various kingdoms, many of which were now ruled by young boys whose fathers had been killed in the battle of Kuru-kṣetra. There they would request the local king or prince to accept the sovereignty of the Pāṇḍavas or fight. It was a very difficult time in the world, and Yudhiṣṭhira gave special instructions to Arjuna to avoid extreme violence at all costs: "People have had enough violence. So, somehow or other, persuade these rulers to cooperate. Because this is *dharma*; we are ruling on the basis *dharma*. And if someone doesn't want to cooperate, use only enough force to persuade them, while doing everything possible to avoid more killing." Yudhiṣṭhira was very explicit on this point. He did not want any more violence in the world. The people had had enough. They needed a break.

So Arjuna went out, following this challenge horse, which roamed freely to every kingdom. And while most of these kingdoms voluntarily fell in line without incident, this was not the case with the Kingdom of Sind, today a province on Pakistan's southern coast. Sind had been ruled by Jayadratha, a fierce rival of the Pāṇḍavas and one of the casualities of the recent war. Jayadratha had once abducted Draupadī to use her for his own pleasure, only to be chased down by the Pāṇḍavas and beaten to within an inch of his life. Then, during the battle of Kuru-kṣetra, he had helped the Kurus kill Arjuna's son, Abhimanyu, and was subsequently killed by Arjuna, who had taken a vow to that effect.

So when Arjuna arrived in Sind, the situation couldn't have been worse. The descendants of Jayadratha, his sons and grandsons, were now in charge, and they were still extremely angry and bitter—especially toward Arjuna. For his part, Arjuna gave them the standard two options: accept King Yudhiṣṭhira or fight. And for them, it would be option two. They would fight rather than submit. Even if it meant their own deaths!

With no other alternative in sight, the battle between Arjuna and Jayadratha's heirs began almost at once. Arjuna, a vastly superior warrior, was doing all he could to avoid using lethal force, trying to fend off these angry youngsters without inflicting serious bodily harm. He even pleaded, "Look, Yudhiṣṭhira told me to do everything possible not to kill you. Can't you just cooperate?" But Jayadratha's kin wouldn't listen and only intensified their attack. Finally, Arjuna had had enough. He'd done his best to follow Yudhiṣṭhira's directive, but this was becoming too much. Playtime was over, and some people were going to have a *"reincarnation experience."*

At that point, a very moving scene takes place. Duḥśalā, the sister of Duryodhana and widow of Jayadratha—this truly great lady who was humiliated by her own husband when he tried to kidnap Draupadī—walks into the middle of this active battlefield. And the very presence of the queen mother in the midst of all the fighting sends an unequivocal message to her children and grandchildren that they should immediately lay down their arms. Of course, they obey at once! Duḥśalā then approaches Arjuna, who immediately lays down his weapons and offers his respects.

Arjuna had been readying himself for a fight to the death, but when his own cousin—practically, his sister—entered the battlefield in that way, his mood changed. Then Duḥśalā simply declared the fight over and made it clear that henceforth the kingdom of Sind would accept the sovereignty of the Pāṇḍavas and cooperate with their rule. It's a very moving, very powerful story of how, by her very presence, this great lady ended a battle.

Now, with only a couple of minutes left, I'd like to start wrapping things up.

At the beginning of these talks I mentioned the reasons that Kṛṣṇa comes to this world, as explained by Kṛṣṇa Himself in the *Bhagavad-gītā*:

yadā yadā hi dharmasya
glānir bhavati bhārata
abhyutthānam adharmasya
tadātmānaṁ sṛijāmyaham

paritrāṇāya sādhūnāṁ
vināśāya ca duṣkṛtām
dharma-saṁsthāpanārthāya
sambhavāmi yuge yuge

"Whenever *dharma* weakens and *a-dharma* surges, I then manifest My Self. To deliver the righteous, destroy the wicked and restore *dharma*, I appear in every age."[104]

Fighting fire with fire in circumstances that demanded violent action, Kṛṣṇa descended with assistants like the Pāṇḍavas to restore *dharma* by military means, thereby establishing the just rule of law once again. And according to *Vaiṣṇava* tradition, if Kṛṣṇa and His associates had not taken birth in *kṣatriya* families to forcefully reestablished *dharma,* the world would be a very different place today, meaning far, far worse in various ways.

Interestingly, according to *Vaiṣṇava* tradition, around 500 years ago, Kṛṣṇa descended to this world again, this time as Caitanya, whose only "weapons" were His associates and the chanting of God's holy names. Kṛṣṇa as Caitanya presented His God-conscious message to the people in a very humble, gentle, and peaceable way. In the *Bhagavad-gītā* Kṛṣṇa asked everyone to give up all illusory activities and simply take shelter of the Him (the Supreme Lord). But because people couldn't understand or somehow couldn't follow this recommendation, Kṛṣṇa came again as Caitanya to set a personal example as a devotee of Kṛṣṇa. His method was entirely non-violent. Indeed, throughout the entirety of Caitanya's mission, no one was ever killed, or even seriously injured—not a single person.

In fact, it's said that Caitanya is Rādhā and Kṛṣṇa combined. In other words, because this age is so fallen, both Kṛṣṇa and His eternal consort Rādhā (the most compassionate form of the Divine) came within the same body—the body of Caitanya. Because it's only through causeless mercy and great compassion that the people of this age can be given a chance to make spiritual progress.

---

104 H.D. Goswami, ch. 4, v. 7-8 of *A Comprehensive Guide to Bhagavad-Gītā with Literal Translation* (Gainesville: Krishna West, Inc., 2015), 165.

Moreover, the chanting of the names of God is considered in these literatures to be the *yuga-dharma*—the most powerful means in this age of awakening our eternal spiritual consciousness and dormant love for God. So let us always remain absorbed in the holy names, forms, and activities of Kṛṣṇa and His devotees, and in this way come closer and closer to the Lord.

I'll end with a very nice verse from the seventh chapter of the *Bhagavad-gītā*:

śrī-bhagavān uvāca
mayy āsakta-manāḥ pārtha
yogaṁ yuñjan mad-āśrayaḥ
asaṁśayaṁ samagraṁ māṁ
yathā jñāsyasi tac chṛṇu

"The Lord said: Hear Pārtha [Arjuna], how by practicing *yoga* at My shelter, with mind fixed on Me, you will know Me fully beyond doubt."[105]

Thank you all again for your hospitality and attention. I hope to see you again soon.

---

[105] *Ibid.*, ch. 7, v. 1, 176.

Works Cited

Ayyangar, Keerthanacharya Sreenivasa. *The Rāmāyaṇa of Vālmīki.* Madras: The Little Flower Co., 1962.

Bühler, George, trans. *The Laws of Manu.* Charleston: BiblioBazaar, 2009.

The Eagles. "Hotel California." *Hotel California*. Asylum Records 6E-103, 1976, LP album.

Goodman, Celia, ed. *Living with Koestler: Mamaine Koestler's Letters 1945–51.* London: Weidenfeld & Nicolson, 1985.

Goswami, H.D. *A Comprehensive Guide to Bhagavad-Gītā with Literal Translation.* Gainesville: Krishna West, Inc., 2015.

Haug, Martin, trans. *The Aitareya Brāhmana of the Rigveda: Translation, with Notes.* London: Government Central Book Depot, 1863.

Monier Williams Sanskrit-English Dictionary (2008 revision). http://www.sanskrit-lexicon.uni-koeln.de/monier/

Rajagopalachari, C. *Valmiki's Ramayan.* London: Bharatiya Vidya Bhavan, 2000.

Patnaik, K.N.S. "The Mahā-bhārata Chronology." Accessed February 20, 2017. http://www.hindunet.org/hindu_history/ancient/mahabharat/mahab_patnaik.html.

Prabhupada, A.C. Bhaktivedanta Swami. *Bhaktivedanta VedaBase*. Accessed January 17, 2017. http://www.vedabase.com/en.

Prabhupada, A.C. Bhaktivedanta Swami. *Caitanya-Caritāmṛta: Madhya-Līlā*. Mumbai: Bhaktivedanta Book Trust, 1996.

Prabhupada, A.C. Bhaktivedanta Swami. *Kṛṣṇa, the Supreme Personality of Godhead.* Los Angeles: Bhaktivedanta Book Trust, 1970.

Prabhupada, A.C. Bhaktivedanta Swami. *Śrī Īsopaniṣad.* Los Angeles: ISKCON Books, 1969.

Prabhupada, A.C. Bhaktivedanta Swami. *Śrīmad-Bhāgavatam.* Los Angeles: Bhaktivedanta Book Trust, 1972.

Shakespeare, William, and Cyrus Hoy. *Hamlet.* New York: W.W. Norton, 1996.

Sukthankar, V.S. *Critical Studies in the Mahābhārata.* Bombay: Karnatak Publishing House, 1944.

Twain, Mark. *Following the Equator: A journey around the world.* Hartford: American Pub. Co, 1897.

van Buitenen, J.A.B.*The Mahābhārata: The Book of the Beginning*. London: The University of Chicago Press, Ltd., 1973.

Quest for Justice
Sanskrit Pronunciation Guide

The English transliterations of Sanskrit in Quest for Justice are in keeping with the standard scholarly system of Sanskrit pronunciation, which is as follows:

Vowels

a – as in b*u*t.

ā – as in f*a*r.

i – as in p*i*n.

ī – as in p*i*que (but held twice as long).

u – as in p*u*ll.

ū – as in r*u*le (but held twice as long).

ṛ – as in *ri*m.

e – as in th*ey*.

o – as in g*o*.

ai – as in *ai*sle.

au – as in h*ow*.

Consonants

Gutterals (pronounced with lips)

k – as in *k*ite.

kh – as in Ec*kh*art.

g – as in *g*ive.

gh – as in a*gh*ast.

ṅ – as in si*n*g.

Labials (pronounced from throat)

p – as in *p*ine.

ph – as in u*ph*ill.

b – as in *b*ird.

bh – as in a*bh*or.

m – as in mother.

Cerebrals (pronounced with tongue against roof of palate)

ṭ – as in *t*ub.

ṭh – as in ligh*t-h*eart.

ḍ – as in dove.

ḍh – as in a*dh*ere.

ṇ – as in *n*ut.

Palatals (pronounced with middle of tongue against palate)

c – as in *ch*air.

ch – as in staun*ch-h*eart.

j – as in *j*oy.

jh – as in he*dgeh*og.

ï – as in ca*n*yon.

Dentals (pronounced like cerebrals but with tongue against teeth)

t – as in *t*ub.

th – as in ligh*t-h*eart.

d – as in dove.

dh – as in a*dh*ere.

n – as in *n*ut.

Semivowels

y – as in *y*es.

r – as in *r*un.

l – as in *l*ight.

v – as in *v*ine

Sibilants

ś – as in the German *s*prechen

ṣ – as in *sh*ine

s – as in *s*un.

Aspirate

h – as in *h*ome.

Anusvāra

ṁ – as in the resonant nasal sound nu*mb* or the French bo*n*.

Visarga (a final h-sound)

ḥ – at the end of the couplet *aḥ* as aha; at the end of the couplet *iḥ* as ihi.